Rural poverty and the policy crisis

Rural poverty and

the policy crisis

Coedited by

ROBERT O. COPPEDGE and CARLTON G. DAVIS

Iowa State University Press / Ames

1 9 7 7

Robert O. Coppedge is Associate Professor and Extension Economist for Economic Development, Cooperative Extension Service, New Mexico State University, Las Cruces.

Carlton G. Davis is Associate Professor of Food and Resource Economics, University of Florida, Gainesville.

This volume is the outgrowth of a conference on "The Poverty Dimension of Rural Underdevelopment in America: New Perspectives" at Gainesville, Florida, February 19–20, 1975. The conference was sponsored by the Department of Food and Resource Economics, the Florida Cooperative Extension Service, and the Center for Rural Development, University of Florida.

Composed and Printed by
The Iowa State University Press

First edition, 1977

Library of Congress Cataloging in Publication Data

Main entry under title:

Rural poverty and the policy crisis.

    Includes bibliographies and indexes.
    1. Rural poor—United States—Addresses, essays, lectures. 2. Economic assistance, Domestic—United States—Addresses, essays, lectures. 3. Income distribution—United States—Addresses, essays, lectures. I. Coppedge, Robert O. II. Davis, Carlton G.

HC110.P688   339.2'1   76-53751
ISBN 0-8138-1220-8

C O N T E N T S

Foreword   *Leo Polopolus*   vii
Introduction   *Carlton G. Davis and Robert O. Coppedge*   ix

Part One   Conceptual Dimensions of Poverty Issues and Problems

1 / Conceptual Framework for Discussing Factors Related to
      Income Distribution   *Robert O. Coppedge*   3
2 / Poverty and Rural Underdevelopment in the United
      States: Where Do We Stand?   *Carlton G. Davis*   11
3 / Economics of Being Poor   *Theodore W. Schultz*   35

**Part Two   Alternative Evaluations of the Cost of Rural Poverty
in the United States**

4 / Economic Cost of Poverty   *Luther Tweeten*
                                    and Neal O. Walker   45
   Discussion   *J. Dean Jansma*   69
5 / Social Cost of Poverty   *Sally Bould-Van Til*   71
   Discussion   *Gerald R. Leslie*   81

**Part Three   Alternative Theoretical Frameworks for Viewing
Rural Poverty and Income Distribution**

6 / Neoclassical Economic Theory, Poverty, and Income
      Distribution   *G. Edward Schuh*   87
   Discussion   *Robert D. Emerson*   111
7 / Radical Political Economics, Poverty, and Income
      Distribution   *Joseph Persky*   114
   Discussion   *Edna T. Loehman*   125

v

8 / Institutional Processing of Human Resources: A Theory
of Social Marginalization   *Harland T. Padfield*
                                      and John A. Young 129
Discussion   *Benjamin L. Gorman* 148
9 / Policy Implications of Alternative Theoretical Frameworks
for Viewing Rural Poverty and Income Distribution
                                      Bobby R. Eddleman 152

Part Four   Institutional Role and Responsibilities on Poverty
            Policies and Issues

10 / Survey of Poverty Issues and Programs: Can We
Improve the Performance?   *Emiel W. Owens* 163
Discussion   *Lynn M. Daft* 181
11 / Future Poverty Programs: Political Prospects and
Implications for the Rural Poor   *D. Lee Bawden* 186
Discussion   *Melvin L. Upchurch* 194
12 / Role of the University in Rural Poverty Programs and
Issues   *Emery N. Castle* 196
Discussion   *W. W. McPherson* 206
Contributors   211
Index   217

FOREWORD

T H I S B O O K represents one of a limited number of original and major publications dealing with rural poverty since the 1968 release of *Rural Poverty in the United States* by the President's National Advisory Commission on Rural Poverty. The subject matter focuses upon conceptual dimensions of poverty problems, the cost of rural poverty in the United States, alternative theoretical frameworks for viewing poverty and income distribution, and institutional policies.

The book was conceived by Dr. Carlton G. Davis and Dr. Robert O. Coppedge of the Food and Resource Economics Department, University of Florida, Gainesville. Participation in a series of rural development conferences in 1974 had been a frustrating experience for the two economists, particularly as they attempted to discuss poverty, human resources, and income distribution. With problems of the rural poor becoming more evident as time passed, they suggested that a national symposium be sponsored by the University of Florida to identify and assess the current dimensions of poverty in rural America.

The game plan of the symposium organizers was to assemble exceptionally competent authorities in the field to discuss the subject. The overall emphasis was to be on economic issues, but the interrelationships of several disciplines were explicitly incorporated into the program format. Thus, in addition to papers by agricultural economists, papers were invited from general economists, anthropologists, sociologists, and academic and government administrators. The fact that such distinguished professionals as T. W. Schultz, G. Edward Schuh, D. Lee Bawden, Luther R. Tweeten, Emery N. Castle, Joseph Persky, Harland Padfield, Sally Bould-Van Til, Emiel W. Owens, and B. R. Eddleman agreed to prepare major papers indicated the general interest and need for such a symposium. The originality, quality, and scope of these papers, presented in February 1975, warranted their publication in book form for wider distribution. Dr. Coppedge and Dr. Davis jointly provided expert leadership and follow-through on all aspects of the symposium and book manuscript editing. Many of the faculty members of the Department of Food and Resource Economics of the University of Florida—Robert D. Emerson, J. Dean Jansma, Edna T. Loehman, W. W. McPherson, and M. L. Upchurch—participated also in this effort. The strong support of Dr. B. R. Eddleman, former Director of the University of Florida Center for Rural Development, is gratefully acknowledged, as well as the financial and logistical support of the Florida Cooperative Extension Service. Dr. Kenneth R. Tefertiller, Vice President for Agricultural Affairs, was among the first to lend his backing to this effort. Finally, we are grateful to Dr. James R. Hildreth and Dr. W. Neill Schaller of the Farm Foundation for their moral and financial support to this project.

This book will be useful not only to teachers and researchers who have a professional interest in the economics of rural poverty, but also to administrators, legislators, and citizens interested in this important problem area of contemporary American society. We trust that it will serve also as a standard reference for follow-up conferences in various regions where proposed policies and action programs are discussed and debated.

LEO POLOPOLUS
Chairman, Department of Food and Resource Economics
University of Florida

INTRODUCTION

P O V E R T Y and underdevelopment are inextricably bound in a complex network of socioeconomic relationships that historically have defied complete codification and eluded pragmatic and effective policy prescription. In the face of an increasing knowledge gap on the subject, this volume attempts to present the beginnings of a multidisciplinary framework for theoretical and empirical analysis of certain issues relating to the major components. In the initial process of doing so, more questions than answers are generated, but the right questions must be asked before the right answers are to be found. If indeed the questions raised as part of this new perspective are the right ones, then the basis is laid for future empirical research designed to backstop remedial programs and policies. The failure of programs to eradicate poverty to date bears testimony to the inappropriateness of questions raised and answered in the past.

The focus in several chapters is on rural areas, but we are concerned overall with the issues and problems of poverty regardless of location. This is as it should be, since the rural-urban analytical framework for poverty evaluation as an effective means for defining appropriate policies has been seriously questioned at times.

The questions and issues of poverty, income distribution, and rural underdevelopment are examined within a dynamic framework that represents a departure from the conventional approach to poverty and underdevelopment problems. The dynamic element is introduced through recognition of and treatment of the poverty and underdevelopment problem as a *process* rather than a *stage*. Within this framework certain key components of the rural political economy are identified as being *poverty and underdevelopment generating*. It is possible to identify the (sometimes subtle) interrelationships of key economic and institutional variables that explain the tendency for persistent poverty and and underdevelopment in rural areas.

Part One presents a cross-disciplinary conceptual framework for viewing problems related to income distribution, reviews definitional and empirical measurement problems, and highlights the complexity of the economic and social-psychological components of the problem. The first chapter examines the assumptions of traditional economic theory about human and market-political-institutional (all other) behavior. Questions are raised about the policy implications of these assumptions in relation to income distribution. Potential contributions of radical political economic theory and other social sciences are discussed in terms of improved model specification in applied economic research as a basis for relevant and effective policy formulation on poverty problems.

The second chapter reviews the major issues surrounding poverty definitions and empirical estimates of poverty. It also analyzes trends exhibited in official poverty statistics over the 1959–73 period and implications of the statistics for welfare gains. Special attention is given to poverty and underdevelopment in rural areas within a comparative analytical framework.

Chapter 3 reviews within an international framework some inconsistencies between the observed facts on income distribution and economic theory. It traces reasons for the inconsistencies and examines some resulting puzzles, particularly as they relate to international poverty problems. Since most of the world's people are poor, if we understand the economics of being poor, we would "know most of the economics that really matter," Focus on domestic poverty problems in isolation from the generalized global poverty problem runs the risk of becoming myopic.

Part Two discusses the cost of poverty in the United States. An empirical estimate of the social and economic cost of poverty and unemployment is seen in Chapter 4, as a necessary condition for intelligent decisions on whether to alleviate poverty. The authors offer the premise that the economic cost of continuing poverty exceeds the cost of alleviating poverty. They then test the premise empirically within a marginal utility framework.

Chapter 5 approaches cost evaluation from a functional sociological perspective. It is argued that the social costs of poverty to the nonpoor must be weighed against the benefits of poverty to this group in determining the feasibility of poverty eradication within a realistic political-economic framework. The nonpoor have both the power and the economic means to support or defeat antipoverty programs.

Part Three reviews and evaluates the policy implications of three alternative theoretical frameworks for viewing income distribution and poverty problems. Chapter 6 provides a thorough review of those elements of neoclassical economic theory that are applicable to the problem of income distribution and poverty. Concentration is on three components of the theory: underlying assumptions, sectoral explanation of rural poverty, and microeconomic theories that appear relevant to rural poverty problems.

Chapter 7 represents a departure from Chapter 6 in its interpretation of the economics of rural poverty. The views of the radical economists are receiving increased attention in the economic literature. This interest is probably related to the general failure of antipoverty policies and programs based on traditional or neoclassical economic theory. The paper criticizes neoclassical theory and presents the radical viewpoint, describes the rural poverty situation within a Marxist framework, and suggests antipoverty measures based on the radical line of reasoning.

In contrast to the preceding two chapters, the approach in Chapter 8 is behavioral rather than deterministic. The focus includes the behavior of institutions that educate and regulate (process) human resources, as well as the behavior of the poor. It is argued that such a focus reveals the tendency of these institutions to segregate people irreversibly into economically peripheral, dependent, and counterproductive modes of activity. This effect of processing human resources is called "social marginalization."

Chapter 9 attempts to trace the policy implications for poverty eradication in relation to the preceding three theoretical frameworks. Emphasis is on the policy implications for two large groups of rural underprivileged classes: the unemployable rural poor and the underemployed rural poor.

Part Four, the final section of the volume, reviews the status of current poverty issues and programs and evaluates the performance of some major antipoverty programs. In addition, public and private institutional roles and responsibilities are suggested within a broad political-economic framework. Chapter 10 reviews and highlights some of the issues involving rural poverty. In addition, it reviews some trends in federal income support programs and how certain changes in these programs affect the target low income population. Chapter 11 focuses on two major poverty programs currently under legislative consideration: a universal cash transfer program and national health insurance. The two programs are income conditioned and thus would have major impact on the poor. The chapter speculates on the political prospects of the two programs and assesses their implications for the rural poor. Chapter 12 presents a three-part argument. The first part makes explicit certain assumptions concerning the nature of the poverty problem and the university. The second part develops a conceptual framework for viewing the nature of the university. The final part of the chapter integrates the two preceding parts in an attempt to make explicit the role of the university relative to poverty issues and programs.

In summary, this book was designed to generate useful information relative to income positions of low income groups. It is hoped the new perspectives offered on the poverty dimension of rural underdevelopment in the United States will be useful in formulating more effective theoretical frameworks for prescribing policies for the poor.

CARLTON G. DAVIS
ROBERT O. COPPEDGE

PART ONE

Conceptual dimensions of poverty issues and problems

Conceptual framework for discussing factors related to income distribution

ROBERT O. COPPEDGE

THIS BOOK explores the role of certain behavioral sciences as contributors to economic theories of income distribution; discusses alternative conceptual frameworks for explaining maldistribution; and makes suggestions concerning policy. This particular chapter presents a conceptual framework reflecting the reasons underlying the organization of the book. A classification scheme is developed for factors or concepts related to income considerations. Some of the implications for expanding economic knowledge are discussed also.

Poverty is generally defined as an inadequate relative income level. While some persons receiving inadequate incomes may not be (or may not have a potential of being) economically productive, others are either "working poor" (underemployed or lacking necessary skills) or unemployed for various reasons. It is this last group, the workers with productivity to offer employers, that is of concern in this chapter.

A brief reminder here of the relationship between poverty and rural development will be useful, because development has implications for relative incomes and because past development has been instrumental in establishing the current situation. Legislation to implement rural development usually has been passed for the purpose of "rural job creation and increasing of rural farm and nonfarm income and business activity" (8, p. 1). The objective of development thus has revolved around economic well-being, which generally is determined by an area's total economic output, per capita income, or incidence of individual poverty.

While development policies and programs often are specific attempts to inject economic betterment, other activities also are categorized as

The author benefited from comments on this chapter by several readers, including K. C. Gibbs, J. D. Jansma, and G. D. Lynne.

development. These include programs related to housing, public facilities and services, and land use. Economists should be aware of the socioeconomic implications of all public decisions (and especially those related to development), even if the decision is a common one of spending tax dollars for a new sewage system or a new road. Such an expenditure of funds may preclude an expenditure for services related to poverty needs.

Development always requires resources and yields economic change; change that has implications for the existing distribution of incomes. Rural development can be directly related to the rural poverty question in the sense that under existing market situations the gains of development could be distributed *away* from a particular group or sector. Perhaps these implications should be considered more directly in community development programs that are not explicitly classified as poverty programs. Poverty is not solely a consequence of previous rural development efforts but some direct relationships may exist. Not considering the poverty implications of all rural development programs has seriously diminished the impact of specific poverty programs.

CLASSIFICATION OF FACTORS POTENTIALLY RELATED TO

INCOME. Brief clarification is given here for the definition of certain terms within the discipline of economics that are sometimes confused.

Assumptions: assumptions are those relationships and conditions relative to potential (significant or insignificant) factors or conditions under which results of a conceptual framework, theory, or model will be as postulated. Some of these factors are assumed to be relevant to the analysis and are included in the model. Factors are not discipline-specific.

Specified assumptions: specified assumptions are those relationships and conditions that have been stated as constituting a portion of the applicable body of knowledge or model of current concern. They include also the implicit assumptions that can be derived from the stated and unstated assumptions recognized as part of the conventional wisdom. Often it is considered unnecessary to restate a commonly accepted condition. However, an unstated condition could be an assumption so far buried in the historical development of the conventional wisdom that it has become, in effect, unrecognized and potentially damaging.

Unspecified assumptions: unspecified assumptions are those conditions and relationships that are unrecognized in the case at hand (for example, a particular economic model purporting to explain income levels). An unrecognized factor is an unknown factor that has not been previously incorporated into the specialized body of knowledge. It may well be outside the subject matter expertise of the economist since factors are not discipline-specific.

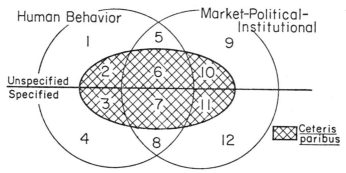

Human Behavior Assumptions
1. Unspecified: not significant
2. Unspecified: has a significant influence that is unrecognized—in effect, a **ceteris paribus** (held constant) condition
3. Specified: has a recognized significant influence but is (perhaps temporarily) held constant for analytical purposes
4. Specified: either has no significant influence or, if significant, is included in the model as a variable.

Joint Human Behavior and Market-Political-Institutional Assumptions
5. Unspecified: not significant
6. Unspecified: significant but unrecognized
7. Specified: significant but held constant for analysis
8. Specified: either not significant or, if significant, included in model as a variable.

Market-Political-Institutional Assumptions
9. Unspecified: not significant
10. Unspecified: significant but unrecognized
11. Specified: significant but held constant for analysis
12. Specified: either not significant or, if significant, included in model as a variable.

FIG. 1.1. *Classification of assumptions about factors in the social sciences related to income.*

Ceteris paribus: ceteris paribus conditions refer to those factors held at a constant or unchanging level for purposes of investigation or interpretation. Some of the economic assumptions concerning factors are that they are held constant; hence *ceteris paribus* conditions are a subset of assumptions.

With the above definitions a Venn diagram can be constructed (Fig. 1.1). In many situations where the conventional wisdom is incomplete, the argument pictured in this diagram may be applied. The underlying argument is not limited to income or to the discipline of economics. As used here, the diagram first postulates that all factors potentially related to income can be divided into two sectors: human behavior and market-political-institutional (all other) factors. Some factors may not be readily categorized as belonging solely to either of the two, and therefore the two classification sets intersect. Other divisions, categories, or sectors can be postulated, but the focus of this book on the nature of human behavior and the poverty question suggests this classification scheme for illustration purposes.

Since *ceteris paribus* conditions were defined as a subset of assumptions, these conditions can be represented by a smaller ellipse placed within the two larger circles. Thus *ceteris paribus* conditions can refer to human behavior factors, market-political-institutional factors, and combinations of the two.

Figure 1.1 now allows any potential factor to be held constant as a *ceteris paribus* condition, incorporated into a theory or model as a hypothetically significant variable, or dismissed as insignificant or irrelevant to the case at hand.

The specified assumptions of mainline economists, otherwise referred to as the conventional wisdom, constitute all factors recognized by economists as potentially related to income. However, since economics is not all-encompassing, the potential factors outside the conventional wisdom are unspecified. This leads to the division of the Venn diagram of Fig. 1.1 into specified and unspecified assumptions about conditions and relationships concerning income questions.

Some assumptions concerning potential factors have been specified by economists (explicitly or implicitly) while others have thus far not been recognized or incorporated into the body of economic knowledge. Some of these assumptions may be irrelevant to explaining income distributions. Others within the unspecified realm may be significant but are unrecognized. If a factor is significant but unrecognized, then it is an unspecified *ceteris paribus* condition. While this unspecified variable is not consciously held constant, its unrecognized influence on the model is such that empirical estimates will be as postulated only when this variable does not change or fluctuate.

To repeat, this diagram is not discipline-specific. The unrecognized factors must be brought to the economist's attention by other disciplines. Economics as a discipline does not exist apart from other disciplines; it is not a closed system. "Predictions in economics are therefore subject to an unspecified *ceteris paribus* condition" (1, p. 164). Discovery of these unspecified conditions and the attendant implications are important areas of inquiry. Although the limit to potential conditions is unknown, the direction of improvement is toward incorporating or recognizing as many of the relevant conditions as possible.

The questions posed in this book may be summarized briefly:
1. What are the assumptions of the conventional economic wisdom?
2. What are the implications of radical economic thought?
3. What contributions are possible from other social science disciplines such as sociology or anthropology?

Represented in the authorships are two noneconomic social science disciplines: sociology and anthropology. Each deals primarily with the realm of the unspecified (unrecognized) in economic models, although some previous interaction with these disciplines has influenced the content of economics. The primary contribution from these disciplines is to increase the scope of economics to include potentially significant factors currently unrecognized.

Current anthropological thought as represented by the paper by Padfield and Young has meaningful implications for economic knowledge in essentially all the unspecified areas. Likewise, an understanding of sociological concepts as represented in the paper by Bould-Van Til increases comprehension of the individual or family in the community and society.

The recognition of unspecified assumptions, however, is not seen as the only need for improvement. Radical economic theory, for example, holds that many specified assumptions of conventional economic theory lack substance or assume away the problem (5, p. 159). To a degree, the radical economist makes statements about unstated but implicitly specified assumptions that have been so far buried in the historical development of conventional economic wisdom that the assumptions have become unrecognized and, in effect, unspecified. Additionally, the radical school comments about some factors unrecognized by the more conventional practitioner of economics. These factors may be broadly classified as the importance of interconnections among all events and institutions, inherent conflicts at the heart of every social problem, and the role of constant change, evolution, and development (7, pp. 6–10). In fact, the radical critique brings into focus a major problem with the Venn diagram in Fig. 1.1: it is static rather than dynamic. Scientific endeavors constantly change the unknown, and the process of change is crucial.

Assumptions that are necessary in one type of research endeavor may not be appropriate for another, and this becomes more critical when the assumptions are unrecognized or unstated. Input from outside disciplines and nonconventional economists may assist in improving the predictive power of economic theory by improving the assumptions related to income levels and distributions. Many of these assumptions center around the concepts of rational "economic men," independent utility functions, perfect knowledge, initial ownership of resources, resource mobility, divisibility of inputs, and externalities.

One type of economic assumption we can question concerns human behavior. When production function analysis relates to physical inputs, many aspects of human behavior are not relevant to the analysis, and the assumptions about human behavior are unstated and usually unnecessary. But when analysis includes the human input, human behavior assumptions become important and perhaps extremely crucial in policy related research. The dynamics of the unspecified assumptions about human behavior are perhaps such that predictive models based on past behavior may not be accurate or even precise. Human input analysis requires consideration of such questions as the conceptual validity of the homogeneous input, the distribution of traits and characteristics, and identical responses to identical economic stimuli. Many of these factors enter the labor supply function and/or the laborer's *demand* for experiences that will increase his productivity or earning capacity (4, pp. 10–11).

It is my belief that new progress on income considerations will occur in the discipline of economics through serious questioning of the conventional wisdom and further inter- or multidisciplinary exploration of the unrecognized relevant factors. Economists may still perform effective partial equilibrium analyses relevant to income considerations without such exploration. But the marginal returns from such activity may be relatively low. Poverty is a problem in this nation, and some say social and economic inequity is approaching a crisis stage. This book implies that economic knowledge to solve problems is also in an incomplete or crisis stage.

> All crises begin with the blurring of a paradigm and the consequent loosening of the rules for normal research . . . and all crises close with the emergence of a new candidate for paradigm and with the subsequent battle over its acceptance. (2, p. 85)

In terms of the above quotation, the three conceptual frameworks examined in this book could be called competing paradigms. They are (1) neoclassical economics, (2) radical economics, and (3) social marginalization. The following chapters considered as a whole will help uncover the extent to which these frameworks are competing paradigms. Perhaps more important is the relationship among the frameworks concerning policy implications (Fig. 1.2). Are policy implications of these three frameworks unrelated? (See part A of Fig. 1.2.) Do they overlap in some respects? (See part B.) Is neoclassical economics a subset of radical economics or vice versa? (See part C.) How does social marginalization intersect with these two? Is radical economics unrelated, and are neoclassical economics and social marginalization closely related? (See Part D of Fig. 1.2.) The possibilities are many.

These questions need to be answered. No one paradigm should be dismissed before the evidence is considered, for each may have significantly different policy implications. Although other bodies of knowledge deserve scrutiny, the concern in this book is to consider the validity of these three conceptual frameworks and to what degree they are related to each other or to some grander scheme. The important goal is improvement of economic knowledge.

ECONOMIC KNOWLEDGE IS POWER. Improvement of economic knowledge is important: first, improved models may be constructed; second, more effective programs may be devised; third, a potential crisis of inequity may be averted.

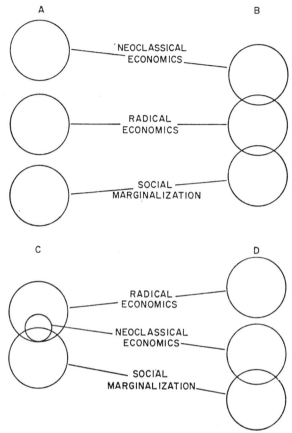

FIG. 1.2. *Policy implications of three conceptual frameworks: how much difference?*

Improved economic knowledge or information may increase the ability to influence income positions significantly, first, by increasing information concerning the individual, social, economic, and political obstacles confronting the poor. Programs also can be improved to serve the poor who are unable to help themselves because of physical infirmity, age, or other unavoidable circumstances. Moreover, the poor can help themselves when they possess greater effective economic knowledge, or power. The poor person, for example, would have more influence over his situation through greater productivity (attained through various learning experiences), increased knowledge of events influencing his income stream, and ability to use this knowledge (moving to the city, training) to better his economic condition. New information "changes the relative power of individuals" (6, p. 230). Individuals become better able to control and influence their economic status.

As public officials or professionals involved in the generation or extension of knowledge, our actions are not neutral. Increased knowledge has the capacity to change lives.

> It is into this context that researchers, teachers, and extension workers, as providers and disseminators of information, are thrust. Willingly or unwillingly, the purveyor of information is cast into the role of an active modifier of power relationships. This being so, it behooves him to consider carefully which kinds of power modifications are consistent with his personal morality, his professional ethics, and the social function of his host institution. (6, p. 230)

In conclusion, social scientists must decrease the disruptive influence of unspecified conditions and make the specified ones more relevant; we cannot simply assume away the problem in the "publish or perish" race to survive in academia. The contribution of radical economists at the least is to cause concern that traditional analyses limit the conclusions to the trivial (3, p. 289) or "kill all relevance and we are left with mere mechanics" (5, p. 159). As educators and providers of information we should continually be aware that our activities are not neutral, that scientific neutrality is a fallacy.

REFERENCES

(1). Grunberg, Emile, "The Meaning of Scope and External Boundaries of Economics," in Sherman Roy Krupp, ed., *The Structure of Economic Science*, Englewood Cliffs, N.J.: Prentice-Hall, 1966.

(2). Kuhn, Thomas, "Paradigms and Some Misinterpretations of Science," in Dudley Sapere, ed., *The Philosophical Problems of Natural Science*, New York: Macmillan, 1965.

(3). Michelson, Stephen, "Distribution Issues: Trends and Policies—Discussion," *American Economic Review* 2 (60): 283–85.

(4). Mincer, Jacob, "The Distribution of Labor Incomes: A Survey with Reference to the Human Capital Approach," *Journal of Economic Literature* 7 (1): 1–26.

(5). Nell, Edward, "Cyclical Accumulation: A Marxian Model of Development," *American Economic Review* 63 (2): 152–59.

(6). Randall, Alan, "Information, Power, and Academic Responsibility," *American Journal of Agricultural Economics* 56 (2): 227–34, May 1974.

(7). Sherman, Howard, *Radical Political Economy: Capitalism and Socialism from a Marxist Humanist Perspective*, New York: Basic Books, 1972.

(8). U.S. Senate, 92nd Congress, 2nd Session, Committee on Agriculture and Forestry, *Rural Development Legislation as Amended by the Rural Development Act of 1972: Analysis and Explanation*, Public Law 92–149, Washington: USGPO, December 12, 1972.

Poverty and rural underdevelopment in the United States: where do we stand?

CARLTON G. DAVIS

THE WORD *poverty* has assumed a multiplicity of meanings at different times and places. Moreover, the term now has different meanings for different persons even within the same academic discipline. The latter trend is growing among social scientists and public agencies concerned with social welfare. However, the general consensus as revealed in the literature is that the term *poverty* attains pragmatic and relevant dimensions only within a relative framework. One economist states:

> It is relative rather than absolute, it is essentially qualitative rather than quantitative; it is to a certain extent subjective rather than objective; it refers to the general condition of man rather than a specific facet of his existence. (7, p. 26)

Another economist observes, "it is primarily for this reason that in the richest country in the world [the United States], one person in eight can be designated as poor" (8, p. 1).

POVERTY DEFINITIONS. Poverty, as far as it can be measured, can be defined as a general lack of those goods and services believed necessary for an adequate standard of living (8, p. 2). A major problem arises, however, when attempts are made to define "adequate" in concrete terms. Standards of adequacy tend to vary in relation to the society's general level of economic well-being and prevailing attitudes toward economic deprivation. The net effect of these two societal elements is to encourage widely divergent definitions of family and individual basic needs.

11

TABLE 2.1.   Poverty income limits for continental U.S., 1973.[a]

Family Size	Residence	
	Nonfarm	Farm
Number		
1	$2,100	$1,800
2	2,725	2,325
3	3,450	2,950
4	4,200	3,575
5	4,925	4,200
6	5,550	4,725
7[b]	6,200	5,275

Source: (20).
[a] 1972 price levels.
[b] Income limits for families of more than seven persons are determined by adding $650 and $550 for each additional person for the nonfarm and farm sectors, respectively.

Poverty is defined by the U.S. Department of Labor in terms of the adequacy of current family income in meeting a constant absolute standard of food consumption. The poverty income line is based primarily on family size, with adjustment for farm and nonfarm residency. In the Census Bureau's definition, additional adjustment is made for sex and age differences of the head of household. Table 2.1 shows the Labor Department's poverty limits for the continental United States for 1973 (a different set of poverty income limits are computed for Hawaii and Alaska).

Aggregate changes in the number of poor are used as social indicators of welfare gain or loss. For example, the Census Bureau estimated the number of poor to be 39.8 million in 1960. This represented 22.2 percent of the total population. The official count of the poor in 1970 was estimated at 25.4 million, or 12.6 percent of the total population. A ratio of 1 poor person in 4 in 1960 compared with 1 in 8 in 1970 would generally be interpreted as a major gain in the federal "war on poverty."

Even within the context of these social indicators, some observers are quick to point out a need for cautious pessimism about actual welfare gains. First, aggregate changes in the number of poor tend to mask significant movements of persons in and out of poverty ranks. For example, 37 percent of the poor moved out of poverty in 1969, but 34 percent of the poor in 1969 were not in poverty in 1968 (8, p. 7). Second, other measures of poverty that go beyond the income based component show no such decline in the absolute number of poor or in the incidence of poverty. Third, the decade-long trend of annual reductions in the absolute number of poor persons came to a halt in 1969. The number actually increased between 1969 and 1971 before declining slightly again in 1972 and 1973.

In general the controversy surrounding the relevance of official poverty definitions and statistics focuses on two central issues: (1) whether official poverty definitions and statistics reflect the full extent of social and economic deprivation, and (2) whether the static nature of assumptions underlying official income based poverty definitions can reflect the dynamic nature of welfare changes over time.

Much of the controversy is related to growing recognition of the multidimensional characteristic of poverty. It has been suggested that the complexity of current poverty status can only be appreciated if viewed within the six broad dimensions of (1) income, (2) assets or wealth, (3) access to basic services, (4) social mobility and education, (5) political power, and (6) status and satisfaction (14). Thus emphasis on any *single* dimension could either understate or overstate the magnitude of the poverty problem, in spite of high correlation between the various dimensions. The general consensus among students of the poverty question is that current poverty statistics, with their primary focus in income, tend to understate the extent of social and economic deprivation. Obviously need exists for a more sensitive and pragmatic definition of poverty, if genuine social welfare gains are to be measured.

The immediate task, however, is to review and evaluate the implications of the major issues surrounding official poverty statistics. Such a review and evaluation naturally draws on the pioneering empirical work of J. Patrick Madden (9, 10, 11, 12, 13). In his writing on the social indicators of welfare gains, Madden proposes two criteria for evaluating poverty statistics (9, p. 3):

1. How accurately do the poverty data for a given year represent the degree of perceived deprivation in that year?

2. How well do the trends in poverty data reflect the changes in the social welfare over time?

Madden applies these criteria to the premises underlying calculation of existing poverty lines. In his view, the four key premises (9, p. 5) are:

1. In the base year, 1963, a family of a given size at the poverty line has enough income to afford the USDA economy food plan for that size family.

2. A family at this subsistence level will spend one-third of its income on food. This expenditure, in relation to the first premise, generates a base year poverty line of three times the USDA economy food budget.

3. Farm families need only 85 percent as much income as nonfarm families of the same size.

4. With the 1963 base year as the starting point, annual changes in purchasing power of the poverty thresholds are reflected in adjustments made for changes in the Consumer Price Index.

Madden's study concluded that the first premise has major shortcomings with respect to his two welfare measurement criteria (9, p. 19). One shortcoming stems from the discrepancy between the historical expenditure pattern of low income families and the assumption of the USDA economy food plan. He argues that, by definition, the poor lack enough resources to afford an adequate diet, since the poverty line is based on the value of the economy food budget. The assumptions of the economy food plan are that the diet represents consumption for short term emergency situations, and that homemakers possess the necessary purchasing knowledge and cooking skills to obtain and prepare the proper foods in an economical and palatable manner for the family. These assumptions are clearly unrealistic in terms of actual circumstances and the observed behavior of homemakers.

Some studies on food expenditure patterns show that low income families with food expenditures at the economy food plan level in nine out of ten cases have poor diets according to the National Research Council allowances of the seven key nutrients (6). Other studies indicate that the incidence of low food expenditures is severe at the lower end of the income continuum and declines gradually in intensity as income rises above the poverty level. Specifically, studies have shown, 80 percent of families with budgets less than three-fourths of the poverty line spent less on food than the economy food budget; 63 percent of families just below the poverty line had food expenditures below the economy food budget, compared with 42 percent of those just above the poverty line; and not until income reached twice the amount at the poverty line did the incidence of low food expenditure drop below 10 percent (9, p. 20). These findings increase the number of questions regarding the reliability of data indicating welfare gains through absolute income changes.

The second premise essentially fixes the base year poverty income threshold of a given family size at three times the value of the USDA economy food budget. The original one-third expenditure ratio was obtained from a 1955 national survey of family expenditure pattern. Thus the ratio was explicitly indicative of a national average. The national average ratio was then assumed to be representative of low income households. A major shortcoming of this premise is that it fixes the annual food expenditure of the poor at the 1955 national average of income expenditure on food. Thus if average income level rises over time and the proportion spent on food declines as reflected in Engel's Law, then the poverty income threshold would rise proportionally. But this certainly has not been the case.

(Engel's Law asserts that the lower the family money-income the greater the percentage of that income spent for food and that the percentage of family income spent for food is therefore the best measure for determining levels of living.)

It is probably of some significance, however, that at least one empirical study of low income household expenditure patterns indicated a spending rate of 30 percent on food, somewhat less than a third of the household income (2). Furthermore, this study by Carlin found significant variability in the food-income ratio, which is important for gauging poverty thresholds since even small variations in the ratio would have major impacts on threshold levels. A major finding from the Carlin study was that an income higher than the established poverty line would be required to afford the economy food plan, given the observed expenditure pattern of low income households.

In light of the questions about the validity of the foregoing assumptions, the adequacy of the level of living of poor families, as represented by the poverty line, assumes great significance. In addition, when dynamic changes over time are ignored by the assumption of a fixed ratio, poverty appears to be static, a condition that could not be further from the worsening plight of the poor in the real world.

The third premise does not appear to cause a major measurement problem in evaluating the relevance of current poverty data. Empirical estimates of farm-nonfarm purchasing power support the premise that a farm-nonfarm ratio of .85 is an adequate reflection of equivalent levels of cost of living for broad categories of farm and nonfarm residents. Possible questions might involve the tendency to mask major variation in the ratio in relation to varying degrees of urbanization and differences in family size.

The fourth premise does not appear to represent any major shortcoming that would tend to invalidate the income poverty indicator of welfare status. One minor deficiency, however, is its failure to reflect regional and locational differences in cost of living. Adjustments made in the consumer price index to reflect these differences would tend to equalize measurements of levels of living and purchasing power in different areas.

Definitional Issues and Welfare Implications. Critical evaluation of official poverty statistics within a social welfare context reveals a number of definitional deficiencies. According to Madden's first welfare criterion, current income poverty data must be judged as inadequate. The official poverty line fails to reflect the true magnitude of either absolute or relative deprivation. On an absolute basis true levels of economic deprivation in our society appear to be above those levels established in official poverty thresholds. On a relative basis the official statistics are equally inadequate, since they fail to reflect rising economic standards of society as these standards might be reflected in increased aspirations and expectations of the poor. Current definitions must also be judged in terms of the second criterion. Madden argues:

> Deprivation is a continuum in several dimensions, such as hunger, sickness, and high death rates. Conditions so widespread among the poor are also visited upon the near poor. Thus, even in an absolute sense, the poverty statistics tend to understate the degree of deprivation associated with inadequate income. While the official poverty statistics serve rather crudely

for the limited purpose of reflecting the degree of absolute deprivation in any one year, these statistics are grossly unsatisfactory as indicators of trends over time in the well-being of society. (9, p. 23)

USE OF POVERTY STATISTICS. In this chapter discussion of social welfare gains is constrained by the limits of available poverty statistics. Use of these statistics may seem contradictory to the preceding evaluation of their inadequacy in measuring social welfare. However, the approach is rationalized on the basis of two considerations. First, despite the weaknesses of current poverty statistics, the virtual absence of acceptable alternative quantitative poverty measures makes any other measurement questionable. Second, recognition of the *direction* of biases in current poverty statistics could encourage formulation of political goals and timetables for national poverty reduction. On the latter consideration, the observation of Tobin is insightful:

> The Federal "war on poverty," whatever else it has accomplished, has established an official measure of the prevalence of poverty in the United States. Adoption of a specific quantitative measure, however arbitrary and debatable, will have durable and far-reaching political consequences. Administrations will be judged by their success or failure in reducing the officially measured prevalence of poverty. So long as any families are found below the official poverty line, no politician will be able to claim victory in the war on poverty or ignore the repeated solemn acknowledgments of society's obligation to its poorer members. A similarly binding commitment to a specific measure of full employment, the adoption of 4 percent unemployment as the "interim target" of the Kennedy administration in 1961, strengthened the political forces on the side of expansionary fiscal and monetary policy in the early 1960's. (4, p. 83)

As stated earlier, concentration on income poverty changes in evaluating social welfare tends to understate both the magnitude of poverty and its multidimensional aspects. An inherent danger exists in any policy or program that overemphasizes the income component of deprivation to the exclusion of other noneconomic components. Often overlooked, however, is the fact that the current income definition of poverty does not inherently exclude noneconomic or cultural considerations as they relate to low income groups. As Lampman points out:

> What it does ignore is a "culture of poverty," i.e., a behavior pattern manifesting alienation from the rest of the community and a short time horizon, which may persist beyond the time income is low. (7, p. 54)

Lampman further argues that income poverty definitions have the advantage over other definitions in that they can be more properly and readily *indicated.* However, current definitions operate under the assumption that changes in income will cause changes in the psychological, social, and political dimension of poverty. As such, the definitions assume that "the subculture of poverty is more often an adaptation to limited opportunity than it is an independent and causal agent of low income" (7, p. 54).

In spite of the limitations of income poverty statistics in portraying the extent of economic and social deprivation, a review of such data can, at least, indicate certain changes in terms of general welfare status. Wherever possible, attempts will be made to review other dimensions of the poverty problem as a means of rounding out the poverty picture.

POVERTY IN AMERICA, 1959–73: AN OVERVIEW

Poverty Incidence. Tables 2.2 to 2.5 show the relative poverty status of persons, percentage distribution by year, race, family status, and place of residence, as well as other selected socioeconomic characteristics for the period 1959–73. (At 1973 prices, the 1973 poverty income threshold separating the "poor" from the "nonpoor" was $4,540 for a nonfarm family of four. It was $4,275 in 1972 and $2,973 in 1959.) Figure 2.1 shows the national trend in the number of poor individuals and the associated annual poverty incidence for the same period. The absolute number of poor persons was 39.4 million in 1959. This figure represented a national poverty incidence of 22.4 percent for that period. Table 2.2 and Fig. 2.1, read in conjunction, dramatize the national poverty picture over the last decade and a half. Beginning in 1960 the absolute number of poor persons declined each year until 1969. In those 9 years the number of poor persons dropped by almost 16 million (from 39.8 to 24.1 million). For the same period, the national incidence of poverty was reduced from 22. 2 percent to 12.1 percent.

It is significant that the most rapid rate of poverty reduction occurred during the mid-1960s. This period was one of major expansion in economic activities and an associated expansion in aggregate employment. During the period the level of unemployment was reduced from more than 6 percent to less than 4 percent (9, p. 2). The recession of 1970–71 and the accompanying increase in the level of unemployment resulted in an increase over the 1969 level of the absolute number of poor persons as well as the incidence of poverty. Specifically, the absolute number of poor persons increased from 24.1 million in 1969 to 25.4 million in 1970, but remained almost unchanged (25.5 million) for 1971. The statistics for 1972 show a slight reduction in the absolute number of poor (24.4 million), as well as in the incidence of poverty (11.9 percent). According to the March 1974 Bureau of the Census Current Population Survey, 22.9 million persons were in poverty in 1973, which represents an incidence of 11.1 percent. The 1973 figure is actually 1.5 million below the 1972 figure, and about 4.8 million families and 4.6 million un-

TABLE 2.2. Persons below poverty level by race and family status, U.S., 1959-72.

No. below poverty level (*thous*) and %

Race and Year	All Persons No.	%	Persons in Families — Total No.	%	Family head Total No.	%	Family head Nonfarm No.	%	Family head Farm No.	%	Related children under 18 years No.	%	Other family members No.	%	Unrelated individuals 14 years and over No.	%
Total																
1959	39,490	22.4	34,562	20.8	8,320	18.5	6,624	16.1	1,696	44.6	17,208	26.9	9,034	15.9	4,928	46.1
1960	39,851	22.2	34,925	20.7	8,243	18.1	6,649	15.8	1,594	45.7	17,288	26.5	9,394	16.2	4,926	45.2
1961	39,628	21.9	34,509	20.3	8,391	18.1	7,044	16.4	1,347	38.6	16,577	25.2	9,541	16.5	5,119	45.9
1962	38,625	21.0	33,623	19.4	8,077	17.2	7,004	16.0	1,073	33.5	16,630	24.7	8,916	15.1	5,002	45.4
1963	36,436	19.5	31,498	17.9	7,554	15.9	6,467	14.6	1,087	35.1	15,691	22.8	8,253	13.8	4,938	44.2
1964	36,055	19.0	30,912	17.4	7,160	15.0	6,058	13.5	1,102	35.6	15,736	22.7	8,016	13.3	5,143	42.7
1965	33,185	17.3	28,358	15.8	6,721	13.9	5,841	12.9	880	29.8	14,388	20.7	7,249	11.8	4,827	39.8
1966a	28,510	14.7	23,809	13.1	5,784	11.8	5,211	11.3	573	20.6	12,146	17.4	5,879	9.5	4,701	38.3
1967	27,769	14.2	22,771	12.5	5,667	11.4	5,093	10.8	574	21.4	11,427	16.3	5,677	9.1	4,998	38.1
1968	25,389	12.8	20,695	11.3	5,047	10.0	4,553	9.5	494	18.8	10,739	15.3	4,909	7.8	4,694	34.0
1969	24,289	12.2	19,438	10.5	4,950	9.7	4,522	9.3	428	17.4	9,821	14.1	4,667	7.3	4,851	33.6
1969b	24,147	12.1	19,175	10.4	5,008	13.8	4,582	9.3	426	17.4	9,501	13.8	4,667	7.2	4,972	34.0
1970	25,420	12.6	20,330	10.9	5,260	10.1	4,822	9.7	438	18.6	10,235	14.9	4,835	7.4	5,090	32.9
1971	25,559	12.5	20,405	10.8	5,303	10.0	4,851	9.6	452	17.4	10,344	15.1	4,757	7.2	5,154	31.6
1972	24,460	11.9	19,577	10.3	5,075	9.3	4,753	9.2	323	12.8	10,082	14.9	4,420	6.6	4,883	29.0
White																
1959	28,484	18.1	24,443	16.5	6,185	15.2	4,915	13.1	1,270	38.0	11,386	20.6	6,872	13.3	4,041	44.1
1960	28,309	17.8	24,262	16.2	6,115	14.9	4,919	12.9	1,196	39.0	11,229	20.0	6,918	13.3	4,047	43.0
1961	27,890	17.4	23,747	15.8	6,205	14.8	5,162	13.3	1,043	33.3	10,614	18.7	6,928	13.3	4,143	43.2
1962	26,672	16.4	22,613	14.7	5,887	13.9	5,090	12.9	797	27.5	10,382	17.9	6,344	12.0	4,059	42.7
1963	25,238	15.3	21,149	13.6	5,466	12.8	4,610	11.6	856	30.5	9,749	16.5	5,934	11.0	4,089	42.0
1964	24,957	14.9	20,716	13.2	5,258	12.2	4,380	10.9	878	31.2	9,573	16.1	5,885	10.8	4,241	40.7
1965	22,496	13.3	18,508	11.7	4,824	11.1	4,163	10.2	661	24.6	8,595	14.4	5,089	9.2	3,988	38.1
1966a	19,290	11.3	15,430	9.7	4,106	9.3	3,685	8.9	421	16.5	7,204	12.1	4,120	7.4	3,860	36.1
1967	18,983	11.0	14,851	9.2	4,056	9.0	3,610	8.5	446	18.1	6,729	11.3	4,066	7.2	4,132	36.5
1968	17,395	10.0	13,546	8.4	3,616	8.0	3,225	7.5	391	15.9	6,373	10.7	3,557	6.3	3,849	32.2

TABLE 2.2 (Continued)

			Persons in Families					Related children under 18 years		Other family members		Unrelated individuals 14 years and over	
	All Persons		Total		Family head Nonfarm		Farm							
Race and Year	No.	%	No.	%	No.	%	No.	%	No.	%	No.	%	No.	%
					No. below poverty level (thous) and %									
White														
1969	16,671	9.5	12,709	7.8	3,555	7.7	3,206	7.3	349	15.1	5,777	9.8	3,377	5.8	3,962	31.8
1969[b]	16,659	9.5	12,623	7.8	3,575	7.7	3,229	7.3	346	15.1	5,667	9.7	3,381	5.8	4,036	32.1
1970	17,484	9.9	13,323	8.1	3,708	8.0	3,351	7.5	357	16.2	6,138	10.5	3,477	5.9	4,161	30.8
1971	17,780	9.9	13,566	8.2	3,751	7.9	3,382	7.5	369	15.2	6,341	10.9	3,474	5.8	4,214	29.6
1972	16,203	9.0	12,268	7.4	3,441	7.1	3,171	6.9	270	11.3	5,784	10.1	3,043	5.1	3,935	27.1
Negro & Other Races														
1959	11,006	56.2	10,119	56.0	2,135	50.4	1,709	45.3	426	91.8	5,822	66.7	2,162	42.5	887	57.4
1960	11,542	55.9	10,663	55.7	2,128	49.0	1,730	44.2	398	93.4	6,059	66.6	2,476	43.3	879	59.3
1961	11,738	56.1	10,762	55.6	2,186	49.0	1,882	45.9	304	85.4	5,963	65.7	2,613	44.8	976	62.7
1962	11,953	55.8	11,010	55.3	2,190	48.0	1,914	45.0	276	90.2	6,248	66.4	2,572	43.2	943	62.1
1963	11,198	51.0	10,349	50.5	2,088	43.7	1,857	41.4	231	81.3	5,942	60.9	2,319	38.9	849	58.3
1964	11,098	49.6	10,196	49.1	1,902	40.0	1,678	37.5	224	79.2	6,163	61.5	2,131	35.7	902	55.0
1965	10,689	47.1	9,850	46.8	1,897	39.7	1,678	37.2	219	82.0	5,793	57.3	2,160	35.3	839	50.7
1966[a]	9,220	39.8	8,379	38.9	1,678	33.9	1,526	32.2	152	68.2	4,942	48.2	1,759	27.7	841	53.1
1967	8,786	37.2	7,920	36.3	1,611	32.1	1,483	30.9	128	58.4	4,698	44.9	1,611	25.3	866	48.2
1968	7,994	33.5	7,149	32.4	1,431	28.2	1,328	27.1	103	58.9	4,366	41.6	1,352	20.9	845	45.7
1969	7,618	31.1	6,729	29.9	1,395	26.7	1,316	26.0	79	51.6	4,044	38.0	1,290	19.4	889	44.9
1969[b]	7,488	31.0	6,552	29.6	1,433	26.9	1,353	26.2	79	51.5	3,834	37.7	1,286	19.4	936	45.5
1970	7,936	32.0	7,007	30.7	1,552	28.1	1,471	27.4	81	55.5	4,097	39.6	1,358	19.5	929	46.7
1971	7,780	30.9	6,839	29.7	1,552		1,469	26.8	83	50.3	4,003	38.7	1,283	18.2	941	44.9
1972	8,257	31.9	7,309	31.0	1,634	27.7	1,582	27.4	53	41.1	4,298	41.3	1,377	19.0	948	40.9

Source: (19, pp. 381–82).
[a] Beginning 1966, data are based on revised methodology for processing income data.
[b] Beginning 1969, data are based on 1970 census population controls and therefore are not strictly comparable with data for earlier years.

19

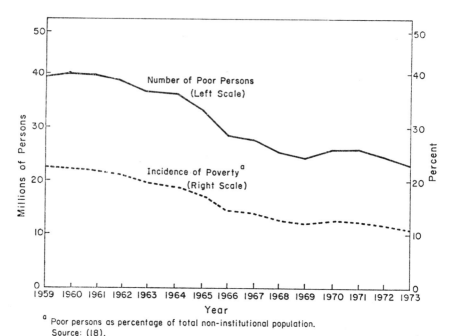

^a Poor persons as percentage of total non-institutional population.
Source: (18).

Fig. 2.1. *Persons below the poverty level and poverty incidence, U.S., 1959–73.*

related individuals were found to be below poverty income levels. Both figures were below the official 1972 levels (18).

Table 2.2 shows a 1959 poverty incidence of 20.8 percent for persons in families. The corresponding poverty incidence for this category of persons was 15.8 percent and 10.3 percent for the years 1965 and 1972, respectively. In 1973 the incidence (not shown in Table 2.2) was 8.8 percent (18). The table shows considerable variability in the poverty status of whites and nonwhites. In 1959 the incidence of poverty for all persons in families was 16.5 percent for whites compared with 56 percent for blacks and other races. Some evidence suggests a tendency for a more persistent poverty status among nonwhite families. Between 1959 and 1965 the poverty incidence among white persons in families declined from 16.5 percent to 11.7 percent. A corresponding decline for nonwhite families from 56 percent to 46.8 percent occurred in the same period. For the period 1965–72, the incidence among white families declined from 11.7 percent to 7.4 percent, while the associated change was from 46.8 percent to 31 percent among families of blacks and other races.

The tendency for persistent poverty status among nonwhite families is evidenced by comparative poverty incidences among the two racial groups at selected time intervals. The incidence among nonwhite families was almost three and a half times that of white families in 1959. By 1965 the incidence for nonwhite families had risen to exactly four times that of white families. Probably of greater significance, however, is the fact that despite rapid reduction in national poverty incidence since the mid-1960s, the incidence among nonwhite families was slightly over four times that of whites in 1972. Similar trends are exhibited for white and nonwhite family heads, related children under 18 years of age, and other family members and related individuals 14 years and over. Few changes have taken place in the relative positions between 1972 and 1973 (18).

Major differences exist in the incidence of poverty among geographical regions of the country (18). The incidence is highest in the South. In 1973 the incidence among persons and families of all races was 11.1 percent and 8.8 percent, respectively. The incidence among persons of all races was 9.1 percent for the North and West, compared with 15.3 percent for the South. The incidence among white persons was 7.6 percent in the North and West and 10.3 percent in the South, compared with 8.4 percent for white persons on a national basis. In contrast, blacks in the South had an incidence of 36.3 percent, compared with 25.9 percent for those in the North and West. The national poverty incidence among blacks was 31.4 percent. White families had a poverty incidence of 6.6 percent on a national basis, compared with 28.1 percent for blacks. However, poverty level white families had an incidence of 5.9 percent in the North and West, compared with 8.2 percent for those in the South. The poverty incidence among southern black families was 32.1 percent, compared with 23.6 percent for those in the North and West (18).

Characteristics of the Poor. One economist has commented that the nation's increasing affluence makes deprivation of those who remain poor both more noticeable and more poignant (8, p. 4). This observation makes it crucial to identify the major characteristics and correlates of poverty status. Table 2.3 shows some of the major socioeconomic and demographic characteristics associated with poverty status in 1971. The table indicates strong relationships among poverty status, age, race, sex of family head, work status, and educational attainment. The 1971 characteristics remain relevant for the present.

From the characteristics listed in the table, the poor can be divided into four major categories (8, p. 7):
1. The elderly poor
2. Working-age persons who are employed
3. Working-age persons who are unemployed
4. Children in poor families

THE ELDERLY POOR. The aged poor have the highest incidence of poverty of all age groups in the population. Poor persons age 65 and over accounted for 12 percent of that age group in families and 42 percent of that age group living alone (Table 2.3). In terms of national ratios, 1 person is in poverty for every 5 for that age group, compared with 1 person in 9 for individuals under the age of 65. Levitan suggests, however, that these ratios might actually understate the magnitude of economic deprivation among the elderly:

If anything, the situation may have been worse than these figures indicated, for the estimate of 4.3 million elderly poor excluded many living in

TABLE 2.3. Characteristics of the poor, U.S., 1971.

Characteristic	Persons in Families		Persons Living Alone	
		Poor as percent of total in group		Poor as percent of total in group
	(thous)		(thous)	
Total	20,405	11	5,154	32
Age Group				
Under 16	4,430	16	39	100
16–64	9,265	8	2,552	25
65 and over	1,710	12	2,563	42
Race				
White	13,566	8	4,214	30
Spanish surnamed	2,217	25	133	36
Black	6,530	31	866	46
Other	309	14	75	35
Family Status				
Head	5,303	10	. . .	. . .
Other adults	4,757	7	. . .	. . .
Children	10,344	15	. . .	. . .
Location of Residence				
Central city	6,693	12	2,218	29
Outside central city	4,450	6	1,199	26
Farm	1,934	20	133	37
Other nonmetropolitan	7,328	15	1,604	43
Sex of Family Head				
Male	12,608	8	1,543	24
Female	7,797	39	3,611	37
Work Experience of Family Head				
Worked full year, full time	1,084	3	292	5
Worked part year or part time	1,725	16	1,330	31
Did not work	2,422	30	3,530	54
Armed forces	72	7	3	3
Education of Family Head				
8 years or less	2,293	18	2,387	48
High school, 1–3 years	947	11	638	32
High school, 4 years	933	6	735	21
College, 1–3 years	268	5	244	17
College, 4 years or more	143	2	201	11

Source: (8, p. 6).

public homes and perhaps 2 million more whose own income would have classified them among the poor but who lived in nonpoor households. (8, p. 7)

Two characteristics appear to be highly correlated with the high poverty incidence among the elderly. These are relatively high levels of unemployment and underemployment, and of infirmities, which tend to affect their ability to seek or maintain gainful employment. Less than two-fifths of the elderly poor male family heads were reported to have worked in 1970, compared with more than 90 percent of younger male family heads. Less than one-fifth of the elderly poor female family heads worked during that year, compared with over two-thirds of the younger female heads (8, p. 9). Interestingly, the number of elderly poor declined by 10 percent between 1972 and 1973. This trend continues a decline observed between 1971 and 1972. However, the observed decline is apparently more a reflection of increases in Social Security benefits since 1970 than of any significant changes in employment status (18).

THE WORKING POOR. Unemployment is a major factor associated with poverty status. However, employment per se does not guarantee nonpoverty status (or for that matter adequate income, however one might define adequacy). It has been estimated that more than one-half of an estimated 5.2 million poor family heads were employed in 1971 (Tables 2.2 and 2.3). This included three-fourths of male family heads in the age group 25 to 64 and one-half of the female family heads in that age group (8, p. 11). Obviously the poverty status of these individuals could not be directly attributed to a lack of employment. In this case their status was more the result of low paying jobs and/or intermittent employment.

While unemployment per se is neither a *necessary* nor a *sufficient* condition for poverty status, unemployment must nevertheless be recognized as a major cause of poverty. The incidence of poverty among family heads who worked full-year on a full-time basis in 1971 was 3 percent for persons in families and 5 percent for persons living alone (Table 2.3). Comparable incidences were 16 percent and 31 percent for family heads who worked part time or part of the year and for persons living alone, respectively. In contrast, the levels were 30 percent and 54 percent for unemployed family heads and for unrelated individuals, respectively. (Within these employment categories, race further affects poverty status. The incidence of poverty among employed family heads and persons living alone is significantly higher for blacks than for whites. This is true for both full-year, full-time employment and for part-time employment. In 1973, the national incidence of poverty was 2.5 percent for all full-time employed family heads and 15.8 percent for those working 1 to 49 weeks. The incidence was 1.9 percent and 12.7 percent among white family heads for the two employment categories, respectively. In contrast, the incidence was 9.3 percent and 36.4 percent respectively among blacks [18].)

The mutual reinforcement of poverty and unemployment is an additional complication. Levitan argues:

> The poor are victims of forced idleness more frequently than the nonpoor. Poor family heads, both male and female, are about three times as likely to be unemployed as were nonpoor family heads. (8, p. 11)

Labor market imperfections and other institutional factors often operate to the disadvantage of the working poor. The combined effects of intermittent employment (as a result of voluntary or involuntary decisions or through disability and illness) and low paying jobs keep many of the working poor permanently locked into poverty situations. Primarily for these reasons, more than one-half of poor family heads and one-third of single poor persons who worked during 1971 remained in poverty. In many instances poverty families have two or more working members of the household. In 1971, for example, one-fourth of all poor families had two or more family members who worked during the year (8, p. 11). In 1973, 20 percent of all poor families had two or more earners (18).

The number of working poor has shown a declining trend since the 1960s. In fact, the rate of decline for this group was faster than the rate of decline for the total poverty population. Despite such status, however, poverty conditions existed in 1971 for 1.1 million family heads, with 4 million dependents, and another 300,000 unrelated individuals who were continually employed during the year (8, p. 12). In 1973, the designated 4.8 million poverty families contained 22.9 million persons (or about 4.7 persons per family). Among the heads of these poverty families, 2.4 million (or one-half) worked the preceding year. Slightly over 1 million of these poor heads of households worked for 50 to 52 weeks. The remaining 1.4 million worked from 1 to 49 weeks. For the latter category, part-year employment was attributed to "unemployment" by 33 percent of the household heads, and to "other" reasons by the remaining 67 percent. Interestingly, 879,000 household heads who worked full time were in poverty (18).

THE NONWORKING POOR. The poverty status of the majority of the nonworking poor can be directly attributed to lack of employment opportunities and the fact that a combination of circumstances make them unemployable. A large proportion of the nonworking poor are victims of varying degrees of physical and mental handicaps that affect their ability either to seek or maintain productive employment. For example, during 1971 more than three-fourths of all poor male family heads age 25 to 64 who were unemployed for the whole year attributed their unemployed status to illness or disability (8, p. 12).

The trend over the 1959–73 period has been a fairly rapid decline in the absolute number of poor families headed by a working male. However, there was a 14 percent *increase* in the number of poor families headed by a female. The implication is clear. The sex of the family head is an important variable in low income status, since families headed by females have become a greater proportion of all low income families. This group represented 23 percent of poverty status families in 1959; 43 percent in 1972; and 45 percent in 1973. Only 7 percent of families headed by females were *above* designated poverty income levels in 1959. The proportion had increased to only 9 percent by 1972 and remained at that level for 1973 (18).

The relatively high level of unemployment among female family heads is highly correlated with the incidence of poverty among this group. A high proportion of female family heads are unemployed for a good proportion of the year. In most cases their unemployment status is a result of child care, home responsibilities, or illness and disability. According to Levitan:

> The presence of children not only increases income needs and the likelihood of poverty, but also hinders the employment of mothers and therefore reduces (or limits) the income available to meet family needs. (8, p. 12)

It appears that the solution to poverty status for many of the non-working poor is not employment. While training and retraining programs can improve the skill structure and hence the employability of some members of this group, for the vast majority jobs are not the answer, and some form of income maintenance program must be devised.

CHILDREN IN POVERTY. The relationship between family size and economic deprivation is well established. The incidence of poverty among families is positively correlated with the number of children in those families. In 1971 2 of every 5 poor people were children under 16 years of age, and 1 of every 6 children was designated as being in poverty. Poverty statistics for 1971 show the following relationships between poverty status and family size: (a) for families with no children under the age of 18, 8 percent of those families were poor and another 3.8 percent were classified as "near poor"; (b) for families with 1 child, the percentages of poor and near poor were 8.4 and 3.1, respectively; (c) for families with 3 children, the percentages of poor and near poor were 12.1 and 4.9; (d) for families with 5 children, the percentages of poor and near poor families were 26.3 and 9.1 percent; and (e) for families with 6 or more children, the percentages of poor and near poor were 33.8 percent and 10.3 percent, respectively (8, p. 10).

As indicated earlier, the incidence of poverty among all families was 8.8 percent in 1973 (18). The incidence was 6.6 percent for white families and 28.1 percent for black families. The incidence among all families with no children was only 5.4 percent, compared with 14.5 percent for families with 3 to 4 children, and 29.5 percent for those with 5 or more children. Furthermore, significant differences appeared in the poverty status of black and white families in relation to number of children in the household. Only 4.7 percent of white families with no related children under 18 years of age were in poverty, compared with 15.4 percent of black families. The incidence for white families with 3 to 4 children was 10.1 percent, compared with 39.8 percent for black families. White families with 5 or more children had a poverty incidence of 19.2 percent, compared with 56.3 percent for black families (18).

POVERTY AND UNDERDEVELOPMENT IN NONMETROPOLI-TAN AREAS: A SPECIAL CASE. The 1967 Poverty Commission's findings regarding the relatively low quality of life in nonmetropolitan and rural America was a major factor in national reaffirmation of commitment to improving the level of living in these areas (21). In spite of the many and varied rural antipoverty programs implemented over the last decade, the net effect of such programs is increasingly being questioned (5, 15, 23). Growing recognition of the limited success of earlier programs in bringing about improvements in the quality of life in rural America was a major factor in the passage of the Rural Development Act in 1972. The act was intended as a reaffirmation of commitment to equalize the levels of living between rural and urban people. This reaffirmation was earlier made in Title IX of the Agricultural Act of 1970, which stated:

> The Congress commits itself to a sound balance between rural and urban America. The Congress considers this balance so essential to the peace, prosperity and welfare of all our citizens that the highest priority must be given to the revitalization and development of rural areas. (22, p. 40)

The 1970 and 1972 acts designated the Secretary of Agriculture as the President's rural development director. In addition to authorizing federal assistance for private and public rural development programs, Title V of the 1972 Rural Development Act authorized federal appropriations to land grant institutions for research focusing on rural development problems. However, funding levels and administrative policies have generated controversy about the seriousness of the government's commitment to rural development.

Recent national focus on the plight of nonmetropolitan and rural areas should not be interpreted as necessarily biased against metropolitan areas. The case for special attention being given to the problems of rural areas is well made by the Council for Agriculture Science and Technology in a recent report:

Rural development is a policy goal. As such it is based on value judgments that human resources in rural as well as other sectors should be fully employed at a reasonable wage level, and that unemployable persons should be provided buying power for a decent living standard. The rural development concept is a response to the existence of large numbers of rural people who are unable to utilize their talents fully for lack of adequate employment and who consequently receive an inferior portion of the opportunities provided by our social system. The main premise of our

TABLE 2.4.   Persons below poverty level by residence, U.S., 1959–73.

Year	All Persons	Metropolitan	Nonmetropolitan
		(thous)	
1959	39,490	17,337	22,153
1960	39,851	. . .	. . .
1961	39,628	. . .	. . .
1962	38,625	. . .	. . .
1963	36,436	. . .	. . .
1964	36,055	. . .	. . .
1965	33,185	. . .	. . .
1966	38,510	. . .	. . .
1967	27,769	. . .	. . .
1968	25,389	12,871	12,518
1969	24,280	12,317	11,963
1970	25,520	13,378	12,142
1971	25,559	14,561	10,999
1972	24,460	14,508	9,952
1973	22,973	13,759	9,214
Percent of Persons in Each Category in Poverty, by Residence			
1959	22.4	15.3	33.2
1960	22.2	. . .	. . .
1961	21.9	. . .	. . .
1962	21.0	. . .	. . .
1963	19.5	. . .	. . .
1964	19.0	. . .	. . .
1965	17.3	. . .	. . .
1966	14.7	. . .	. . .
1967	14.2	. . .	. . .
1968	12.8	10.0	18.0
1969	12.2	9.5	17.1
1970	12.6	10.2	17.0
1971	12.5	. . .	. . .
1972	11.9	. . .	. . .
1973	11.1	9.7	14.0
Percent of All Persons in Poverty, by Residence			
1959	100	43.9	56.1
1968	100	50.7	49.3
1969	100	50.7	49.3
1970	100	52.4	47.6
1971	100	57.0	43.0
1972	100	59.3	40.7
1973	100	59.9	40.1

Source: (1, Table 4, p. 60; 18).

TABLE 2.5. Nonmetropolitan persons below poverty level by family status, U.S., 1959, 1968–73.

Year	Total Nonmetropolitan Persons in Poverty	Persons in Families							Unrelated Individuals 14 Years of Age and Older
		Total	Heads of families			Family members under 18 years of age	Other family members		
			Total	Nonfarm	Farm				
				(thous)					
1959	22,153	19,686	4,718	3,022	1,696	9,293	5,675		2,467
1968	12,518	10,765	2,629	2,135	494	5,257	2,879		1,753
1969	11,963	10,019	2,533	2,105	428	4,789	2,697		1,944
1970	12,142	10,322	2,561	2,125	436	5,080	2,681		1,820
1971	10,999	...	...	...	...	...	...		...
1972	9,952	...	...	...	...	...	...		...
1973	9,214	7,522	1,990	...	...	3,564	1,968		1,692

Source: (1, Table 4, p. 60; 18).

report is that the purpose of rural development programs is to serve people rather than places. Industrialization, new jobs, manpower training, education, health care delivery, housing, roads, and water and sewer systems are only means to the end of having a more effectively contributing rural citizenry. The resulting indirect benefits to other areas and population groups cause rural development to be in the broad national interest. (3, pp. 3–4)

Tables 2.4 and 2.5 provide some basic indicators of the relative income positions of metropolitan and nonmetropolitan areas from 1959 to 1973. The term *metropolitan* refers to all counties having a city of 50,000 or more. *Nonmetropolitan* refers to all counties not containing any city of more than 50,000. *Rural* refers to all open county areas and cities of less than 2,500 population. Focus on rural and nonmetropolitan areas provides a better picture of the plight of small cities than could be gained by examination of rural areas alone.

Table 2.4 shows that a dramatic decline has occurred in the absolute number of poor persons in nonmetropolitan areas since 1959 and that the incidence of poverty is higher in nonmetropolitan areas than in metropolitan areas. In 1973 nonmetropolitan residents made up 31 percent of the U.S. population, but they accounted for 40 percent of the U.S. poor (18). In addition, 14 percent of all poverty-income individuals were nonmetropolitan residents, compared with 9.7 percent among residents of metropolitan areas.

The majority of poverty-stricken nonmetropolitan residents are white. In 1973, 6.7 million nonmetropolitan poor were white, compared with 2.4 million blacks. However, the poverty incidence among black nonmetropolitan residents was almost 4 times as high as that of whites (41 percent for blacks, compared with 11 percent for whites). The majority of the poverty-stricken blacks are located in the South (18).

Slightly less than 2 million nonmetropolitan family heads were in poverty in 1973 (Table 2.5). Although the table does not show the poverty distribution among farm and nonfarm family heads, we may assume that a relatively small proportion of nonmetropolitan poverty family heads actually lives on farms. This assumption appears reasonable, since in 1970 only about 16 percent of such family heads actually lived on farms. The majority of the rural poor families were found in small towns and cities or in the open country.

The existence of a relatively high poverty incidence in nonmetropolitan America is only one facet of the general underdevelopment of these areas. Housing quality, educational attainment, and health facilities and services are other generally accepted indicators of relative levels of development. All three indicators consistently show nonmetropolitan areas come out second best when compared to metropolitan areas.

Table 2.6 shows the percentage of substandard housing units in the U.S. by residence and major geographical areas for 1970. The table in-

TABLE 2.6.   Substandard housing units by residence and region, U.S., 1970.

Region	Nonmetropolitan Housing	Rural Housing	All Housing
		(%)	
East South Central	25.2	31.4	17.7
West South Central	14.8	19.1	9.0
Mountain	8.0	11.2	5.2
Pacific	4.8	5.3	2.9
New England	7.4	7.2	4.7
Middle Atlantic	5.7	7.2	4.1
East North Central	8.6	9.6	5.1
West North Central	9.8	12.3	7.2
South Atlantic	18.9	21.7	10.8
United States	12.8	15.0	6.8

Source: (16).

dicates the relatively disadvantaged position of nonmetropolitan and rural areas as to adequate shelter. The relatively high incidence of inferior housing in these areas and the associated impact on the quality of life for residents led the Select Committee on Nutrition and Human Needs of the 92nd Congress to conclude:

> In housing as in hunger, it is clear that greatest need parallels lowest income. Nonwhites, including blacks, Indians and Mexican Americans, occupy a disproportionate share of the Nation's bad housing. Between 1960 and 1970, the share of substandard housing occupied by black households actually increased . . . the experts' best estimate is that almost 60 percent of America's inadequate housing is in rural areas. If a "decent home" is what the Nation's accepted housing codes say is the minimum essential for health and safety, then our official housing goal of 26 million units over a 10 year period is far too low and could be as much as 45 million units. (23, p. 17)

Nonmetropolitan areas lag behind metropolitan areas in both the level of educational attainment and the diversity of educational programs. In 1970, for example, 22 percent of white students in metropolitan areas terminated their education with eight years of schooling or less, compared with 32 percent of nonfarm and 43 percent of farm white students in nonmetropolitan areas. The proportions were considerably higher for nonmetropolitan farm and nonfarm black students (1, pp. 66–67). A significantly lower proportion of nonmetropolitan youths graduated from high school, compared with metropolitan youths. Furthermore, the relatively low per pupil investment in nonmetropolitan areas, and the associated inadequate educational facilities, tended to place rural youths in a disadvantaged position vis-à-vis metropolitan youth in regard to effective earning potential.

Health related statistics consistently indicate the following characteristics of nonmetropolitan and rural health services: limited access to poor quality health care; high incidence of health problems; and low usage of health care facilities and services (1, pp. 68–69). In all three general health characteristics, metropolitan areas rank consistently better. The use of physician and hospital services and the extent of physical disabilities are considered to be reliable indicators of the health profile of a community. These reflect, to a much greater extent than a physical count of personnel and facilities, the occupational and environmental risks associated with various residential areas (15, p. 10). Nonmetropolitan residents of all age categories tend to have fewer visits to physicians and dentists, as well as lower insurance coverage, compared with their metropolitan counterparts. Farm residents generally have the lowest number of visits and the lowest coverage (15, pp. 10–11). In 1968, for example, metropolitan residents 25 years of age and older averaged 4.8 physician visits per year, compared with 4.4 visits for nonmetropolitan-nonfarm residents, and 3.9 for nonmetropolitan farm residents. Farm residents in nonmetropolitan areas visited the dentist an average of .7 visits per year, compared with 1.5 visits for metropolitan residents. Nonmetropolitan-nonfarm residents averaged about .9 visits to the dentist per year (1, p. 70).

Nonmetropolitan and rural areas tend to have more but smaller hospitals than metropolitan areas. The smaller sized hospitals explain the similarity in the number of beds per capita for the two regions, despite the larger number of hospitals in nonmetropolitan and rural areas. Of some importance, however, is the existence in nonmetropolitan and rural areas of a relatively high incidence of inadequately staffed hospitals, unsophisticated equipment, and a lack of extended care facilities. The net effect of these deficiencies is that a large number of nonmetropolitan hospitals are unaccredited (1, pp. 69–70; 15).

The incidence of persons with activity-limiting chronic health disabilities is higher in nonmetropolitan and rural areas. These conditions occur about 50 percent more often in these areas compared with metropolitan areas. Infant mortality, postnatal mortality, and undetected nutritional deficiencies (which show up later) suggest that poverty-stricken nonmetropolitan and rural residents receive inadequate health services. Reports show that the number of draft rejectees for health deficiencies from nonmetropolitan and rural areas is much greater, proportionally, than the number from metropolitan areas. This observation has led to the conclusion that at some point in their lives, a large proportion of nonmetropolitan and rural residents have not received proper medical attention (15, p. 26).

SUMMARY AND CONCLUSIONS. Since the 1960s major strides have been made in combating poverty and other elements of social and economic deprivation in the United States. The accelerated rate of poverty reduction in the mid-1960s was the direct result of sustained economic growth, tight labor markets, and antipoverty legislation emanating from the federal war on poverty. Failure to sustain or expand these efforts in the latter part of the 1960s and conscious reduction in national antipoverty efforts in the 1970s have resulted in a decline in the rate of poverty reduction. The absolute number of poor persons actually increased between 1969 and 1971. The early years of the decade of the 1970s appears to be in a stable state in which poverty has assumed dynamic persistency.

The Great Society philosophy of the Johnson administration and its associated war on poverty saw major budgetary outlay to combat poverty. Under the first Nixon administration, national programs in aid of the poor continued to expand and flourish. However, the nation opted for loosening the demand for labor as a means of reducing inflationary pressures. Rising unemployment contributed significantly to the decline in the rate of poverty reduction. The second Nixon administration saw massive dismantling of antipoverty programs. The decision was made that because of the high cost of eradicating poverty and its competition with other national goals, poverty eradication should be a low priority item on the national agenda. The war on poverty had assumed, as one economist puts it, "the status of a historical phenomenon, with a secure little chapter of its own in the history textbooks" (17, jacket).

At the end of 1973 about 23 million persons were experiencing income poverty. This represented a national poverty incidence of 11 percent. More than 9 million (40 percent) of these poor individuals were residents of nonmetropolitan areas, while about 14 million (60 percent) were residents of metropolitan areas. The relatively disadvantaged income status of nonmetropolitan residents is highlighted by the fact that they are 31 percent of the total population but they have among them 40 percent of the nation's poor.

A high incidence of inferior housing, poor health facilities, and low educational attainment goes hand in hand with a high poverty incidence among the poor, the near poor, and nonmetropolitan and rural areas. The relatively higher incidence of all four dimensions among nonmetropolitan and rural areas is indicative of both the relative level of economic well-being and the underdeveloped status of these areas compared with metropolitan areas.

The historical record of successful reduction in both the absolute level and the incidence of income poverty on a national basis is impressive and commendable. The fact is, however, that at this time, poverty and social deprivation are both *immediate and real* for some 23 million individuals and 5 million families. The historical record offers very little consolation (if any) to these groups. There is even a question as to whether the record might not in fact generate a feeling of futility and hopelessness for those individuals caught up in the vicious cycle of poverty.

The persistence of poverty and underdevelopment for a significant percentage of the nation's population and certain geographical areas, in a period of declining support for the war on poverty, raises a key question regarding national policy consensus about economic equality. This policy has historically been predicated on the value judgment that reduced economic inequality is, by definition, a necessary part of a more ideal social arrangement (7, p. 17). In this regard, the Council for Agriculture Science and Technology in a 1974 report made the following observation:

> How equal do we want our people to be? In the area of civil rights, the answer is becoming a clear statement of equal access. In the area of economic equality, however, the answer is less enthusiastic. In the political sphere, the picture is obscured by contending forces of centralized authority and constitutional separation of powers. Rural development is a move towards greater equality of economic opportunity and status. To what extent is there support for this move? (3, p. 9).

The report went on to conclude that the question of economic equality has not been settled, and until this is done, ambiguous, ambivalent, and ineffective programs are likely. Furthermore, the report continues, shortlived and underfunded programs are simply the manifestation of failure to achieve policy consensus.

If the observation of the Council is correct, strong grounds exist for pessimism regarding future national commitments to eradicating poverty and other forms of economic deprivation. To reverse the current trends will demand major efforts from all segments of the society. The academic community, historically, has led the pace for innovative thinking, problem identification, and policy prescription. It has the opportunity to do so again by taking a leadership role in this very crucial policy issue of the poverty problem in America.

REFERENCES

(1). Brinkman, George, "The Condition and Problems of Nonmetropolitan America," in George Brinkman, ed., *The Development of Rural America,* Lawrence: The University Press of Kansas, 1974.

(2). Carlin, T., "The Economic Analysis of the Predicted Effects of Alternative Family Assistance Programs on Selected Household Expenditures," Ph.D. dissertation, Pennsylvania State University, 1971.

(3). Council for Agricultural Science and Technology, *Rural Development,* Report No. 35 (prepared for the Honorable Hubert H. Humphrey), November 19, 1974.

(4). Gordon, Kermit, ed., *Agenda for the Nation,* Washington: The Brookings Institution, 1970.

(5). Hansen, Niles M., *Rural Poverty and the Urban Crisis: A Strategy for Regional Development,* Bloomington: Indiana University Press, 1970.

(6). Herrmann, Robert O., "Discussion of Food Costs of Families," paper, 136th meeting, American Association for the Advancement of Science, Washington, December 28, 1969.

(7). Lampman, Robert J., *Ends and Means of Reducing Income Poverty,* Chicago: Markham Publishing Company, Institute for Research on Poverty Monograph Series, 1971.

(8). Levitan, Sar A., *Programs in Aid of the Poor in the 1970's,* Baltimore: © 1973 by Johns Hopkins University Press.

(9). Madden, J. Patrick, *Poverty Statistics: A Guide to Interpretation,* Department of Agricultural Economics and Rural Sociology, Pennsylvania State University, revised October 16, 1972.

(10). ———, "Poverty by Color and Residence—Projections to 1975 and 1980," *American Journal of Agricultural Economics* 50 (5): 1399–1412.

(11). ———, "Poverty Measures as Indicators of Social Welfare," In *Anticipating the Poverties of the Poor,* Institute for Social Welfare Research, University of Kentucky, November 1971.

(12). ———, "Poverty Projections in Relations to Aggregate Demand, Economic Growth and Unemployment," *Rural Poverty in the United States,* Washington: USGPO, May 1968.

(13). Madden, J. Patrick, J. L. Pennock, and C. M. Jaeger, "Equivalent Levels of Living: A New Approach to Scaling the Poverty Lines to Different Family Characteristics and Place of Residence," in *Rural Poverty in the United States,* Washington: USGPO, May 1968.

(14). Miller, S. M., Martin Rein, Pamela Roby, and Bertram M. Gross, "Poverty, Inequality, and Conflict," *Annals of the American Academy of Political and Social Science* 337:16.

(15). National Academy of Sciences, *The Quality of Rural Living: Proceeding of a Workshop,* Washington, 1971.

(16). Rural Housing Alliance and Housing Assistance Council, Inc., Second National Rural Housing Conference, Washington, November 28–30, 1972.

(17). Sundquist, James L., ed., *On Fighting Poverty,* New York: Basic Books, 1969.

(18). U.S. Department of Commerce, Social and Economic Statistics Administration, "Characteristics of the Low-Income Population: 1973," in *Current Population Reports: Consumer Income,* Bureau of the Census, Series P–60. No. 94, July 1974.

(19). U.S. Department of Labor, Manpower Administration, *Manpower Report of the President,* Washington: USGPO, 1974.

(20). U.S. Department of Labor, Manpower Administration, *Manpower Technical Exchange* 5:1 Washington: USGPO, January 12, 1973.

(21). U.S. National Advisory Commission on Rural Poverty, *The People Left Behind,* Washington: USGPO, September 1967.

(22). U.S. Senate, Committee on Agriculture and Forestry, 92nd Congress, 2nd Session, *Rural Development Legislation as Amended by the Rural Development Act of 1972: Analysis and Explanation,* Public Law 92–149, Washington: USGPO, December 12, 1972.

(23). U.S. Senate, Select Committee on Nutrition and Human Needs, *Promises to Keep: Housing Needs and Federal Failure in Rural America,* Washington: USGPO, revised April 1972.

CHAPTER THREE

Economics of being poor

THEODORE W. SCHULTZ

S I N C E most of the people in the world are poor, it would appear that if we knew the economics of being poor, we would know most of the economics that really matter. But how much does economic theory tell us about poverty? Since Ricardo the winding path of theory and its ever-changing income distribution implications have challenged many. (Harry Johnson has cogently elucidated them in his published course notes on the theory of income distribution [8]. In addition, Jan Pen in his now translated study of income distribution [14] has pointed out the numerous gaps and inconsistencies between observed facts and received theories.) I am particularly struck by puzzles in our understanding of the size distribution of income and the secular changes in factor shares and in personal shares. Seeing these puzzles, I have become increasingly uneasy about the state of our knowledge of poverty. In this chapter I will consider why our perspective on poverty keeps us from explaining these puzzles, and I will suggest new questions that we need to ask.

A major problem with our perspective on poverty is that it is too narrow; often we think only in terms of our own economy and our own culture. It is very difficult for us in the United States, with our astronomically high incomes, to perceive what the economic implications of low incomes are in the rest of the world. Our life style and national data thwart our perception of how poor people in nonwestern countries manage to live and how in times past western people, when they too were very poor, maintained their households and families. Our highly skilled federal statisticians now provide us with a sophisticated measure of poverty, and we see that the poverty threshold of a nonfarm family of four in the United States is presently about $5,200 and of a farm family of the same size, about $4,400 (22).* I am not going to evaluate the under-

* In 1973 these two poverty thresholds were $4,540 and $3,859, respectively. I have adjusted them in line with the increase in consumer price index since then. See 22 (Table A-1, p. 160) for the procedure.

lying assumptions and technical accuracy of these statistics, since that has been done elsewhere in this volume. Suffice it to say that if the poorest billion in the world had a fifth as much real income as these poverty thresholds imply, they would be rich indeed compared to what they now live on.

Two recent studies are useful in acquiring a broader historical perspective on the micro attributes of poverty. First, the essays in Peter Laslett's book (13) are especially rewarding in showing the size and structure of households and the state of family life over the past three centuries in England, France, the Netherlands, Serbia, Japan, and colonial North America. Second, a rare body of agricultural production and household consumption data appears in the *Resurvey of Matar Taluka* by Vimal Shah and C. H. Shah (21) of the University of Bombay. (Along with the study by Shah and Shah the all-too-brief lectures by M. L. Dantwala [3] should be read.) These data are cogently analyzed to show what took place between 1930 and 1967 when the population doubled and per capita expenditure in real terms increased by only a fourth. In general, however, studies of poverty in low income countries should be approached with caution. Currently available per capita income data for these countries are subject to large errors, and the real value of the income per dollar is unknown for lack of a standard for measuring the consumption value of these income statistics. I place more reliance on what one observes while moving about in low income countries.

Observation within different countries has the advantage of putting economic facts into a cultural context. One observer who emphasizes this advantage is the distinguished anthropologist Lloyd Fallers. In his book *Inequality* (4) Fallers writes that his thinking on income distribution has been "tempered and rendered more mature by my direct experience in East Africa and Turkey." In Fallers' view the income inequality on which economists concentrate is a subset within the cultural domain of inequality. Since it is not a stationary domain and since changes in it affect our subset, we would be well advised to take account of such changes. Fallers is also very effective in showing that we are culturally bound in our views about inequality.

Within this cultural context, I have contended, the actions of the poor are finely attuned to marginal costs and returns, and they tend to make the most out of what they have. Accordingly, for me it is an axiom that poor people tend to live close to their economic optimum given their circumstances; it follows from this that being poor does not imply being inefficient (19).

We have to look, then, beyond our own culture, our own economy, and our own history to get a true picture of the economics of being poor. In the process we see worldwide economic trends that narrower perspectives miss. We see also that economic theory has often ignored long-range international trends, at its peril. I would like to consider some of these long-range developments here, in particular the changing relationship of poverty to land, life span, human capital, and personal income shares.

POVERTY AND LAND. In economics the relationship between poverty and land is unclear. Although the shadow of Henry George and the Single Tax is now dim, the emphasis is still on land reform as a means of alleviating rural poverty in most of the world. Meanwhile, the current doomsday pronouncements project increasing poverty and famine as world population grows while the land suitable for growing crops remains virtually fixed. In retrospect, however, we see that the households and families in Western Europe, according to Laslett (13), were in general very poor, despite the fact that the population was much smaller then and the natural endowment of land was what it is now. This observation suggests the first puzzle with which I am concerned.

Within the very low income heart of Asia are two city-states with virtually no cropland or minerals, with only human resources, in which personal incomes are far above Asian standards. Although Hong Kong is crowded with more than 4 million people, the per capita gross domestic product (GDP) is equal to about $1,000, U.S. dollars. Singapore has more than 2 million people and a per capita GDP equal to about $1,200, U.S. dollars. The study by Geiger and Geiger (7) is a major contribution in analyzing and in explaining the remarkable economic success of these two city-states.

It is evident that in many countries with a *low* population-land density ratio the rank and file are very poor, and that they are similarly poor in many countries with a *high* population-land density ratio. The puzzle is, why has this difference in the ratio of people to cropland in these countries not produced a difference in incomes? Until we have the answer to this question, it behooves us not to treat land as a key variable in explaining income differences among all low income countries.

INCOME INEQUALITY AND LIFE SPAN. It is clear from historical records and from current data that the difference in the life spans of human beings is a critical index of the difference in their well-being. This index has been rising rapidly in low income countries. Since 1950 the life expectancy in low income countries has risen about 40 percent; from 35–40 years to approximately 52 years (2, p. 7). By this important measure of human well-being the gap between the low and the high income countries has been substantially reduced. The puzzle is that there are all kinds of data on the per capita availability of food and of the state of housing and of unemployment that presumably show that the standard of living has not improved and that conditions have become worse when it comes to finding employment. Since I am quite convinced from various evidence that life expectancy has risen in most low income countries, I have begun a search for the explanatory factors. Early English history provides some clues, but none of the western countries, to the best of my knowledge, ever came close to matching the above gains in life span. In this context I am fascinated by the economic logic and the quantitative importance of Dan Usher's attributing changes in life expectancy to the measure of economic growth (23). In the case of Ceylon his analysis shows that the growth rate of GNP is more than doubled when the value of the increase in life expectancy between 1946 and 1963 is taken into account. The point to ponder is the inconsistency between this rise in life expectancy and our "data" on food supplies, nutrition, and health in low income countries.

FACTOR INCOME SHARES FOR PROPERTY AND HUMAN CAP-ITAL. In the rhetoric on factor shares, capitalists are rich and workers are poor. Analytically, however, we deal with two forms of capital, property assets and human capital. In western countries the stock of human capital has been increasing relative to that of property assets, and it is a well-established fact that the share of national income accruing to labor has become much larger than it was when the early English economists had their say. As this share has increased, the level of family income has risen and the personal distribution of income has become less unequal. Simon Kuznets (9, 10, 11, 12), taking the long view of economic processes in western countries, sees labor's share as having risen from 55 to 75 percent in the last century, while the share accruing to property assets has declined from 45 to 25 percent. But the reasons for these secular changes in factor shares have received too little attention in economics. I will examine two aspects: the decline in the income share accruing to landlords and the rise in the value of human time.

At the time when Ricardo wrote, about half the income of the rank and file of people in England went for food. Wages were very low and the rents accruing to the owners of farmland accounted for 20 to 25 percent of the national income. Thus, according to Kuznets' estimates cited in the previous paragraph, about half the income accruing to property assets at that time consisted of farmland rent. What we observe in many nonwestern countries today is a similar economic picture. Since Ricardo's day, however, landlords as an economic class in western countries have been fading away. Economic theory has litttle to offer in explaining why this has occurred; what we know we learn from the data. Since I have dealt at length elsewhere on what the secular evidence reveals (16, especially Chapter 8), here it will suffice to say that the increases in productivity of cropland are largely man-made and that a vast array of substitutes for cropland has been developed. In terms of theory we fail to see these developments because our theoretical approach rests on Hicks's Law. No one has been as cogent as Jan Pen (14, especially pp. 208–14) in showing the limitations of Hicks's Law in analyzing the historical decline in farmland rents as a share of income.

In connection with this decline, I cannot resist noting the current lack of perspective in what is being said and written about farm products, raw materials, energy, and oil. I foresee that the trends of the decades prior to 1972 will again prevail: the owners of natural resource assets will lose income as man-made substitutes for these assets are developed, and as ways of exploiting natural resources are improved. Even the oil lords who are now collecting large rents will see their rents diminishing for the same basic reasons that account for the decline of landlords as an economic class.

One thing is certain: in the western countries, as the income share accruing to farmland has declined, the income share accruing to labor has increased, and the economic lot of poor people has improved. It is this increase in the income share accruing to labor that holds the key to the secular rise in income for most families. If we knew the economic reasons for the marked, persistent rise in the value of human time in western countries, we would be able to explain in large part why the income share of labor has been increasing (17).

What determines the long-term changes in the supply of and the demand for labor? Recent advances in economic thought have supplied a substantial portion of the theory which functionally relates changes in the supply of labor to the *quality attributes* of labor. The useful abilities people acquire should be viewed as forms of human capital. The investment in these abilities or skills occurs in response to favorable investment opportunities. Individuals, families, and public bodies build up the supply of skills through their expenditures (sacrifices) on education, health, on-the-job training, the search for information, and geographical migration to take advantage of better jobs or consumption opportunities. People are willing to make these sacrifices because the return in future earnings and personal satisfaction is high. And it is high because there is a continuing demand for skilled work in western countries.

But the demand side is still largely an unexplored frontier. The puzzle is, why does the demand for a highly trained work force increase so persistently in the advanced economies, notably in the United States? This growth in demand is implicit in the fact that between 1929 and 1957 the educational capital embodied in the labor force of the United States increased at an average annual rate twice as high as that of reproducible tangible wealth. We know the simple answer to the implied question of why the accumulation of human capital occurs at a higher rate than that of nonhuman capital. Theory and empirical analysis both imply that this difference is a response to the difference in rates of return.

But this response to the difference in rates of return sheds no light whatsoever on why the rate of return to human capital has tended to be relatively high. The basic question is this: what is it about these economic processes that increases the demand for skilled labor services and why have those services long maintained a relatively high rate of return to human capital investment?

Thinking about the demand problem considered here, I am convinced that we can explain simultaneously two critical factual puzzles. The first is that diminishing returns to capital have not occurred generally despite the vast accumulation of capital in advanced economies. The second fact is the relatively high rate at which the formation of human capital has occurred. The resolution of the first puzzle also provides a solution for the second.

The key to both puzzles is the continuous growth of knowledge. The acquisition, adoption, and efficient utilization of new knowledge provides new sources of investment opportunities, so it maintains the growth process and keeps the returns to capital from diminishing over time. Furthermore, these additions to the stock of knowledge increase opportunities for human capital more than investment opportunities for material capital.

Studies of the last decade tell us that people in the United States who are poor over their life span possess relatively little skill, or human capital. Lack of training limits not only the job skills they might invest, but also their skills in coping with a complex modern environment. The consequences are that their lifetime earnings are low, that they are especially vulnerable to unemployment, that they experience the most disabilities for reasons of poor health, that they are relatively inefficient in their financial affairs, in household production, in searching for information, and in dealing with economic disequilibria during their life span. In this context it is important to take into account the differences in entrepreneurial ability of housewives, laborers, students, farmers, and businessmen. The economic value of the ability to deal with disequilibria is substantial, and the effects of education and experience in enhancing this particular ability are strong and clear (20).

HUMAN CAPITAL AND PERSONAL INCOME. Lastly, I come to personal income: how it is distributed and how it is spent. Conceptually, personal income is beset with ambiguities. Decisions about the use made of personal income are not vested equally among all members of the family. Consumer units are very heterogeneous. Theoretically, the economic interactions between functional and personal income are far from clear. In going from relative factor shares, modified by private and public transfers to personal income shares without theory as a guide, one soon becomes lost. What would be the consequences for personal income shares if the economy were open and competitive, if total national income were rising secularly, and if there were no public income transfers? Not having enough theory to generate implications, we are short on economic explanations that have been tested. We know very little about the economics of intergenerational transfers of property assets or about the effects of differences in family wealth on the investment that parents make in the human capital of their children. Empirically, we can learn much from Dorothy Projector and Gertrude Weiss (15). As expected, the ownership of investment assets, which accounted for 33 percent of the total wealth in their 1962 survey, is distributed very unequally, despite progressive inheritance taxes. But, quite unexpectedly to me, 27 percent of our total wealth consisted of owners' equity in their homes, and this form of personal wealth was distributed almost equally among consumer units by income classes.

Most of the story of personal income shares is linked to human capital and its personal distribution. Gary Becker (1) has advanced a theoretical approach to analyze the function of human capital in this context. Empirical tests of its implications are still fragmentary. There are plenty of difficulties in using the theory. Several issues need to be considered further if we are to explain the relationship of human capital to personal income: personal priorities affect the jobs that people take, since among those with the same human capital, some more than others prefer pleasanter jobs with fewer earnings; transitory earnings should be distinguished from permanent earnings; the life cycle of earnings is important; and the measure of full returns to human capital should not omit the value of time devoted to household production, the value of entrepreneurial skill, the value of human capital after retirement, and the value of skill in making consumer choices. (Bruce Gardner, in his study of recent changes in rural poverty in the United States [6] has made commendable progress in analyzing several of these issues.)

There are many mansions in the economics of being poor. But most of them are unoccupied.

REFERENCES

(1). Becker, Gary S., *Human Capital and the Distribution of Personal Income: An Analytical Approach,* Woytinsky Lecture No. 1, Institute of Public Administration, University of Michigan, 1967.

(2). Berelson, Bernard, and staff, "World Population: Status Report 1974," in *Reports on Population and Family Planning,* New York: Population Council, 1974.

(3). Dantwala, M. L., *Poverty in India—Then and Now, 1870–1970,* Bombay: Macmillan Co. of India, 1973.

(4). Fallers, Lloyd A., *Inequality: Social Stratification Reconsidered,* Chicago: University of Chicago Press, 1973.

(5). Furniss, Edgar S., *The Position of the Laborer in a System of Nationalism,* Boston: Houghton Mifflin, 1920.

(6). Gardner, Bruce L., "An Analysis of Recent Changes in Rural Poverty in the U.S.," unpublished paper, State University of North Carolina, August 1974.

(7). Geiger, Theodore, and Frances M. Geiger, *Tales of Two City-States: The Development Progress of Hong Kong and Singapore*, Washington: National Planning Association, 1973.

(8). Johnson, Harry G., *The Theory of Income Distribution*, London: Gray-Mills Publishing, 1973.

(9). Kuznets, Simon, "Economic Growth and Income Inequality," *American Economic Review* 45:1–28.

(10). ———, *Economic Growth and Nations*, Cambridge: Harvard University Press, 1971.

(11). ———, *Modern Economic Growth*, New Haven: Yale University Press, 1966.

(12.) ———, "Quantitative Aspects of the Economic Growth of Nations: VIII. Distribution of Income by Size," *Economic Development and Cultural Change* 2 (2): 1–80.

(13). Laslett, Peter, assisted by Richard Wall, *Household and Family in Past Times*, Cambridge, Eng.: Cambridge University Press, 1972.

(14). Pen, Jan, *Income Distribution: Facts, Theories, Policies,* translated from the Dutch by Trevor S. Preston, New York: Praeger, 1971.

(15). Projector, Dorothy S., and Gertrude S. Weiss, *Survey of Financial Characteristics of Consumers*, Washington, Board of Governors of the Federal Reserve System, 1966.

(16). Schultz, Theodore W., *The Economic Organization of Agriculture*, New York: McGraw-Hill, 1953.

(17). ———, "The Increasing Economic Value of Human Time," *American Journal of Agricultural Economics* 54 (5): 843–50.

(18). ———, "Public Approaches to Minimize Poverty," in Leo Fishman, ed., *Poverty Amid Affluence*, New Haven: Yale University Press, 1966.

(19). ———, *Transforming Traditional Agriculture*, New Haven: Yale University Press, 1964.

(20). ———, "The Value of the Ability to Deal with Disequilibria," *Journal of Economic Literature*, in press. (Human Capital Paper No. 74:1, revised December 20, 1974, University of Chicago.)

(21). Shah, Vimal, and C. H. Shah, *Resurvey of Matar Taluka*, Bombay: Vora and Co., 1974.

(22). U.S. Department of Commerce, Social and Economic Statistics Administration, *Current Population Reports: Consumer Income,* Bureau of the Census, Series P-60, No. 98, January 1975.

(23). Usher, Dan, "An Imputation to the Measure of Economic Growth for Changes in Life Expectancy," in Milton Moss, ed., *Measurement of Economic and Social Performance*, National Bureau of Economic Research, New York: Columbia University Press, 1973.

Alternative evaluations of the cost of rural poverty in the United States

Economic cost of poverty

LUTHER   TWEETEN
and
NEAL   O.   WALKER

R A T I O N A L decisions by society about whether or not to alleviate poverty await measures of the social cost of continuing poverty and the cost of alleviating it. Before estimating the social cost of poverty, we must define poverty and social cost. Because absolute deprivation has been largely eliminated from this nation and because demoralization, alienation, and other psychic tolls taken by poverty are functions mainly of relative rather than absolute deprivation, we define poverty as relative deprivation. It is relative to the well-being of other classes within a society. That is why attitudes associated with poverty are not generally found among foreign nation middle classes who have lower buying power than America's poor. Within America, social welfare outlays have increased up to $19 billion per year while the measured poverty gap (between income of the poor and the official poverty threshold) has remained steady at about $10 billion per year for a decade. (The gap would largely disappear if imputed returns to assets and huge payment-in-kind programs were included in income of the "poor." The remaining gap is disproportionately concentrated among the rural poor.) Alleviating poverty, then, requires raising incomes at least to the poverty threshold while narrowing the difference of income between classes.

The social cost of poverty can be viewed from two perspectives: the cost of allowing poverty to continue and the cost of eliminating poverty. Measuring the social cost of allowing poverty to continue is almost impossible. (For example, how do you measure the influence of poverty on crime and the attendant *net* social cost in money or psychic terms of property transferred through theft?) Therefore, we emphasize here the

Comments of Gerald Doeksen, Dean Schreiner, and Leo Blakley are deeply appreciated. The authors, of course, are solely responsible for the contents of this chapter.

social costs and benefits of alleviating poverty. However, in the first section of the chapter we do measure one cost of continuing poverty associated with underutilized human resources—the foregone earnings and output of rural workers because of underemployment.

Examining the least-cost mix of public programs to alleviate rural poverty and underemployment, we find that the major public cost is for income maintenance welfare) programs. Accordingly, the middle section of the chapter discusses the social cost measured in foregone earnings and national output of income maintenance programs, summarizing the now vast results of labor-supply-earnings response as well as new results on investment response.

The chapter concludes with the most appropriate measure of the social cost of poverty—utility foregone. In the long run, total national income is sacrificed as the distribution of income becomes more equal, because income is transferred from persons with high propensities to invest to persons with low. But total *utility* is not necessarily correlated with national income. Change in the well-being of society depends on the marginal utility of income to gainers and losers. Estimated representative or typical marginal utility curves reveal the appropriate distribution of income to maximize satisfaction in society.

FOREGONE EARNINGS FROM RURAL UNDEREMPLOYMENT.

Poverty and underemployment (including unemployment) are inseparable, and so one measure of the cost of poverty is earnings (and value of production of goods and services) foregone by underemployment. Three independent estimates (30, p. 130; 16; and 25) each placed underemployment in nonmetropolitan counties (whose cities have 2,500 to 50,000 people) at 3 million full-time person-year equivalents. This figure, 12 percent of the nonmetropolitan work force, is modest in view of underemployment rates of over 30 percent in many rural counties (where cities have less than 2,500 people).

Using earnings of production workers in private nonagricultural industries as measures of opportunity cost, we find the value foregone per person-equivalent is $144 per week or $7,505 in 1973. Multiplied by 3 million underemployed, the cost of nonmetropolitan underemployment is $22.5 billion annually in foregone value of goods and services produced as reflected by lost earnings. Stated differently, the potential benefit from jobs for these 3 million underemployed would be $22.5 billion. (We caution that the above data are for a relatively full employment economy and fall far short of measuring lost earnings and output in 1975.)

These potential benefits of utilizing underemployed rural human resources cannot be realized without incurring some public costs. Research increasingly documents that in a disturbing number of instances the costs of placing the underemployed poor in productive employment outweighs monetary benefits derived from a stream of earnings generated by the new jobs.

A STRATEGY TO MINIMIZE PUBLIC OUTLAYS TO ALLEVIATE POVERTY AND UNDEREMPLOYMENT.

A recent simulation study by Nelson and Tweeten (15) examined the impact of rural development programs on a low income rural area similar to many depressed rural areas in the nation. Objectives were to:

1. Estimate technical efficiency coefficients for six public rural development programs.

2. Devise a computerized simulation model depicting economic-demographic processes and how these are influenced over time by public programs. (The simulation model can be used in the classroom as a rural development game and can also provide information for local, state, and national public policy decisions.)

3. Evaluate the effectiveness of past and potential rural area development policies (program packages) in alleviating poverty and underemployment in the low income, seven-county Eastern Oklahoma Development District located in the Ozarks Region.

The district's population of 114,104 nonpoor and 77,090 poor was divided into 21 categories based on age, education, income, and other factors relating to eligibility for employment. The impact, with appropriate income and employment multipliers, on each of these population categories was estimated for six public programs: (1) public assistance or income maintenance, (2) school dropout prevention, (3) vocational training, (4) family planning, (5) industrial location incentives to generate local jobs, and (6) labor mobility subsidies to bring workers to outside jobs.

One or more of the six public programs can be initiated, in simulation over and above conventional public investments. (Roads, schools and other services, and infrastructure appeared to be adequate in the area under study, so spending extra development funds on them would have had low economic payoff.) Of course, the area is free to tax the additional economic base generated by economic development programs to provide additional services as residents see fit.

Background Data on Specific Programs. A brief background of coefficients used in the study is presented below.

LABOR MOBILITY SUBSIDIES. Nelson and Tweeten (14) estimated that training, counseling, and moving persons from areas with excess labor supply to areas of excess labor demand brought an average return of 15 percent on the public investment (averaging approximately $1,000 per relocated worker). A most discouraging aspect of the large number of these subsidized mobility projects sponsored by the U.S. Department of

Labor (68 studies were used to derive coefficients) is that approximately two out of three relocatees returned home. Hence, the cost per worker permanently relocated is approximately $3,000, and providing adequate local jobs and incomes to those who return home remains an issue.

The success of these programs decreases as the programs serve more disadvantaged clientele. The Job Corps and Work Incentive program (WIN) had placement rates averaging only about 20 percent, and the rate of return on the investment was near zero. The Manpower Development and Training Act (MDTA) served a less disadvantaged group, had placement rates of approximately 50 percent, and the rate of return on investment averaged roughly 15 percent (see Goldstein, 7, for evaluation of several programs). Finally, the mostly state run vocational-technical programs that trained less disadvantaged youngsters had placement rates of approximately 75 percent, and the social rate of return on investment averaged approximately 20 percent. However, placement and investment returns vary widely among schools, geographical areas, and programs.

EDUCATION. Schultz (19) estimated that education contributed at least three-tenths and perhaps more than one-half the growth in U.S. national income between 1929 and 1956. Bowman (3) reduced that proportion to one-seventh, a figure in line with Denison's (4) estimate for the contribution of education to economic growth between 1950 and 1962. While these data reflect early trends away from the more extravagant claims of those who embraced education as the panacea for economic ills, subsequent findings are even more discomfiting. Generally it cannot be said that nonmetropolitan schools are inadequate, although many of them can be improved, particularly for minority students. Unfortunately, it is increasingly clear that the process by which resources are converted to favorable student outcomes in school achievement and future economic success is not well understand.

Some analysis provides direction but also reveals that rates of return on additional investment to improve schools for the disadvantaged are not large. The Rand Corporation (Averch, et al., 2) reviewed a large number of studies including controlled experiments in schooling techniques, processes, and practices. The report concluded that parents' income, education, and occupation are the consistent, significant predictors of student outcomes. Studies show no consistent and significant evidence that teachers with more experience, more degrees, and more salary are more (or less) effective in producing favorable student outcomes. Little evidence suggests that expensive facilities and equipment, live teachers (compared to television), smaller classes, team teaching, ability grouping, track systems, desegregation, enlarged curriculum, individualized instruction, computerized instruction, or decentralization of school control increase (or decrease) student success. Private contractors (presumably free to discard old myths and obsolete practices) who were hired to run schools had little more success than public school administrators. While results point to no single practice that consistently produced favorable outcomes, *schools can be improved*. But improvements tend to be unique to each situation, and require in-depth analysis, school by school (28).

To be sure, studies of the payoff from private and public investment indicate social rates of return averaging approximately 10 percent for high school and college (28). But these rates are averages for a grade or group of grades and do not indicate where to invest the next dollars— they are not marginal rates of return.

Several studies have examined payoffs from specific programs for the disadvantaged. Weisbrod (32) evaluated the economic payoff from a counseling program used in St. Louis to reduce dropout rates. The program in fact reduced rates, but it cost an average $8,200 to obtain benefits of $5,673 from having one less dropout.

Ribich examined data from a number of compensatory programs, most derived from controlled experiments with one group of children receiving special services. Summarizing several earlier studies, he stated:

> The calculations indicate some interesting differences in payoff rates among various types of programs, but what was most interesting was the generally low ratio of estimated total income gains that appeared (on average) for *each* basic type of educational change considered. The typical relationship was for income gains to be around 60 percent of costs. (18, p. 226)

Title I of the Elementary and Secondary Education Act of 1965 (designed to assist disadvantaged children in common schools) and the Head Start Program (a preschool program for the disadvantaged begun in 1964) stimulated either no significant achievement test gain or gains soon lost, according to reports released in 1969 (18, p. 227).

We make no call for less spending on schooling. In fact, spending will increase because teachers and other resources used in education need remuneration competitive with other uses to hold their services. But vastly expanded additional resources devoted to general schooling would probably give a disappointing payoff. Part of the problem is that while additional schooling improves mean incomes, it tends to shift the entire distribution of income upward, leaving the variance of income and hence relative deprivation essentially unchanged.

INDUSTRIAL LOCATION INCENTIVES. Although rural communities made great efforts to seek industry in the 1960s, economists viewed such efforts as not only ineffective but also inappropriate from the standpoint of national economic efficiency (1, 9, 23). These studies implied that the public cost of generating new jobs in rural areas was infinite. Not only did empirical studies indicate that tax incentives and other inducements to bring industry had no significant influence, but economists reasoned that industry required skilled labor, a nearness to markets, and agglomeration economies not found in nonmetropolitan communities. In 1971, however, in a comprehensive article on industry location incentives, Singer (21) concluded that the public cost of bringing jobs to nonmetropolitan communities was in fact finite: subsidies of approximately $17,-000 were required to generate each new job. Later, data revealed that industry indeed is decentralizing and that profit rates are not significantly different by size of community (10). Major net economic benefits were found to accrue to communities attracting industry (20), and off-farm jobs were found to be the major source of economic gains to farmers in the 1960s.

Data from the Economic Development Administration (5) led EDA to conclude that the public cost of generating a new job averaged approximately $7,000, the same figure estimated earlier by Tweeten (23, p. 445) based on data for the investment tax credit. However, much of the assistance provided by EDA to attract industry was for improvement of public services that in many cases did not result in permanent new jobs. With more cost-effective approaches such as grants or tax write-offs tying assistance more closely to actual industrial development, cost-effectiveness of industrial subsidies can be even higher.

Comprehensive studies of 250 job development projects by the EDA indicated that the public outlays per job generated may be even less than indicated above. Analysis of these EDA data (22) supports the wisdom of locating jobs in or near growth centers of approximately 25,000 population in areas with a high proportion of underemployment and blue collar labor force, but within reach of hinterland rural workers. Additional analysis at Oklahoma State University (10) of the cost per capita of providing public services, comparative profit rates of private industry, and attitudes relating to well-being suggests that policies to attract industries might well concentrate in cities of 20,000 to 1 million. Reviewing a substantial number of case studies, Janssen (10) concluded that from 25 to 50 percent of the workers hired in new industry will come from the low income population; therefore, in the simulation results reported later in this chapter, one-third is assumed to come from the poor.

Subsidies to industry need not necessarily be regarded as a social cost. If the subsidies only encourage industry to do what a more perfect market would do in the absence of externalities and rigidities limiting growth of nonmetropolitan industry, then subsidies may be regarded as a social gain rather than a social loss. In short, industry location incentives can be a more effective and efficient development tool than once was thought, with cost-effectiveness estimates trending down through time from an infinite cost to as low as $5,000 per job generated. In the simulation results reported later in the chapter, the public cost was considered to be $10,000 per direct job generated.

INCOME MAINTENANCE. Because Public Assistance payments do not generate multiplier effects through private investment, or future earnings as large as those generated by other programs, these payments are generally not regarded as a cost-effective means to increase incomes. Yet in many cases the payments are more cost-effective than investment in training programs that goes to middle class program administrators and instructors but eludes the poor participants who are unable to generate a future stream of earnings from their own human investment in the programs.

A number of proposals would reform welfare to include the working poor, eliminate incentives for family disintegration, and encourage employment. Costs and benefits of income maintenance programs deserve more treatment than can be given here and are discussed later.

Results. The simulated development strategy containing only welfare, subsidized labor mobility, and industrial development programs was most cost-effective in minimizing public funds to alleviate poverty and underemployment (15). This simple strategy entails Public Assistance grants to provide minimum nonpoverty incomes for the unemployable poor and job development activities (labor mobility and industrial development) to eliminate underemployment. Given the assumptions of the model, underemployment can be alleviated in the study area in 15 or fewer years by annually allocating fewer public funds to nonwelfare development activities than were allocated in 1970 (approximately $5 million). But it is necessary to use nonwelfare funds more cost-effectively than in the past.

Political considerations might reduce or eliminate labor mobility programs on grounds that they encourage outmigration of an area's youth, deplete a surplus labor pool, or are inconsistent with programs to create jobs within the area. The findings of this research indicate that a strategy including welfare and industrial development but excluding labor mobility programs would be less cost-effective but could still eliminate poverty and yield returns in excess of public costs. While subsidized labor mobility is the single most cost-effective program for the employable poor in the short run, it cannot substantially reduce underemployment because of high return migration. But it complements industrial development because it is a useful "holding action," providing earnings and upgrading skills elsewhere while jobs are being developed locally.

Simulated results of strategies including school dropout prevention and family planning activities were not found to differ greatly from strategies excluding such activities. Such programs, as considered in this study, are quite shallow (affect relatively few people and require minimal funding), so if they are considered socially desirable, they should not necessarily be avoided even though they are neither very efficient nor effective in the time horizon considered. These human resource investments over and above existing programs have low payoffs indeed unless accompanied by programs to provide jobs locally by expanding the economic base or elsewhere by assisting labor outmigration.

Strategies containing post–high school technical training programs were less effective in eliminating poverty or generating income than equal-cost strategies with technical training excluded. On-the-job training programs with established and new industry along with existing high school and post–high school training programs currently are highly developed in the area and are assumed to operate at past levels over the years simulated. With some realignment of programs, existing technical programs can provide an adequate base of trained personnel to support the industrial development in the area.

For the study area, Public Assistance grants totaling almost $72 million per year (compared to $50 million in 1970) in the early years of a development plan are required to bring incomes of all unemployable poor to the poverty threshold. These funds constitute the vast bulk of "development" funding and emphasize the fact that the greater part of the poor is not employable. The comparatively small annual allocation of under $5 million annually to other development activities, mainly to job development, would alleviate underemployment in less than 15 years and could probably be phased out as the critical mass of development becomes self-sustaining.

SOCIAL COSTS AND BENEFITS FROM TRANSFER PROGRAMS TO NARROW INCOME DIFFERENCES.

Human capital development programs can be efficient in generating future income streams that cover costs, hence they warrant funding in their own right. But alone they are totally inadequate to alleviate poverty. Such programs benefit the least disadvantaged of those eligible and often widen rather than narrow income differences. In this light, the major focus in the remainder of this chapter is on costs and benefits of efforts to make the income distribution more nearly equal. Particular emphasis is on income maintenance programs, especially the negative income tax. The following discussion summarizes results of massive past research on the labor effects of a negative income tax. But while millions of dollars have been spent to learn the labor effects, scandalously little has been spent to research the investment effects. The principal original contribution of this chapter is to estimate the investment effects of income redistribution and the implications for an optimal income distribution based on the marginal utility of money.

Labor Supply Response. This discussion of labor effects is divided into two parts: previously unpublished results for marginal wage earners in the Iowa-North Carolina rural income maintenance experiment, and comprehensive summaries of research on labor response to transfer payments, applicable mainly to urban areas.

EFFECT OF NEGATIVE INCOME TAX ON MARGINAL RURAL WORKERS. The following results from a sample of unemployment-prone male wage workers show response of wages, employment, and earnings to tax rates and income guarantees under a negative income tax (NIT) program (26). The analysis from data obtained in a three-year rural income maintenance experiment in Iowa and North Carolina is included because that experiment provides perhaps the most reliable data from any of the income maintenance studies; because the statistical model is structurally detailed, including provision for payments to raise wages through more effective job search as the NIT reduced the opportunity cost of search; and because the conclusions are for a subsample of marginal male wage workers considered to be of major concern to society, as evidenced by past exclusion of a majority of this group from eligibility for Public Assistance.

One objective of the empirical analysis was to test the hypothesis that the negative income tax, by allowing families money to live on while the wage head looks for work, enhances the search effort so that wage gains more than offset wage losses (through temporary unemployment) and result in added earnings. Self-employed males and wives generally have less rigid work schedules than male wage workers, and wives may experience less opportunity cost of search than their spouses to the extent that husbands provide continuing household earnings. Therefore, this hypothesis was expected to be most relevant to wage heads, and the analysis was confined to that subsample.

The study found clear differences in effect between five negative income tax plans (Table 4.1). The employment disincentives associated with high tax rates and high guarantee levels more than offset potentially more effective job search stemming from reduced opportunity cost of search. The result was a net loss from search. But low tax rates and low guarantees generated effective job search that more than offset disincentives for employment, causing wage gains. For the standard plan (T50/G75) featuring a tax rate of 50 percent and income guarantee

TABLE 4.1. Estimated percentage change in wages, frequency and duration of unemployment, and earnings for unemployment-prone male workers, under various negative income tax plans, U.S.

Program Plan[a]	Wages		Unemployment			Earnings	
				Duration			
	Per search	Total	Frequency	per search	Total	Per search	Total
			(%)				
T70/G75	−11.4	−20.7	25.5	35.5	61.0	−54.0	−93.9
T50/G100	−22.6	−41.1	93.8	16.6	110.4	−42.5	−173.6
T50/G75	3.6	6.5	6.7	19.7	26.4	−20.0	−25.2
T30/G75	18.5	33.6	−11.9	3.8	−8.1	13.9	43.3
T50/G50	29.8	54.2	−80.3	22.8	−57.5	2.4	123.2

Source: (26).
[a] T refers to the tax rate and G to the guarantee as a percent of the poverty threshold.

of 75 percent of the poverty threshold, the effect of greater search effort dominated slightly, causing net wage gains from job hunting and associated unemployment of 3.6 percent per search. The frequency of unemployment increased 6.7 percent under the standard plan. Disincentives to employment seemed to dominate for high tax and guarantee levels, but were overshadowed by other factors at low tax and guarantee levels, so unemployment frequency was reduced by low tax rates and guarantees.

Each of the plans increased the duration of unemployment, but the plan with a tax rate of 30 percent and guarantee of 75 percent (T30/G75) had the smallest influence. It increased the duration of each unemployment period only 3.8 percent.

The total percentage change in unemployment is the sum of the percentage changes in frequency and duration. Using the standard plan as the most reliable estimate, the NIT increased unemployment of this subsample of marginal male workers by 26 percent.

Wage changes per search were adjusted for the distributed lag effect of repeated search, in order to derive the long-term or total impact on wages of repeated search. Sharply diminishing returns from search were apparent—repeated search resulted in long-range wage gains only 1.82 times the short-term gains. The long run is not very distant—90 percent of the adjustment is made in only 2.9 search periods, approximately one year for this subsample. The study predicts that the standard plan will raise wage rates 6.5 percent in total (long run).

The standard plan is estimated to reduce earnings 20 percent in the short run (approximately two months of search-unemployment and two months of employment), and 25 percent in approximately one year (half unemployment, half employment). Higher tax rates and guarantee levels substantially reduce earnings, and lower tax rates and guarantee levels substantially increase total annual earnings. Although the 100 percent guarantee is shown to reduce total earnings more than 100 percent, the actual limit is, of course, 100 percent.

The marginal rate of substitution of the guarantee for tax rate is —1.7 along the total annual iso-earnings line; that is, earnings do not change as the guarantee is raised (lowered) 1 percentage point and the tax rate is lowered (raised) by 1.7 percentage points. On the average, annual earnings increased by 5.9 percentage points with each percentage point decrease in the guarantee. Hence, a plan with a tax rate of 50 percent and a guarantee set at 71 percent of the poverty threshold would not change total earnings based on these estimates. On the average, each percentage point decrease in the tax rates increased total earnings 3.4 percentage points. Hence, a plan with a tax rate of 43 percent and a guarantee of 75 percent of the poverty threshold would leave earnings unchanged in approximately one year. As the time period is extended, small additions to earnings could occur under each of these plans through wage gains from repeated search, but this effect is almost zero because of diminishing return from repeated job search. It would be offset by additional unemployment. A principal conclusion is that the negative income tax with appropriate tax rate and guarantee levels would not materially influence earnings for this subpopulation.

The subsample of unemployment-prone male wage heads analyzed herein was composed of 12 percent of the male wage head sample population. If the remaining male wage head population had similar wage rates and displayed no earnings response to the negative income tax, then the standard plan (T50/G75) would reduce overall earnings of all male wage heads only .12 (25.2) = 3.0 percent, and slightly lower tax rates or guarantees would bring no change in earnings based on this analysis. Of course, if society values equity, it might prefer generous plans offering high guarantees even with some loss in earnings and associated national output.

LABOR EFFECTS OF NEGATIVE INCOME TAX ON OTHER GROUPS. After reviewing a large number of studies of the impact of transfer payments on the labor supply, Garfinkel reported:

> Empirical studies based on cross-sectional sample survey data, experimental data, and income transfer program data confirm the a priori prediction derived from economic theory that income transfer programs will induce program beneficiaries to work less. While almost all studies of the labor supply of wives, female family heads, and older men indicate that transfer payments will lead (or have led to fairly sizable reductions in their labor supply, most of the more reliable studies of the labor supply of prime-aged husbands indicate that transfer programs would lead to relatively small reductions in their work effort.
>
> Even though new government income transfer programs might induce some substantial work reductions among certain groups of beneficiaries, such as wives, it is important to bear in mind that the effects of the national economy will be very small. This is the case because the families that would be eligible for most proposed income payments constitute a relatively small proportion of the existing work force and their output represents an even smaller proportion of total output. (6, p. 30)

The largest controlled negative income tax experiment was carried out primarily in New Jersey, encompassed 1,350 families, and cost $7 million, of which $2.8 million was for cash payments to participating families. Tom Murray summarized findings:

> There was no widespread withdrawal from work by the experimental group. Average benefit payments to the experimental families over three years increased by less than the cost-of-living correction built into the benefit calculation. In the first year of the experiment the average weekly payment was $23; in the third year this had increased to $24.
>
> The effect for able-bodied males with family responsibilities was almost undetectable. Over the central two years of the experiment, the employ-

ment rate for male family heads on the experimental group was only 1.5 percent less than for the controls.

The change in employment of wives was more pronounced, with experimental wives working 23 percent fewer hours than the controls. However, these wives had an average of four children, so their spending more time at home might be seen as valuable. Also, the average work figure for these wives was only 4.4 hours a week, so the change in family labor supply and national costs are not large in the overall picture.

As for total family labor supply, the experimental families worked about nine percent less than the controls. The average earnings per week were about the same in the two samples.

The disincentive, as indicated above, came mostly from the work withdrawal by wives who decided to work at home and teenagers who may have been able to stay in school longer (12, pp. 27–28).

Some Comments. The impact of an income maintenance program on labor supply and earnings is large for some groups but small in national perspective. For example, the program proposed by the President's Commission on Income Maintenance Programs (17) would cost an estimated $5 billion over current programs in the late 1960s, would reduce hours worked by 1.9 percent in the population most influenced but would reduce production loss as a percent of total earnings of the labor force by only .6 percent (unadjusted rate from 8, p. 62). The conclusion is that the labor effect of a negative income tax with a guarantee set at 75 percent of the poverty threshold and 50 percent tax rate would reduce national output by substantially less than 1 percent.

Investment Response. Income transfers could equalize incomes per person, but society is not necessarily made better off simply through equality. If the redistribution toward low income persons reduces investment and economic growth sufficiently, society may be worse off because of the resulting lower national income, even if marginal utility is greater for low than for high income persons. Welfare measures must consider utility gains from both the distribution and total amount of goods and services produced and consumed by society.

In 1974 Walker (31) quantified the trade-offs between income redistribution and economic growth, using 1960–69 as a study period. The steps involved in this process were as follows:

1. Determine the distribution of social welfare benefits among income classes by farm, rural nonfarm, and urban sectors.

2. Determine the distribution of social welfare costs among income classes by sectors.

3. Specify an investment function and combine the distributions obtained in steps one and two to determine the effects of income transfers on investment spending and income growth.

4. Use measures of distributional inequality to measure the trade-offs between income redistribution and growth.

A simulation model was constructed to process the data and derive summary measures reflecting the effects of public transfer program expenditure. Input into the model included distribution of population, income, investment, consumption, and benefits and costs of public transfer expenditures. Output from the model included net transfer effects of program expenditures, investment effects, income growth, and summary measures of distributional inequalities.

The urban, rural nonfarm, and farm sectors of the population were further divided into ten income classes (after taxes). Dollar amounts unless indicated otherwise (including income classifications) are reported in constant 1961 dollars below.

Three base years provided data for the simulation model to allocate benefits from social welfare programs and taxes necessary to pay for such programs. Data for base year 1961 were derived from the Survey of Consumer Expenditures. Data for base years 1965 and 1966 were derived from the Survey of Economic Opportunity. Distributions for the remaining years of the 1960–69 study period were linearly interpolated from base year data. Data reflecting the distribution of income were derived from issues of *The Statistical Abstract of the United States*. Table 4.2 shows expenditures under social welfare programs considered in the study.

Initially, two income distributions were determined by the model (by class and by sector). The first, called *posttransfer* income, was the actual distribution of income including benefits from social welfare programs and the corresponding taxes supporting these programs. The second, called *pretransfer* income, was the income distribution which would have occurred in the absence of income from social welfare expenditures and in the absence of taxes needed to pay for such. Pretransfer income plus income from investment of net transfers is referred to as *simulated* income, income that would have occurred in the absence of social welfare programs.

INVESTMENT FUNCTIONS. Investment schedules were developed from U.S. Bureau of Labor Statistics data. Alternative investment schedules with higher marginal propensities to invest were tried but judged less realistic because of large investment effects from income redistribution. Schedules of marginal investment rates by income classes for the population by economic sectors were used to determine the impact of income redistribution on income growth. Negative investment was common to each of the investment schedules in lower income levels and was accompanied by consumption levels which temporarily equaled or exceeded income. It can be argued that income transfers to low income groups (with high marginal investment rates) tend not to be spent on productive investment opportunities but rather are used to offset negative investment used for consumption purposes. Accordingly, in the simulation

TABLE 4.2. Expenditures under selected social welfare programs, U.S., 1960–69.[a]

Program	1960	1961	1962	1963	1964	1965	1966	1967	1968	1969
						(mil dol)				
OASDHI (Social Security)	11,153	12,161	13,831	14,975	15,578	16,114	18,692	22,025	24,695	27,212
Railroad Retirement	935	992	1,022	1,048	1,064	1,069	1,116	1,145	1,217	1,264
Railroad Unemployment	217	213	161	120	89	73	48	35	40	37
Railroad Disability	70	58	56	52	48	44	40	34	31	47
Public Employment Retirement	2,598	2,870	3,155	3,508	3,856	4,286	4,739	5,289	5,654	6,108
Unemployment	2,860	4,310	3,804	3,291	3,162	2,847	2,542	2,467	2,515	2,407
State Temporary Disability	347	382	403	435	463	458	467	475	493	528
Public Assistance	4,145	4,441	4,877	5,148	5,365	5,957	6,724	7,920	9,528	10,773
Health and Medical	4,390	4,757	3,261	3,315	3,456	3,656	4,007	3,988	4,220	4,212
Other Welfare	1,174	1,248	1,602	1,719	1,864	1,956	2,159	2,605	2,828	3,127
Veterans' Pensions	3,464	3,690	3,733	3,852	3,869	3,940	4,075	4,043	4,051	4,050
Total	31,354	35,122	35,905	37,464	38,804	40,400	44,517	50,025	55,272	59,765

Source: (29, 1961 and later issues).
[a] Expenditures are adjusted to constant dollars by the index (CPI) of purchasing power of the dollar (1961 = 100).

runs, marginal investment rates were considered zero where negative investment occurred.

Economic Growth. One objective of this study was to estimate the effect of income transfers on the growth of private income accruing to individuals. During the study period, personal income (in constant dollars) increased at an average annual rate of 5.06 percent. Net investment (gross private domestic investment less capital consumption allowance) increased at an average annual rate of 4.78 percent.

Several adjustments were made in the income and investment data to estimate the return on net investment. A portion of "return on investment" is retained by corporations in the form of undistributed corporate profits and inventory valuation adjustments. To allow for this, corporate profits (total) and inventory valuation adjustments were added to personal income, and dividends were subtracted (to avoid double counting). To remove the influence of such government investment, personal income was adjusted to reflect a 10 percent return on investment for schooling expenditures and a 50 percent return on investment for research expenditures (24, ch. 5).

A portion of the increase in aggregate personal income was due to growth in population and labor force. After adjustments were made for the foregoing factors, an average annual return on investment of 50 percent was required to account for the growth in real income. It was assumed that investors receive a 15 percent return (before taxes) on their investments. The remaining 35 percent return on investment was distributed among income classes according to their consumption expenditures in accordance with the concept of consumer surplus. Investment to classes and sectors was cumulative over time.

The simulation model, run by years from 1960 to 1969, revealed that the $4,000–$5,000 income class would have had about the same income in 1969 with or without transfer payments. For all classes above $5,000, simulated income exceeded posttransfer income in all years. Income in the higher classes would have been considerably greater in 1969 in the absence of social insurance programs. Simulated income for the highest class (above $15,000) was 13 percent greater than 1969 posttransfer income.

Distributional Inequality. The summary measure of income inequality utilized by Walker was the Gini ratio, defined in the standard way as the ratio of (a) the area between a Lorenz curve and the line of perfectly equal distribution (45° line) and (b) the area under the line of perfectly equal distribution. The measure ranges from a limit of zero, for an equal distribution, to one.

Gini ratios (based on per capita income) are presented in Table 4.3. The Gini ratios for posttransfer income averaged 0.2130 while those of pretransfer income averaged 0.2634. Gini ratios for posttransfer and

TABLE 4.3. Gini ratios for adjusted personal income, U.S., 1960–69.

Year	Posttransfer Income[a]	Pretransfer Income[b]	Simulated Income[c]
1960	0.2082	0.2593	0.2593
1961	0.2085	0.2612	0.2615
1962	0.2089	0.2592	0.2634
1963	0.2046	0.2585	0.2590
1964	0.2046	0.2578	0.2581
1965	0.2060	0.2576	0.2575
1966	0.2237	0.2660	0.2616
1967	0.2180	0.2669	0.2665
1968	0.2220	0.2716	0.2705
1969	0.2254	0.2763	0.2741

[a] Income including social welfare expenditures less taxes paid.
[b] Income minus net transfer effects of social welfare expenditures.
[c] Income with transfer effects treated as investment.

pretransfer income differed by 0.05 in 1969. Although there was little difference between Gini ratios of pretransfer income and simulated income (which accounts for investment), results suggest that in the absence of these social welfare programs income would have been less equally distributed.

Because of special interest in Public Assistance (PA), these expenditures were separated from total social expenditures to isolate their effects. Expenditures in the PA program ranged from 12.7 percent of total social welfare expenditures in 1961 to 18.1 percent of such expenditures in 1969 (see Table 4.2). The costs of PA expenditures in terms of foregone income growth rose to $15.3 billion in 1969 compared to a 1969 income loss of $22.2 billion for all social insurance programs. Thus of the 3.64 percent loss in income due to all social insurance programs, more than two-thirds (2.41 percent) was due to PA expenditures. This suggests that while total social insurance transfers were concentrated in the middle income levels, PA expenditures tended to transfer funds from upper income levels where high investment rates resulted in greater investment losses.

Though PA programs were relatively costly in terms of foregone income growth, they were more effective than total social welfare programs in promoting distributional equality. The 1969 Gini ratio of 0.2763 for pretransfer income was lowered to 0.2254 by total social welfare transfers but to 0.2377 by income transfers from PA programs alone. Thus, through use of the Gini ratio, we see that 76 percent of the distributional equality effected by social welfare programs was due to PA expenditures.

In summary, Pa expenditures (which amounted to a small portion of total social welfare expenditures) were relatively costly in terms of foregone income growth but were much more effective than other types of programs in redistributing income. Both results stemmed from the tendency of PA programs to transfer income from upper income groups to lower income groups as opposed to social insurance programs which mainly transfer income from upper middle income classes to lower middle income classes.

The simulation model has not yet been applied to estimate the impact of a negative income tax, but some crude estimate of the impact can be made from the above data. The negative income tax with a $2,400 guarantee and 50 percent tax rate for a family of four would have added approximately $5 billion to public assistance costs in the late 1960s based on data from the President's Commission on Income Maintenance Programs (17). This is equivalent to approximately half of PA expenditures. If the tax expenditure pattern among income classes followed that of PA, the simulation analysis suggests the cost in foregone income would be approximately .5(2.41) = 1.2 percent of personal income in the nation. Thus the investment effect on national output of redistribution may be greater than the labor effects depicted earlier. A negative income tax would require much greater outlay of funds today than in the late 1960s, but the relative real cost over time in foregone personal income through investment would not be expected to be markedly different.

Graduated Equality Model. The above data give some idea of the effects of actual transfer patterns. However, a generalized transfer scheme was desired. Under the Graduated Equality Model (GEM), the transfer pattern was altered to move all persons a given percentage toward the mean per capita income. Thus in the first run of GEM, the difference in per capita income and mean income was decreased by 5 percent for all persons (this was called a "5 percent GEM"). In the second run, the difference between per capita income and mean income was decreased by 10 percent for all persons (a "10 percent GEM"). By increasing the percentage to 100 percent, all persons have the same posttransfer income in a given year and the posttransfer Gini ratio is zero. Thus GEM shows the results of graduated shifts toward income equality and provides a comparative model for the transfer pattern of existing and proposed social insurance programs.

Results in Fig. 4.1 are for the final year of ten years (1960–69) simulated income adjustment to the respective income distributions. That is, income is invested at the respective marginal propensities to invest with a return of 15 percent on investment for ten years. The ten-year intermediate run is shown because random events and other factors severely distort results as the time period is extended. On the other hand, income in the short run may perform the opposite of that shown. Lack of aggregate demand rather than capital may limit income in the short run, for example, in 1975 when lag of aggregate demand and unemployment were serious problems. Hence income redistribution to low income people with a high propensity to consume can increase income

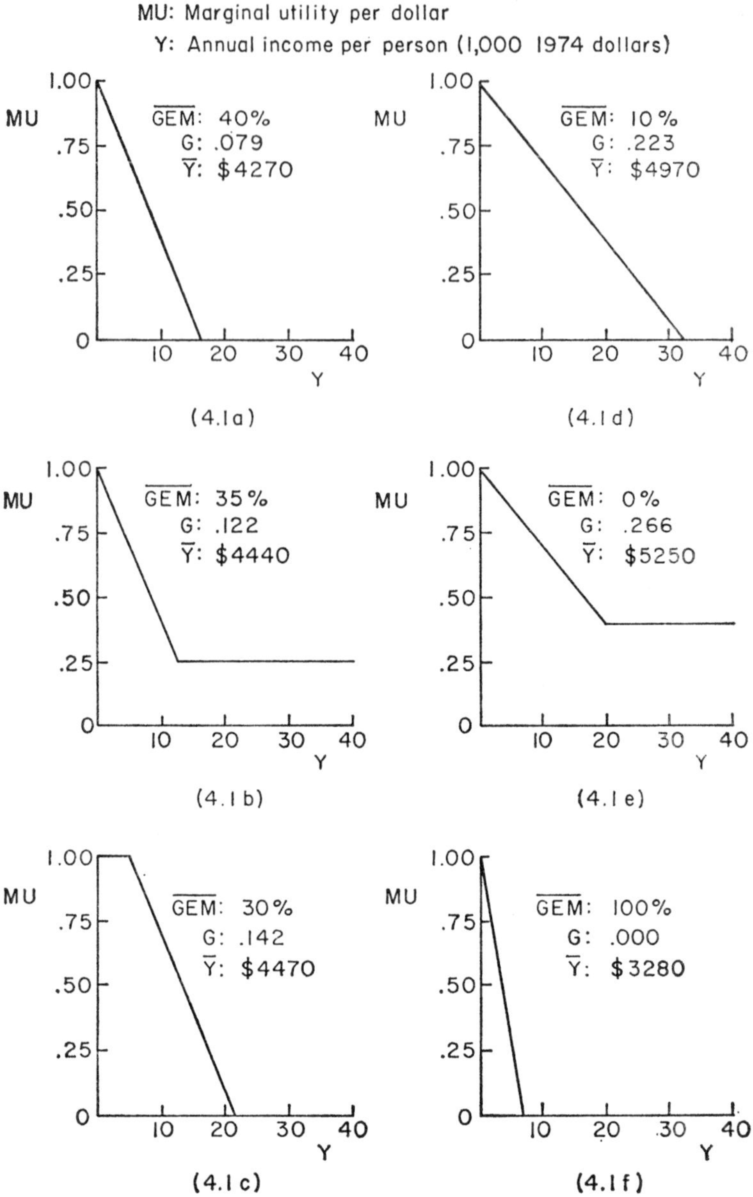

MU: Marginal utility per dollar
Y: Annual income per person (1,000 1974 dollars)

(4.1a)

$\overline{GEM}$: 40%
G: .079
$\overline{Y}$: $4270

(4.1d)

$\overline{GEM}$: 10%
G: .223
$\overline{Y}$: $4970

(4.1b)

$\overline{GEM}$: 35%
G: .122
$\overline{Y}$: $4440

(4.1e)

$\overline{GEM}$: 0%
G: .266
$\overline{Y}$: $5250

(4.1c)

$\overline{GEM}$: 30%
G: .142
$\overline{Y}$: $4470

(4.1f)

$\overline{GEM}$: 100%
G: .000
$\overline{Y}$: $3280

FIG. 4.1. *Marginal utility schedules and associated maximum utility points.*

in the short run. But in a long run, investment in the neoclassical tradition rather than aggregate demand in the Keynesian tradition is considered to be the principal determinant of economic growth.

Net transfer effects of a 10 percent GEM ranged from $11.9 billion in 1960 to $23.0 billion in 1969. This compares to actual net transfers of $16.6 billion in 1960 and $28.2 billion in 1969. In terms of net transfer effects, actual social welfare programs were approximately equal to a 13 percent GEM.

In terms of foregone income, a 10 percent GEM would have lowered 1969 income by 4.31 percent of simulated income. Thus while a 10 percent shift toward mean income would have involved a smaller net transfer of funds than actual social welfare expenditures, the costs of such a transfer would have been greater.

Income redistribution of actual social welfare programs lowered the 1969 Gini ratio from 0.2763 to 0.2254. Income redistribution under a 10 percent GEM would have resulted in a 1969 Gini ratio of 0.2230. This suggests that actual social welfare programs were about equal in redistributing income to a 10 percent GEM.

TOTAL UTILITY UNDER THE GRADUATED EQUALITY MODEL. Society presumably desires both a high mean income and a low level of distributional inequality. However, the GEM specified an inverse relationship between distributional equality and mean total income. Other things equal, greater income equality reduces total income and utility. But if the transfer is from the wealthy with low marginal utility of income to the poor with high marginal utility of income, total utility in society can rise even as national income falls. Thus for a specified utility function, there should exist a level of transfer $\overline{GEM}$ that maximizes the total utility of society. A Gini ratio G, mean personal income $\overline{Y}$, and optimal $\overline{GEM}$ associated with six different schedules of marginal utility are presented in Fig. 4.1. Results were computed for 1969, the end year of a decade of simulated redistribution of income, but were converted to 1974 dollars in Fig. 4.1.

With a linear marginal utility schedule going from 1.0 at no income to 0.0 at $16,500 per capita and above, total utility was maximized with a 40 percent $\overline{GEM}$ (Fig. 4.1a). Though mean income was only 82 percent of the original, gains in distributional equality compensated for the loss (inequality, measured by the Gini ratio, was lowered from a Gini ratio of 0.274 before transfers to a ratio of 0.079 after the 40 percent $\overline{GEM}$ transfer). By putting a "floor" of 0.25 on marginal utility, the maximum utility point was moved from a 40 percent $\overline{GEM}$ to a 35 percent $\overline{GEM}$ (Fig. 4.1b). The higher level of marginal utility in upper income classes made it more difficult for utility from greater equality to compensate for utility sacrificed from a smaller national income.

A linear marginal utility schedule from 1.0 at the $5,000 income level to 0.0 at the $21,450 level and above resulted in the maximum total utility point being obtained with a 30 percent $\overline{\text{GEM}}$ (Fig. 4.1c). This low level of transfers resulted from the fact that marginal utility was constant (MU = 1.0) for more than half the population (mean income equaled $4,472 in 1974 dollars, $2,710 in 1961 dollars).

Changing the slope of the marginal utility curve from −1.0 to −0.5 resulted in maximum total utility being obtained with a 10 percent $\overline{\text{GEM}}$ (Fig. 4.1d). Putting a floor on the marginal utility schedule of 0.25 at the $24,750 level and above did not change the results significantly. This was because there were very few people earning over $24,750 per year. However, a floor of 0.4 at the $19,800 and above income level resulted in the maximum utility point being obtained with a zero percent $\overline{\text{GEM}}$ (Fig. 4.1e). With such a utility schedule, increases in distributional equality did not compensate for any losses in the mean income level.

The slope of the marginal utility curve was then shifted in the opposite direction (made steeper) until a point was reached at which maximum utility corresponded to a completely equal income distribution. This point was reached with a marginal utility schedule from 1.0 at zero income to 0.0 at $6,600 income (Fig. 4.1f). At this point, per capita income was equal for all persons in the population and the Gini ratio was zero. It is apparent that if Fig. 4.1f is the appropriate marginal utility curve for society, satisfactions are maximized with equality of income even though income drops 27 percent.

Few data exist to determine which is the appropriate marginal utility curve for society and hence what is the appropriate distribution of income to maximize satisfactions. Numerous sociological studies of well-being or satisfactions indicate that, as measured, these attitudes do not increase in proportion to income, implying diminishing marginal utility of income. Perhaps the most scientifically objective measures of marginal utility of money are from attitudes such as personal effectiveness regressed on income and other control variables. One such study by Tweeten and Lu (27) yielded a marginal utility function derived from a personal effectiveness index regressed on income divided into three segments. Because the "marginal utility" was derived from coefficients of dummy variables, the curve is not fully defined. It falls between Fig. 4.1a and 4.1f, implying that considerably greater income equality would be socially advantageous (reduce real social cost) in this nation even with a sacrifice of total money income.

One might hypothesize that federal policymakers are in a favorable position to interpret the social welfare function and have within their grasp an instrument, the federal personal income tax, to carry through their interpretation. While progression applies, it falls far short of leveling down incomes from the top. If the intent is to implement equal absolute sacrifice, it is possible to derive a social marginal utility curve prevailing in the personal income tax schedule. Such a curve derived by Mera (11) touches neither axis and lies below the curve in Fig. 4.1f throughout all but the extreme ends of that figure. This implies that Fig. 4.1f is the most realistic of any curves in Fig. 4.1 and that policies to redistribute income from the rich to the poor would increase total utility even as national income substantially declines.

It may be reasoned that overall rather than federal personal income tax rates are the appropriate measure of marginal utility although factors such as convenience, stable year-to-year revenue, and other advantages are apparent in tax rates along with measures of equal sacrifice among income groups. Overall local, state, and federal tax rates are nearly a constant proportion of income at all income levels. If this constant rate implies equal sacrifice from loss of a dollar at all income levels, then the marginal utility of income declines very slowly. Since some concentration of income among high income groups results in greatest growth of income over the long term in a free enterprise society, this implies income and utility are maximized by considerable concentration of wealth. By this measure, 4.1e would be most realistic of the marginal utility schedules displayed in Fig. 4.1.

To gain further insight and to reflect the disparate judgments of marginal utility likely to be found in society, Fig. 4.1 (without $\overline{GEM}$, G, and $\overline{Y}$ data) was shown to 20 agricultural economics faculty members and to the 20 graduate students in rural public policy at Oklahoma State University. They were asked to rank the six curves from most to least representative of typical Americans. The rankings were as follows: (a) 4.1e, (b) 4.1b, 4.1c, 4.1d (tie), (c) 4.1a, and (d) 4.1f. Faculty and graduate students gave the same rankings, and there was comparatively little variation in responses among individuals. (Both groups seemed to be unduly distracted by points where "kinks" in the marginal utility curves occurred, rather than concentrating on the slope of the curves. Future sampling of "informed" opinion would be more reliable if this distraction were avoided.) While the low income group (graduate students) and relatively high income group (faculty) displayed strikingly similar judgments, it may be argued that graduate students are also a high income group measured by present value of expected future earnings. We would expect a sample of the "real" poor to give very different results, probably favoring Fig. 4.1f.

These observations from social-psychological studies, federal personal income tax rates, total tax rates, and faculty and graduate students provide widely divergent guidelines for income distribution. Total tax rates and the faculty-student sample imply that satisfactions would not be enhanced in society with a more equal distribution of income whereas federal income tax rates and the social-psychological study of personal effectiveness suggest that satisfactions in society would be enhanced with a more nearly equal distribution of income even as total income fails considerably.

This preliminary analysis provides no clear mandate for public policy. It demonstrates that equity and efficiency trade-offs in the social welfare function are susceptible to analysis. Marginal utility schedules, though elusive, can be used in public policy research. The typical ivory tower approach of economists—assuming constant marginal utility for all persons at all income levels—seems no longer necessary nor justified.

Congress and the Executive might stipulate an explicit marginal utility schedule which could then be used to formulate tax and expenditure policies (13, p. 204). On that basis, evaluation of past and proposed public policies might entail weighing costs and benefits according to the marginal utility weight assigned to those who pay for and benefit from the projects or policies, with funding priorities based on highest benefit-cost ratios.

SUMMARY AND CONCLUSIONS. This chapter begins with the premise that the social cost of continuing poverty exceeds the social cost of alleviating poverty (a premise tested in the preceding section of the chapter). Although foregone earnings and output from underemployed rural workers appear high, numerous studies indicate that human resource investment programs to generate a future stream of earnings from the poor give a disappointing payoff. To determine the public cost of alleviating underemployment and poverty, a least-cost combination of public programs was estimated for the simulated economy of a substate multicounty development district in eastern Oklahoma with sociodemographic characteristics reasonably representative of other low income rural areas of the nation. *Additional* spending on education and training programs had comparatively little impact on poverty; transfer payments constituted the overwhelming bulk of additional public outlays required to end poverty and underemployment.

Subsidized mobility for labor, even though highly cost-effective with a restricted program size, had only limited ability to end poverty and underemployment because most of the poor could not move to jobs, and approximately two out of three who move return home, often to low incomes and underemployment.

In addition to income transfer programs, the heart of a cost-effective policy for rural development was industrial development. Analysis of the economic efficiency of industrial development within a national context (20) revealed that approximately four out of five eastern Oklahoma workers employed in new industry would need to migrate to the metropolitan jobs for national economic efficiency to be enhanced by locating jobs in the metropolis instead of eastern Oklahoma. Since such high migration rates cannot be expected, national economic efficiency (raising national real income by using public funds to raise earnings of the employable poor) seems to benefit from generating jobs in growth centers in eastern Oklahoma.

Other resource development programs also can be economically efficient, according to research conducted at Oklahoma State University. While national output can expand from public funds committed to programs for the *employable* poor, real output contracts with major additional commitment of public transfer payments to the unemployable poor. The labor supply response and investment response to transfers were examined in detail because income transfer programs so completely overshadowed all others in public cost. Under a negative income tax of modest objectives (income guaranteed at 75 percent of poverty threshold, tax rate 50 percent), the labor effect would be less than 1 percent and the investment effect approximately 1 percent of national income. Together these two economic costs or foregone output of goods and services would total an estimated 2 percent of national income.

But the real social cost must consider not only the size but the distribution of income. The net social cost depends on marginal utilities of gainers and losers. A crude attempt was made to estimate the marginal utility of income for a representative American. If the proportional rates characteristic of total taxes in this country or the sampling of graduate students and faculty of agricultural economics at Oklahoma State University are taken as the social welfare function reflecting equal sacrifice, then transfer programs could be deemphasized and economic efficiency pursued irrespective of equity. But it is the authors' opinion that the federal personal income nominal tax schedule and the somewhat objective social-psychological study of personal effectiveness are the more reliable reflections of the marginal social welfare function. These latter sources of information indicate that failure to alleviate poverty represents a massive social cost (utility foregone), and movement to a more nearly equal distribution of income would minimize social cost even as national income is reduced. Obviously, empirical estimates of marginal utility are in a primitive state—this analysis is intended to probe the frontier with more fruitful development to follow.

REFERENCES

(1). Advisory Commission in Intergovernmental Relationships (ACIR), "State-Local Taxation and Industrial Location," A–30, Washington, USGPO, 1967.

(2). Averch, Harvey, et al., *How Effective is Schooling?* Report to the President's Commission on School Finance, Santa Monica: Rand Corporation, 1971.

(3). Bowman, Mary Jean, "Schultz, Denison and the Contribution of 'Eds' to National Economic Growth," *Journal of Political Economy* 72:450–64.

(4). Denison, Edward, *Why Growth Rates Differ*, Washington: The Brookings Institution, 1967.

(5). Economic Development Administration, *Program Evaluation: The EDA Growth Center Strategy*, Washington: U.S. Department of Commerce, 1972.

(6). Garfinkel, Irwin, "Income Maintenance Programs and Work Effort: A Review," Reprint 118, Institute for Research on Poverty, University of Wisconsin at Madison, 1974.

(7). Goldstein, Jon, "The Effectiveness of Manpower Training Programs," Paper No. 3 of Joint Economic Committee, 92nd Congress, Washington: USGPO, 1972.

(8). Greenberg, David and Marvin Kosters, "Income Guarantees and the Working Poor," R–579–OEO, Santa Monica: Rand Corporation, December 1970.

(9). Hansen, Niles, "Regional Development and the Rural Poor," *Journal of Human Resources* 4:205–14.

(10). Janssen, Larry, "Comparative Profit Rates of U.S. Manufacturing Firms by City Size," master's thesis, Oklahoma State University, 1974.

(11). Mera, Koichi, "Experimental Determination of Relative Marginal Utilities," *Quarterly Journal of Economics* 88:464–77.

(12). Murray, Tom, "Negative Income Tax," news release, Institute for Research on Poverty, University of Wisconsin at Madison, 1975.

(13). Musgrave, Richard and Peggy Musgrave, *Public Finance in Theory and Practice*, New York: McGraw-Hill, 1975.

(14). Nelson, James and Luther Tweeten, "Subsidized Labor Mobility—An Alternative Use of Development Funds," *Annals of Regional Science* 7:57–66.

(15). ———, "Systems Planning of Economic Development in Eastern Oklahoma," unpublished manuscript, Agricultural Experiment Station, Oklahoma State University, 1975.

(16). Office of Economic Opportunity, "Public Employment: Policy Issues and Data Needs," Office of Planning, Research and Evaluation, OEO, 1971.

(17). President's Commission on Income Maintenance Programs, *Poverty Amid Plenty: The American Paradox*, Washington: USGPO, 1969.

(18). Ribich, Thomas, "The Effect of Educational Spending on Poverty Reduction," in *Economic Factors Affecting the Financing of Education*, National Educational Finance Project, Gainesville, Florida, 1970.

(19). Schultz, T. W., "Investment in Human Capital," *American Economic Review* 51:1–17, 1961.

(20). Shaffer, Ron and Luther Tweeten, "Economic Changes from Industrial Development in Eastern Oklahoma," Bulletin B–715, Agricultural Experiment Station, Oklahoma State University, 1974.

(21). Singer, Neil M., "Federal Tax Incentives for Regional Growth," *Southern Economic Journal* 38:230–37, 1971.

(22). Smith, Jackie and Luther Tweeten, "Determinants of the Cost Effectiveness of Public Funds Used to Generate Jobs Through Industrial Development Projects: The EDA Experience," unpublished paper, Department of Agricultural Economics, Oklahoma State University, 1975.

(23). Stinson, Thomas, "The Effects of Taxes and Public Financing Programs on Local Industrial Development," Agricultural Economics Report No. 133, U.S. Department of Agriculture, 1968.

(24). Tweeten, Luther, *Foundations of Farm Policy*, Lincoln: University of Nebraska Press, 1970.

(25). ———, "Manpower Implications of the Rural Development Act of 1972," *Manpower Planning for Jobs in Rural America*, Proceedings of conference sponsored by Center for Rural Manpower and Public Affairs, Michigan State University, 1972.

(26). ———, "Job Search Behavior and Its Impact on Earnings," unpublished manuscript P–157, Institute for Research on Poverty, University of Wisconsin at Madison, 1974.

(27). Tweeten, Luther and Y. C. Lu, "Attitudes as a Measure of Optimal Place of Residence," *Social Science Journal* 13:2.

(28). Tweeten, Luther, et al., "The Economics of Elementary and Secondary Schooling in Oklahoma," Bulletin B–714, Agricultural Experiment Station, Oklahoma State University, 1974.

(29). U.S. Department of Commerce, *Statistical Abstract of the United States,* Washington: USGPO, 1961.
(30). U.S. Department of Labor, Manpower Administration, "Rural Manpower Dilemmas," in *Manpower Report of the President,* Washington: USGPO, 1971.
(31). Walker, Neal, "Effects of Major Social Insurance Programs on Income Distribution, Investment and Growth," Ph.D. thesis, Oklahoma State University, 1974.
(32). Weisbrod, Burton, *External Benefits of Public Education: An Economic Analysis,* Princeton: Princeton University Press, 1964.

Discussion

J .   D E A N   J A N S M A

T H E focus of this discussion will be on the areas of disagreement or difference in emphasis from that suggested by Tweeten and Walker. Perhaps unfairly, I will not discuss the many positive contributions of the Tweeten and Walker chapter.

In considering two perspectives on the economic cost of poverty—the cost of permitting poverty to continue and the cost of alleviating poverty—the authors suggest that they took the second approach. In reality, the chapter is based on a mixture of the two perspectives.

Tweeten and Walker believe "absolute deprivation" has in a large measure been eliminated. This is good news to the 25 million plus people in poverty in 1970. Also the current economic conditions must be having a major reversal effect on the "progress" made in the decade of the 1960s.

The authors also suggest that the most appropriate measure of poverty is utility foregone. This tends to limit measures of poverty to those factors with direct economic utility. An examination of infant mortality statistics or the less precise morbidity measures shows these to be directly related to the economic cost of poverty. Similarly, the finding that educational achievement in children is directly related to parents' income tends to be deemphasized in the authors' economically oriented evaluation of the cost of poverty.

The authors discuss the appropriateness of measuring alleviation of poverty in terms of narrowing income differences within society. They suggest that a decrease in income of high income individuals—with higher marginal propensities to investment—will decrease total income within the economy. I think this "negative effect" needs to be examined within the framework of offsets in aggregate demand which are related to the higher marginal propensity to consume of the lower income families.

A minor area of disagreement involves the procedures used by Tweeten and Walker to compute foregone earnings. Their procedure is based on average productivity. I think it is generally safe to assume that the unemployed are somewhat less skilled, and thus the estimate of $22.5 billion is probably an overestimation of foregone earnings.

In addition to considering policy alternatives, there is the problem of determining the appropriate strategy for implementing the proposed policy. Tweeten and Walker suggest a modified version of Schultz's industrial-urban hypothesis as a guide to *where* investments should be undertaken. They suggest that investment in local areas (industrial development) is an appropriate "cost effective" strategy. This is in disagreement with the basic Schultz formulation. However, Tweeten and Walker retain the 25,000 minimum size requirement for attaining efficiency in investment returns. More and more of the current literature is suggesting the inappropriateness of this rule-of-thumb guideline. Size of community needs to be included as a variable rather than specified ex ante as a constraint. We need to consider size in our research design —not assume the problem away on the basis of a theoretical "economy of size" argument that may or may not be true.

A related problem, inherent in most regional analysis, is the problem of generalizing results from the seven-county research area discussed by the authors. The problems of interregional leakages and changes in comparative advantage, for example, need to be considered.

Finally, a major section of the chapter examines the conceptual and empirical basis for considering trade-offs between maximum economic growth and more equitable income distribution. Although interesting, the approach is hard to evaluate because we are not permitted enough background to the analysis to make informed judgments. In general the approach is neoclassical rather than Keynesian, but one needs the supporting thesis of the coauthor Walker before making judgment on this section of the chapter.

Although this discussion may seem overcritical, it is meant to convey a need for considering alternative conceptual approaches. I want to commend the chapter and the entire program of work at Oklahoma State in this important and complex area of research.

Social cost of poverty

S A L L Y   B O U L D - V A N   T I L

A T the outset two problems are inherent in conceptualizing the costs of poverty on a nonmonetary as well as a monetary basis. The first problem is that economic costs and noneconomic costs are not always separate and distinct categories. For example, in riots, economic costs interact with social (noneconomic) costs. The second is that noneconomic costs could not be easily quantified even if the data were available. This chapter, therefore, focuses upon an interpretation of the meaning of the private and social costs of poverty and how the persistence of poverty can be understood in light of these costs. For purposes of definition, the unit of analysis for private costs will be the individual and for social costs, the collectivity. As the analysis proceeds, however, this distinction will be blurred because of the difficulties inherent in the concept of the collectivity.

In addition, this chapter focuses upon the costs of poverty which specifically affect the nonpoor. This approach contrasts with the conceptualization of the noneconomic costs of poverty during the sixties which emphasized the misery, unhappiness, degradation, marginality, and high rates of mental illness that the poor experience. This chapter examines, rather, the suffering of the nonpoor that is attributable to poverty. For example, a comparable case would be the suffering that the nonpoor experience from having to observe the acute suffering of the poor. Traditionally, such private noneconomic costs of poverty were relieved by giving to charity which permitted the nonpoor to reduce their own discomfort. The poor and ragged beggar learned how to play upon the sympathies of passersby in order to increase his take.

Although this private noneconomic cost eludes measurement, most observers would agree that such a cost of poverty is not particularly widespread in modern society. This is due, in part, to the shifting of

The author thanks Alan M. Horowitz for his comments and suggestions.

71

the obligation from private charity to public responsibility. Furthermore, once such public responsibility is accepted, then social insurance becomes the system by which the rich and prudent can protect themselves from the poor and careless (21, p. 31). Additionally, the direct experience of such a cost on the part of the nonpoor implies a high degree of empathy in the sense that "there, but for the grace of God, go I." This perspective implies that poverty is a random, natural phenomenon and that those who happen to be poor are not responsible for their condition. While this idea fitted well with the social philosophy of colonial America (with the notable exception of slaves), the industrial revolution brought a new idea to the fore: poverty increasingly began to be viewed as an unnatural phenomenon, a sign of a fall from grace. To be poor was a sign of being less fit in the social darwinian race for survival, which was the fault or the responsibility of the poor themselves (25, pp. viii ff.). Under this philosophy, the nonpoor would no longer empathize with the experience of suffering on the part of the poor. Indeed, quite the reverse was the case for those who were not poor; they could pride themselves on the fact that they, not having fallen into poverty, must have had the biological and/or moral capacity to rise above it.

When poverty is defined as the responsibility and fault of those who are poor, what was once a cost to the nonpoor becomes a benefit. These benefits have been explicitly acknowledged by Daniel P. Moynihan in an address to a group of affluent political liberals. He clarified for his listeners their place in the present system of stratification; each of them was "a person who has shared considerably in the rewards of American life, and can look forward to continued sharing and, if anything, on more favorable terms." But such benefits could not continue if poverty, were, in fact, to be eliminated and a more nearly equal society created:

> There are doubtless those among us so ungrateful, or so idealistic, as to wish or to be willing to give it all up in favor of a regime not yet more generous in its distribution of worldly and psychic goods, but there is none of us, I repeat, who would not in fact have something considerable of both to lose in the exchange. (quoted in 32, p. 41)

For Moynihan more than money is at stake. A more nearly equal society would mean a loss of relative status, as well, for those currently benefiting from existing inequalities (see also 8, p. 281). Furthermore, those who lost money and status could no longer view their material rewards as reflections of their inherent worth.

In this chapter, not only will the focus be upon the nonpoor, but the costs of poverty to the nonpoor will always be weighed against the benefits of poverty to the nonpoor, in order to judge whether the costs are greater than the benefits.

NONECONOMIC COSTS AND BENEFITS FOR THE NONPOOR

Costs. The predominant noneconomic social cost of poverty is the cost
of social disruption in terms of violence, riots, and social disorder.
Riots and social disruptions of the sixties were an urban phenomenon,
although historically there are instances of social disorder among the
rural poor. Nevertheless, the quieter rural areas of the sixties have not
been unaffected, since the influx of dollars for welfare and for other
social programs was, to a great extent, influenced by the need to quell
social disorders in cities (4). Violence and disruption in one area of society are likely to have negative consequences for other areas of society.

Benefits. In the case of riots and public disorder, it would appear that
the situation is one of overwhelming noneconomic social costs and
no social benefits. Nevertheless, the recurring eruption of social disorder
on the part of the poor indicates that society is willing to tolerate such
social disorder, dealing only with its symptoms rather than trying to
eliminate it entirely. A closer look at such social disorder in the analysis
of Piven and Cloward (23) indicates that it may be the result of aggregate benefits to the nonpoor for which the poor have been forced to
accept the costs. As Gans points out, the poor "can be made to absorb
the economic and political costs of change and growth" (8, p. 28). The
Report of the National Advisory Commission on Rural Poverty estimated, for example, that technological innovations decreased farm employment by 45 percent during the two previous decades (22, p. ix).
Furthermore, as Piven and Cloward note, this burden of technological
change that fell upon the rural poor was unrelieved; no commensurate
increase in welfare benefits provided for the needs of the rural unemployed. One consequence of this unrelieved burden was, according to
Piven and Cloward, the social disruptions of the sixties (23, pp. 219 ff.).
    Another dimension to the argument of Piven and Cloward is that
one of the functions of welfare is to regulate the labor of those in the
lowest stratum of the society. According to Gans, having a social group
to get the "dirty work" done is an important positive function of poverty
(8, p. 278). From quite a different policy perspective, Walter Miller also
shares the same analysis in his concern over policies aiming at "eliminating the low-skilled laboring class":

> How large a low-skilled laboring force does our society require? . . . From
> what sources are we to get incumbents of these jobs, and where are they to
> receive the socialization and training needed to execute them? Under ex-
> isting circumstances, the female-based child-rearing unit is a prime source
> of this essential pool of low-skilled laborers. It brings them into the world,
> and it furnishes them the values, the aspirations, and the psychic makeup
> that low-skilled jobs require (e.g., high tolerance of recurrent unemploy-

ment; high boredom tolerance, high flexibility with respect to work, residence, relational patterns; capacity to find life gratifications outside the world of work). (quoted in 15, pp. 227–28)

The problem is not simply one of getting the dirty work done, but of getting it done cheaply. Here the nonpoor may benefit in economic terms through lower prices (33, p. 188), while the low skilled worker is left to the ravages of the free market. This is especially characteristic of rural areas where underemployment as well as unemployment abound and where welfare and income protection programs are less likely to protect rural citizens (22, pp. 21 ff. and pp. 85 ff.; 31). Thomas's analysis suggests that those in the worst circumstances are rural workers in the South where general assistance is negligible, AFDC-Unemployed Parent programs nonexistent, Unemployment Compensation benefits limited, and minimum wage legislation minimal (29, pp. 73–74).

The importance of poverty in providing cheap labor for the South explicitly entered the debate over the key antipoverty program of the Nixon administration. Although the Family Assistance Program (FAP) did not receive widespread liberal support, I would concur with Moynihan that the primary reason for its failure was strong opposition by southerners on the Senate Finance Committee (19, pp. 225, 529). Indeed, those most likely to benefit from FAP would have been low wage workers in the South, especially the rural South, since the grant amount was too low to have had much impact on the distribution of income in other parts of the country. Columnist Kevin Phillips saw this issue clearly: "Poor people would be better off but the middle class . . . could be badly hurt" as well as the "Southern cheap-labor industry" (quoted in 19, p. 377). Lester G. Maddox, then Governor of Georgia, indicated "you're not going to be able to find anyone willing to work as maids or janitors or housekeepers if this bill gets through, that I promise you" (quoted in 19, pp. 378–79). Chairman Russell Long of the Senate Finance Committee evinced concern throughout the debate over FAP as to who would iron his shirts should FAP be implemented (reported in 34, p. 16).

The real issue was, of course, more than an economic one. It was also a question of "the rural socioeconomic powerbase of Dixie's conservative Democrats" (Phillips in 19, p. 377). A clever reporter explained exactly how the situation in the South might operate in terms of its effect on one family in one rural community, indicative of potential reverberations throughout the South:

In one of the most dilapidated of the shacks . . . four rooms hammered together from old boards and patched in spots with cardboard, Mrs. Adie Powell lives with her nine children, her parents, her sister and her sister's six children. All of these nineteen people now manage somehow to survive on $50 a week that Mrs. Powell makes on the assembly line at a local wood-processing plant, the sister's welfare check of $104 a month and the $192 old-age and social-security pension that Mrs. Powell's parents receive. . . . Under President Nixon's family-assistance program . . . things would get quite dramatically better for Mrs. Powell and all her kin. As a member of the "working poor," Mrs. Powell could draw $3,552 in cash and food stamps to augment her earnings of $2,500 at the mill. Her sister, as an unemployed welfare mother, could draw $3,316 in cash and stamps, and the parents would collect $2,640. Thus, on the effective date of the bill, July, 1971, annual household income would almost double overnight from $6,052 to $12,008, the sort of money now enjoyed only by the white merchant and landowner class in Alabama's black belt. (1, p. 66)

The welfare director of Georgia estimated that more than half the families in 80 rural Georgia counties would be eligible for FAP (1, p. 67). Throughout the deep South there would have been a large influx of federal dollars—an estimated $134 million in Georgia alone. Yet in the debate the southern cities ignored the potential benefits of such a program that would have poured money into the South, especially the rural South. For them the costs of change apparently overshadowed any possible benefits.

A more localized example is the case of ten rural Alabama counties' reaction to a proposal on the part of the federal government to invest much needed dollars for rural economic development. For the local community the economic costs would have been zero and the economic benefits $600,000. Furthermore, one could assume that certain noneconomic benefits would accrue to the local community from the upgrading of the local economy these investments were likely to foster. Nevertheless, the implementation of this program was strenuously resisted by city and county officials as well as local businessmen (20, p. 40). Clearly, in this case the benefits of the status quo were perceived as greater than the benefits that might have accrued with the program; this was true in spite of the fact that the economic balance sheet was one of zero cost and substantial benefits. A large part of the explanation lies in the fact that those arguing against economic development were really arguing against any change in the status arrangements between the better-off white population of the local community and the poor black population, since it was the latter who were to be the direct beneficiaries of the program. If the poor black community were to improve its position vis-à-vis the white community, then the latter would be in a position to lose status.

More important than status in the minds of the city officials would be the potential power redistribution and power loss resulting from a realignment of economic resources in the local communities. Prosperous black farmers would be in a better position than poor black farmers to organize political opposition challenging the county and city officials. In other words, local officials and businessmen had a political and social stake in the local status quo which included local poverty. This fear was especially real in this case since the grant was to go to the Southwest Alabama Farmers Cooperative Association, a potential political base. Moreover, those in a position to perceive the preponderance of costs over benefits for them in this program were also in a position to influence the final funding decision of the Office of Economic Opportunity (OEO) (16, pp. 47–48). A delegation of Alabama's senators and four of its eight representatives expressed their opposition to the program "on behalf of 'many of the county and city officials' . . . as well as the owners of the major packing companies in the area" (20, p. 40). The result was a reduction of funding by one-third and "a quid pro quo understanding" to sustain the governor's veto of another OEO grant to the National Sharecroppers' Fund.

In these examples, the factor of race obviously plays a key role; indeed, one might argue that the analysis should be more one of racism than of poverty. It is no accident, however, that there is a tremendous overlap between race and poverty. Furthermore, in cases of rural antipoverty programs that do not involve race, similar problems emerged. In his analysis of the Chenango Development Project conducted in Chenango County, New York, Stockdale concludes that "attempts to significantly alter the distribution of goods, services, power or prestige in rural communities will result in at least some conflict regardless of the methods used," and quite consistently there was evidence of "continual pressure for power actors in the county and some administrators in Cooperative Extension and the Agricultural Experiment Station at Cornell to minimize the use of approaches which might generate conflict" (27, pp. 14–18). Clearly, those in power in Chenango County did not wish to see any challenges to the status quo, which currently benefited them. Not unpredictably, local elites were successful in moving the program away from serious antipoverty efforts into the more conservative hands of the Cooperative Extension and the Administration of the College of Agriculture (28, p. 10).

How is it possible for local elites to justify their reluctance to change a status quo that entails a good deal of poverty? Such justification is accomplished by beliefs of the nonpoor that the poor do not really want to see any changes in their life styles; they, too, prefer the status quo. Thus, in opposing federal manpower programs, the Executive Committee and the staff of the Cooperative Extension Service of Mifflin County, Pennsylvania (40 percent rural and 24 percent poor), considered the poor to be "lazy" (20, p. 43). Further evidence suggests that the belief that the poor choose their poverty because they do not wish to work is not limited to Mifflin County but is, in fact, widespread among the nonpoor (10, 35). This resistance to manpower programs because the poor are "unwilling to work" may be critical in light of Hansen's review of the programs to combat poverty in rural areas, which concludes that "the greatest relative need of residents of depressed areas is for more investment in human resources and for expanded manpower programs" (11, p. 157).

NONECONOMIC COSTS AND BENEFITS: A FUNCTIONAL CAUSAL INTERPRETATION. From the examples above it can be inferred that the nonpoor, or at least certain subgroups of the nonpoor, want the persistence of poverty and that functional analysis similar to that presented by Gans (8) is relevant to a causal analysis of poverty. The basic element for a functional explanation is, according to Stinchcombe, that the consequences of a social arrangement are essential elements of the causes of that social arrangement, or, in other words, the consequences of poverty are essential elements of its causes (26, p. 80). Central to this type of functional analysis is the concept of want; the consequences form the essential elements of the cause because they are wanted. Those who benefit from the consequences of a social arrangement are thereby motivated to act in such a way as to bring about its existence or persistence.

The popular approach to poverty in the sixties can be understood in terms of a functional explanation: poverty persists because it is the way of life wanted by the poor. The value placed upon a culture of poverty by the poor then causes poverty. The poor are socialized into a motivational structure that leads them to want the life style of poverty and to ignore existing opportunities by which they could lift themselves out of poverty (14, p. 188). Banfield (3), similarly, sees that poverty is caused by the desire for a present oriented life style among the lower class. In this vein Walter Miller criticizes the government's antipoverty programs precisely because they are attempts to wipe out a way of life which is indeed wanted by those who are in it (18).

In spite of the publicity given to the "culture of poverty causes poverty" argument, critics have developed a rather substantial amount of evidence to indicate that there exists no aspirational culture of poverty (7, pp. 207–9). As Goodwin (9) has shown, poverty life styles are no more highly valued in the ghetto than outside of it. It is not necessary to assume, however, that all aspects of lower class culture are disvalued; indeed some aspects may be quite highly valued—for example, the norm of sharing. But, in examining the roster, it is clear that the costs of poverty far outweigh the benefits for the lower class participants. Thus, seeking an explanation of poverty, it is invalid to assume that poverty is a structure that is *desired* by the poor. It is the nonpoor, rather, whose structure of costs and benefits from this social arrangement is likely to motivate them to want the persistence of poverty.

According to Stinchcombe, one important indication of a phenomenon for which functional analysis is relevant is a case in which "the end is achieved in spite of causes tending to keep it from being achieved"

(26, p. 83). Poverty is certainly such a situation. As early as 1909, Lloyd George, in announcing his budget to wage warfare against poverty, said, "I cannot help believing that before this generation has passed away, we shall have advanced a great step toward that good time when poverty and the degradation which always follows in its camp will be as remote to the people of this country as the wolves which once infested its forests" (quoted in 17, p. 185). Economists today might question this statement of 1909 as being somewhat premature, for there are certain economic constraints to the elimination of poverty. Nevertheless, in the U.S. in 1964, when President Johnson declared a total war on poverty, one of the justifications was that "for the first time in our history it is possible" (12).

In June 1966, Shriver's plan for the elimination of poverty predicted total victory by 1976—to provide a historic precedent for the bicentennial (2, pp. 56, 61). It is clear that no such victory will accompany the bicentennial. Furthermore, no such victory looms on the horizon in the next decade—and no political commentators are making such rash predictions. The situation has reversed itself, so that advice being offered by Moynihan and Banfield, among others, implies that poverty will always be with us, that little can be done about it, and that politicians ought not to promise the poor anything other than their poverty—since such promises only lead to frustration (3, p. 245).

It is no doubt true that antipoverty efforts of the sixties were hampered by the usual inefficiencies, ineptitudes, and bureaucratic bunglings at the local level as well as the federal level. Furthermore, a generalized hostility toward federal intervention is especially prevalent in rural areas. However, this local level bungling and hostility seem to be reserved primarily for programs that might change the status quo—in other words, those programs which would increase the political and economic power of the poor. There appears to be no problem of local support for other federal programs aimed at improving the standard of living in rural areas. The "successful" programs such as the Farmers Home Administration (FmHA) and the farm price supports are those that provide substantial benefits to the better-off farmers with minimum assistance to the poor (24, pp. 289–90). Of FmHA loans or grants, ranging from $349 million to $160 million during the years 1961–66, one estimate is that only $50 million annually benefited the poor (5, p. 454). In fact one effect of the FmHA program among Spanish-Americans was to increase the poverty of the poor farmer due to land foreclosures (13, p. 11).

The original intention of the farm programs developed during the 1930s was to help the needy farmer. There is some evidence, in fact, that these original programs operated first by the Resettlement Administration in 1935 and later by the Farm Security Administration in 1937 were successful in reaching poor farm families (6, p. 195). Unfortunately for the rural poor these programs were probably too successful; their reorganization, creating the Farmers' Home Administration in 1946, basically eliminated the radical features of the original programs (30, p. 398). One feature eliminated was the possibility of loans to cooperatives, a fortuitous choice for the political and economic elite of the South in light of the development of rural cooperatives among poor blacks.

In conclusion, the basic reason that the FmHA programs "worked" and the OEO programs did not was that the latter presented a challenge to the status quo while the former did not. Furthermore, this pattern of action and reaction suggests that the balance sheet of the structure of society that includes poverty is a favorable one for the nonpoor. For the poor the balance sheet appears to be clearly unfavorable. One further difference between the poor and the nonpoor is that the latter have the power to influence the social structure in their favor whereas the former do not. By the nature of the balance sheet the nonpoor have both the wants that are met by the persistence of poverty and the power to have their wants reflected in the system of social arrangements. Together these elements form the basic explanation for why poverty has persisted in spite of all attempts to eliminate it. Thus the consequences of poverty, from the perspective of those who have the power to make changes, explain poverty. Antipoverty programs of the sixties failed not because the society could not afford a full-scale war on poverty, but because the middle and upper classes did not wish to see such a beneficial social arrangement eliminated.

This analysis suggests clear implications for the future of antipoverty programs. The first would be to seek an alternative set of social arrangements or functional alternatives that would provide the same benefits for the nonpoor as poverty currently does. As Gans has pointed out, this route is a difficult if not impossible one (8, pp. 284 ff.). The second implication would be to change the balance sheets so that poverty is more costly for the nonpoor. The position which Gans takes is that "phenomena like poverty can be eliminated only when they become sufficiently dysfunctional for the affluent" (8, p. 288). A third alternative would be to change the structure of power in the society so that the poor could exert a greater influence upon social arrangements or, in Gans' terms, so that "the poor can obtain enough power to change the system of social stratification" (8, p. 288).

The last alternative is that of economic growth. Although this has always been a popular slogan for antipoverty programs among economists, it is important to recognize here that what is involved is neither very simple nor very cheap. A simple logic of economic growth suggests that the growth dividend be appropriated for the poor, thereby bringing them above poverty standards; that process in itself, however, would significantly affect the distribution of income as in the example of the Family Assistance Plan (although the latter's benefits would have been below the poverty line). Thus an economic growth approach could succeed in bringing everyone out of poverty and preserving the present balance only by, in effect, moving everyone significantly forward on the economic ladder, leaving overall economic inequalities, as well as status and power inequalities, intact. This would, of course, require tremendous economic growth and would also raise the issue of poverty as relative deprivation even after such hypothetical growth occurred.

REFERENCES

(1). Armstrong, Richard, "The Looming Money Revolution Down South," *Fortune,* June 1970, pp. 66–69, 152 ff.
(2). Arnold, Mark R., "The Good War That Might Have Been," *New York Times Magazine,* September 29, 1974, pp. 56–76
(3). Banfield, Edward C., *The Unheavenly City,* Boston: Little, Brown and Co., 1968.
(4). Betz, Michael, "Riots and Welfare: Are They Related? *Social Problems* 21 (3): 345–55.
(5). Bonnen, James T., "Rural Poverty: Programs and Problems," *Journal of Farm Economics* 48 (2): 452–65.
(6). Cochrane, Willard, *City Man's Guide to the Farm Problem,* Minneapolis: University of Minnesota Press, 1965.
(7). Gans, Herbert J., "Culture and Class in the Study of Poverty: An Approach to Anti-Poverty Research," in D. Moynihan, ed., *On Understanding Poverty,* New York: Basic Books, 1968.
(8). ———, "The Positive Functions of Poverty," *American Journal of Sociology* 78:275–89.
(9). Goodwin, Leonard, *Do the Poor Want to Work?* Washington: The Brookings Institution, 1972.
(10). ———, "How Suburban Families View the Work Orientations of the Welfare Poor," *Social Problems* 19:337–48.
(11). Hansen, Niles M., *Rural Poverty and the Urban Crisis,* Bloomington: Indiana University Press, 1970.
(12). Johnson, Lyndon B., "Message on Poverty," *Congressional Record,* May 16, 1964.
(13). Knowlton, Clark S., "An Analysis of Certain Selected Causes of Poverty in San Miguel County," paper, annual meeting, Rural Sociological Society, Montreal, August 22–25, 1974.
(14). Lewis, Oscar, "The Culture of Poverty," in D. Moynihan, ed., *On Understanding Poverty,* New York: Basic Books, 1968.
(15). Liebow, Elliot, *Tally's Corner,* Boston: Little, Brown and Co., 1967.
(16). Marshall, Ray and Lamond Goodwin, *Cooperatives and Rural Poverty in the South,* Baltimore: Johns Hopkins Press, 1971.
(17). Miliband, Ralph, "Politics and Poverty," in D. Wedderburn, ed., *Poverty, Inequality and Class Structure,* London: Cambridge University Press, 1974.
(18). Miller, Walter, "The Elimination of the American Lower Class as National Policy: A Critique of the Ideology of Poverty Movements in the 1960s," in D. Moynihan, ed., *On Understanding Poverty,* New York: Basic Books, 1968.
(19). Moynihan, Daniel P., *The Politics of a Guaranteed Income,* New York: Vintage Books, 1973.
(20). Munk, Michael, *Rural Youth-Work Programs: Problems of Size and Scope,* Center for the Study of Unemployed Youth, New York University, 1967.
(21). Musgrave, Richard A., "The Role of Social Insurance in an Overall Program for Social Welfare," in W. Bowen et al., eds., *The Princeton Symposium on the American System of Social Insurance,* New York: McGraw-Hill, 1967.

(22). National Advisory Commission on Rural Poverty, *The People Left Behind,* Washington: USGPO, 1967.

(23). Piven, Francis Fox and Richard A. Cloward, *Regulating the Poor,* New York: Pantheon Books, 1971.

(24). President's Commission on Income Maintenance Programs, Background Papers, Washington: USGPO, 1970.

(25). Rothman, David J. and Sheila M. Rothman, *On Their Own: The Poor in Modern America,* Reading, Mass.: Addison-Wesley, 1972.

(26). Stinchcombe, Arthur L., *Constructing Social Theories,* New York: Harcourt, Brace and World, 1968.

(27). Stockdale, Jerry D., "Rural Organization and Poverty Action," paper, Society for the Study of Social Problems, Montreal, August 25, 1974.

(28). ———, "The University and Purposive Social Change: Selected Issues and Analyses of an Anti-Poverty Effort," Working Paper No. V, Cornell University, 1973.

(29). Thomas, George, *Poverty in the Nonmetropolitan South: A Causal Analysis,* Lexington, Mass.: Lexington Books, 1972.

(30). Tweeten, Luther, *Foundations of Farm Policy,* Lincoln: University of Nebraska Press, 1970.

(31). U.S. Department of Agriculture, Economic Research Service, *The People Left Behind—Four Years Later,* Washington: USGPO, November 30, 1971.

(32). Valentine, Charles A., *Culture and Poverty,* Chicago: University of Chicago Press, 1968.

(33). Wachtel, Howard M., "Capitalism and Poverty in America: Paradox or Contradiction," *American Economic Review* 62 (2): 187–94.

(34). Welsh, James, "Welfare Reform: Born, August 8, 1969, Died, October 4, 1972," *New York Times Magazine,* January 7, 1973, pp. 14–17.

(35). Williamson, John B., "Beliefs About the Motivation of the Poor and Attitudes Toward Poverty Policy," *Social Problems* 21:634–48.

Discussion

GERALD R. LESLIE

I N the space of a few pages I will try to suggest here some alternative approaches to the issues raised by Dr. Bould-Van Til. Her analysis is cast essentially in functionalist terms and argues that poverty persists in part because the benefits it provides to powerful segments of the society outweigh the costs to those same powerful groups and, perhaps, to the society at large. The costs are borne largely by the poor themselves and remain somewhat hidden. That the poor are disproportionately black and have little political power helps keep the problem hidden.

This idea receives some support from the analysis of race relations in the United States done by Gunnar Myrdal and his colleagues at the time of World War II and published under the title *An American Dilemma*. These scholars emphasized the moral conflict created by prejudice and discrimination in the breasts of white people who could not wholly reconcile such discrimination with their professed ideals of democracy. Evidently this partly suppressed moral conflict still exists; witness the necessity to construct a "culture of poverty" concept to explain that "poor people really prefer it that way." On the face of it, the explanation is absurd. No one wants his children to be bloated by malnutrition, to be mugged on the streets, or to become heroin addicts. Strong evidence exists, as Bould-Van Til points out, that the poor share the same values of achievement, work, and acquisition of material goods as the rest of us. The rationalization is necessary, however, to justify perpetuation of the status quo.

The so-called federal "war on poverty" was, of course, not more than a minor skirmish because virtually none of its proponents was prepared to endorse or endure major changes in the institutional structure of the society. Those few programs that offered some hope of sharing political power with the poor—such as the Community Action Program and Legal Services to the Poor—were widely attacked, budgetarily undercut, and stripped of their potential for inducing change.

Bould-Van Til is not optimistic about the possibility of eliminating or even seriously reducing poverty in the future. Not only is there resistance to change, but we quickly become ensnarled in problems of whether poverty should be defined, for example, in terms of absolute income levels, shares of income going to various segments of the population, or the income level received by some lowest fraction of the population.

But the emphasis in this chapter is on noneconomic private and social costs. To me this emphasis requires that we focus not only on the fact that poverty is beneficial to some, but also on the costs to those who bear them. As Bould-Van Til points out, this is difficult because we, as social scientists, have not adequately defined those costs, let alone found ways to measure them. Possibly we are part of those who benefit from poverty and have had little incentive to do analyses that would threaten our own favored positions.

Functionalism, as Bould-Van Til indicates, has been a very widely used framework in sociology and can be used to indicate the obstacles to change. The use of more than one framework in so short a chapter would not be feasible. Indeed, Bould-Van Til accomplished a great deal in the space afforded her. But other theoretical frameworks in sociology can and should be employed in analysis of the social costs of poverty. One of these frameworks is social-psychological and one is purely sociological.

The social-psychological framework is that of symbolic interaction and uses the concepts of status, role, and the social self to focus upon the ways that people learn to function in society. Status refers to position in the social structure and differentiates between statuses that are ascribed to individuals at birth and those that may readily be changed during the individual's lifetime. Poverty basically is an ascribed status. There is downward social mobility in the stratification system, but few people move far enough downward to go from nonpoverty to poverty, and fewer yet do so early enough in life to change the "life chances" of their children. Poor people typically are the offspring of poor people who were the offspring of poor people, and so on. Technically we do not have a caste system with a disprivileged class condemned to perpetual poverty, but terms like "underclass" that do seem to fit the facts suggest that there are castelike elements in the system.

People at all social levels learn early in life that they are more or less worthy essentially according to the status of their parents. The higher the parental status, the more favorable ("healthy") the self concept. Unfavorable self concepts, by contrast, are often referred to as "damaged" or "unhealthy." The general wisdom recognizes that poor children are likely to develop unfavorable conceptions of themselves that severely handicap them in their efforts to compete for whatever goods the society has to offer.

In personal terms, this has the makings of tragedy. All but the totally insensitive among us must suffer with these unfortunate individuals. Socially, there is tremendous cost here. Depending on the estimate of the extent of this hard core poverty, some 12 percent or more of the population is prevented from developing anything like their potential for becoming productive members of the society. I speak not only of the poor who will never become managers or officials but also of the Picassos, the Einsteins, and the Tebaldis who will never be.

Lest this seem too mawkish for toughminded economists, these costs should be susceptible to translation into hard data through the concept of social indicators. The concentration of disease and malnutrition among the poor is subject to measurement. Crime, which has received much public attention in recent years and is a very serious problem, can be shown to be linked to poverty. Low educational achievement, divorce and desertion, and one-parent families are other potential indicators. If we as social scientists were so inclined, over a period of years we could document private and social costs of poverty both to the poor and to the society at large that might far outweigh the advantages in having someone to iron our shirts and do our other dirty work.

In this limited space I have barely scratched the surface of applying this approach, but I need still to suggest a few possibilities of assessing social costs through use of a conflict framework. Essentially, this approach argues that harmony is not the natural relationship among the various groups and categories that make up a population. Instead, their interests are directly opposed; one can profit only at the expense of the others, and social integration is maintained only as a tenuous equilibrium among the competing forces.

The poor appear to be composed of several such segments of the population, some of whom are potentially powerful and some of whom are not. One segment is black. Poverty among blacks is suffered by proportionately three times as many people as among whites (34 percent to 12 percent in 1970). The approximately 7 million black people living in poverty probably can be identified with up to 7 million more "near poor" blacks who fall above the official poverty line but still live in substantial deprivation.

Nearly 5 million poor people are over 65 years of age. Theirs is not so much inherited poverty and lack of skills as it is a function of the inadequacy of the Social Security and social welfare programs upon which they depend for most of their incomes.

Another 4 million farm people live in poverty, but their situation is better analyzed through Bould-Van Til's functionalist framework. Marginal farm operators and farm laborers appear to be firmly under the control of prosperous and politically powerful rural interests.

Blacks and the aged are unlikely to wield enough power to force the society to deal with their poverty directly, but they have ultimately a far more devastating power: the power to factionalize and disrupt. Complex modern societies are incredibly susceptible to disruption. Strikes by groups of employees from steel workers to hospital employees to school teachers provide evidence enough. The rampant inflation which has been gripping much of the world has economic causes obviously, but many of those factors stem from the extremely sensitive dependency of one segment of the economy on others. Many of those organizational factors are not, in a strict sense, economic.

To oversimplify, society can no longer afford the exploitation of certain groups because increasingly they can and do fight back. Governments increasingly formulate policies that try to provide something for everybody and, consequently, satisfy nobody. One seldom hears anybody these days talking about the United States as a superpower. It would be too much to attribute our decline as a world power to our failure to solve the poverty problem. Failure to provide justice for all in the distribution of goods and services in the near future, however, can only hasten our further decline.

Alternative theoretical frameworks for viewing rural poverty and income distribution

Neoclassical economic theory, poverty, and income distribution

G . E D W A R D S C H U H

T H E points of departure for the neoclassical theory of income distribution are that factor markets matter, that marginalism is useful for understanding how resources are allocated and in turn the value of resources, and Joan Robinson and her colleagues notwithstanding, that some sense can be made of the production function, so it can be used as the basis of a marginalist theory of production (for recent works on neoclassical theory, see 12 and 16). Neoclassical theory is distinguished from classical theory in that it treats the value of resources symmetrically to the value of products, with the explanation made in terms of a common set of demand and supply forces. Classical theory, in contrast, had an ad hoc theory for explaining the price of land, labor, and capital. Neoclassical theory is also distinguished from Keynesian distribution theory by its emphasis on the factor markets rather than on the product markets.

Neoclassical theory is often referred to as the marginal productivity theory of distribution, probably because of the extent to which the traditional theory of marginal productivity is applied to the special cases of wages, rent, interest, and profits. However, as Friedman has pointed out (19), the theory of marginal productivity is only a theory of demand for factors. The "scissors" are completed with theories of supply, and here the unity is lost, for the set of factors that determines the supply of labor offered to the market differs from the set that determines the supply of other factors. The difference exists because human beings provide labor services and hence tastes and preferences matter.

The neoclassical theory of income distribution has serious limitations, perhaps the most serious being that in its static formulation it takes the distribution of assets as given. However, extensions of the theory can and have been made to handle this problem in part. Moreover, investment theory can help in the understanding of accumulation of assets by an individual, so we are not as limited as the usual statements of the basic theory would imply.

The theory of income distribution is probably the most underutilized part of neoclassical theory. This is puzzling, for the analytical apparatus is comprehensive and powerful. Some have ascribed this neglect to the aforementioned problem that it takes the distribution of assets as given and hence is of limited value. Others say it is because the inability to make interpersonal comparisons of utility limit what one can say in a normative way about one distribution of income compared to another, with the result that the income distribution question is sterile. But clearly the inability to compare the "goodness" or "badness" of alternative distributions of income should not preclude us from attempting to understand the forces determining the distribution of income.

A more plausible explanation for the underutilization of the theory is that economists have just not taken an interest in income distribution problems. Whether this is because of a lack of sensitivity to the income distribution problem or because of a fear of being labeled a radical or a revolutionary is beyond us here. What I hope to show in this chapter is that there is an ample body of theory to draw on if the motivation is present to use it. The need is for more empirical research designed to test and extend the theory, and to improve our knowledge of the parameters that describe the world we live in.

This chapter is divided into four parts. The first is a brief statement of the assumptions of the neoclassical theory. This is followed by a description of two commonly accepted sectoral theories or explanations of rural poverty. The third section covers more limited bodies of micro theory that can be drawn on for an explanation and understanding of rural poverty. And the final part deals with some of the policy implications of the neoclassical theory.

No attempt is made to lay out a textbook exposition of the theory.

ASSUMPTIONS OF NEOCLASSICAL DISTRIBUTION THEORY.

The usual assumptions of neoclassical distribution theory include those of perfect competition: a large number of competing units; perfect knowledge and foresight on the part of decision makers; profit and utility maximization; homogeneous factors of production; and fixed institutional arrangements. Resources are assumed to be perfectly mobile, wage rates and other "prices" are assumed to be flexible both upward and downward, and resources are assumed to be fully employed. Finally, individual decision-making processes are assumed, in contrast to decisions based on class or race.

Many of these assumptions can be relaxed and the theory can still remain useful. Or perhaps to put it more accurately, the theory becomes more useful when the usual textbook assumptions are relaxed and the implications of so doing are traced. We will see below that important causes of rural poverty are due to the failure of markets to work perfectly, or due to the assumptions of the theory not being fulfilled in the empirical world. Important policy implications may in some cases have to do with attempting to establish the conditions for more efficient and perfectly functioning markets.

SECTORAL EXPLANATIONS OF RURAL POVERTY. Two neoclassical theories deal with the problem of *relative* poverty in agriculture. One deals with the secular tendency of the incomes of farm people to lag behind those of nonfarm people as an economy develops, and the other deals with the spatial distribution of incomes within agriculture. Both theories are rooted in the factor markets and depend importantly on assumed imperfections in those markets.

The explanation for the secular lag in incomes in agriculture traces, I believe, to Book IV of Mill, although it was brought into post–World War II discussions of the farm problem by T. W. Schultz in his book on the *Economic Organization of Agriculture* (43). The income elasticity of demand for agricultural products is low relative to the demand for nonfarm goods and services, and declines as per capita incomes rise because of Engel's Law. If product supply curves were shifting to the right at the same rates, the difference in income elasticities of demand would in themselves require the transfer of resources from agriculture to the nonfarm sector, largely because countries start the development process with the bulk of their resources in agriculture.

This need to transfer resources would itself cause relative incomes in the farm sector to be below those in the nonfarm sector. But a number of factors act to aggravate the problem. First, reproduction rates of the farm population tend to be higher than the nonfarm population because the costs of production of children are lower and institutional restrictions against children participating in the labor force are not strong. Hence, the agricultural sector becomes a net producer of children, in the sense that it contributes more labor to the sectors' labor force than can be absorbed by it. Second, as countries invest in new production technology for the agricultural sector, the product supply curve shifts to the right more rapidly. Moreover, this new production technology tends to be embedded in new modern inputs, making the rate of return to capital investments relatively high and shifting the proportion among inputs. And finally, land has only limited opportunities, so the extent to which it is shifted out of agriculture is limited. Asset values may be written down, but at the margin the price of land can fall to quite low levels before it is withdrawn from production.

The consequence of this combination of factors is that the agricultural labor force has to bear the burden of the adjustment process. This characteristic transfer of labor from the farm to the nonfarm sector as an economy develops has been referred to as the agricultural transformation. (For an excellent survey of the literature dealing with this subject, see 23.) The problem becomes especially serious because product demand shifts to the right only slowly, the fertility rates of farm people tend to be relatively high, there is little adjustment in land, and rates of return are such that capital increases and new, more highly productive inputs are introduced into the farm sector. The returns to labor in agriculture decline in a relative sense, although they may be increasing absolutely.

If factor markets were perfect, of course, there would be no decline in the relative returns to labor. But agricultural labor markets are far from perfect. The agricultural labor force tends to be widely dispersed geographically and hence its members are not always well informed about urban labor markets. To take alternative employment often requires geographic moves, with the associated risks and pecuniary costs as well as the nonpecuinary costs of leaving family and friends. And the agricultural labor force tends to be ill equipped for employment in the nonfarm sector. Governments tend to underinvest in formal education for rural people and in vocational training programs as well.

The greater the adjustment required, and the greater the imperfections in the labor market, the more will labor incomes in agriculture lag behind those in the nonfarm sector. The size of the adjustment required will depend largely on the rate of technological improvement in agriculture and the relative size of the fertility differential. The seriousness of the imperfections will depend on relative differentials in education, the geographic dispersion of nonfarm activities, and the development of communications and transportation. In Brazil, a semi-industrialized country, the nature of the problem is such that even in 1970 the average labor income in the agricultural sector was only one-third that in the nonfarm sector, and this for the most part represents real income differentials (42). The differential has never been as large in the United States, although during the 1950s the differential in some regions, especially the South, was quite large (39).

The rather large geographical differences in per capita income within the agricultural sector complicate the problem of relative rural poverty. To explain this phenomenon, Schultz postulated a theory of spatial development that has come to be called the urban-industrial impact hypothesis (43). This hypothesis has been extensively tested with the U.S. data (for a survey see 40), with somewhat mixed results—the model seems to have greater explanatory power for data from east of the Mississippi River than for data from states west of the river. The model has also been tested with data from other countries (37).

The hypothesis can be summarized in three propositions: (1) economic growth in a community occurs at different locations and at different times, in contrast to a generalized phenomenon that proceeds constantly over time, (2) the centers of growth are primarily urban–industrial in composition, and (3) the existing economic organization functions best at or near the center of a particular matrix of development, and also in those agricultural zones located favorably in relation to such a matrix.

A number of implications follow from these propositions. First, the income level of agriculture in a community that experiences urban-industrial growth can be expected to increase relative to that which does not experience such growth. Second, because of a spatial adjustment lag, the closer a community is to an urban-industrial center, the higher the level of agricultural income in the community will be.

From his original three propositions, Schultz argues that three factors associated with industrial growth create regional income disparities. First, industrialization causes an increase in the proportion of the population engaged in productive work. Second, productivity of the labor force increases, based on such factors as increased investments in education. And third, impediments to factor-price equalization are reduced. Put differently, there is a reduction in the imperfections in the factor and product markets faced by agriculture as a result of the urban-industrial development.

Keith Bryant (13) has extended, tested, and reinterpreted the original Schultz formulation of the model. He argues that the effect of urban industrialization on agricultural development operates through somewhat different channels and in a somewhat different way than Schultz originally postulated. In the first place he believes that the role of market imperfections has been overplayed, both by Schultz and by later researchers who tested the theory. He shows that in the United States most of the observed relationships can be understood as a simple influx of capital from the industrial sector and that, contrary to what others have argued, the evidence for a reduction in market imperfections is not present.

Second, Bryant argues that the effect of urban-industrial development on agriculture is largely a consequence of agglomeration and involves at least four factors. Expansion of the nonfarm labor market increases the numbers and kinds of jobs available to prospective migrants, availability that speeds up the migration process. The price of labor in agriculture rises as a consequence, and this in turn encourages a reorganization of factors in agriculture to make labor more productive.

A similar set of forces works in the capital market. The urban-industrial complex mobilizes savings that become available to agriculture at a lower interest rate. The combination of changes in the labor and capital markets shifts the labor-capital price ratios, fostering the substitution of capital for labor and in turn raising the productivity of labor, other things being equal. With new production technology embedded in the capital goods, a further impetus to improvements in labor productivity is provided.

The local demand for farm products also expands as the urban population grows and is spatially concentrated through agglomeration. This expanding market fosters specialization in production, which permits the realization of economies to size and/or scale. In addition the high income levels in the urban center tend to create a market for labor-intensive, high income cash crops. The cash flow on farms is increased, which in turn reduces the amount of capital rationing.

Finally, the agglomeration results in more social overhead capital in the form of roads, an improved communication system, more abundant sources of power, and an expanded and improved education system. The latter, of course, leads to increased labor mobility and to an increase in productivity of the labor that remains in agriculture

Bryant's recasting of the Schultz theory does not remove it from neoclassical tradition, but it does focus the analysis on a somewhat different set of variables, and it leads to somewhat different policy implications. Both models are disequilibrium theories, however, and provide explanations consistent with the neoclassical theory of why geographic differences in per capita incomes exist within agriculture. Bryant's interpretation deemphasizes the importance of institutional factors, but still focuses in large part on developments in the factor markets.

Martin Katzman (24) has recently developed a neoclassical formulation of the Von Thuenen paradigm and compared it to the urban-industrial impact model. He points out that to the extent spatial variations in commodity and factor prices reflect transfer costs, the urban-industrial impact model logically reduces to a Von Thuenen model. The urban-industrial paradigm genuinely differs from the Von Thuenen model, however, in its emphasis on market imperfections associated with monopoly and monopsony in rural areas dominated by small towns. The evidence from his tests suggests that a synthesis of the Von Thuenen and urban-industrial impact models will provide a stronger explanation of the relationship between urban and rural development.

To summarize, the explanation of the secular lag of farm incomes behind those in the nonfarm sector rests inherently on the problem of imperfect factor markets, especially for labor. One explanation for spatial differences in per capita incomes within agriculture also gives a major role to factor market imperfections, although the problem is more general than just the labor market. The revisionist interpretation of the spatial-lag model, however, gives more emphasis to price differentials related to distance and differentials in transportation costs. The policy implications that flow from these alternative interpretations are somewhat different.

MICRO THEORIES. Recent developments in economic theory have far outrun our empirical knowledge and empirical research. This new theory, which could perhaps better be described as extension and reformulation of old theory, holds much promise of understanding poverty and of offering prescriptions for policy. Until improved data are generated, however, and we make greater strides in quantifying the parameters, the contribution of the theory to improved policy will be limited.

The problem is not just that those inclined to empirical work have not taken up the task. Rather, major contributions to economic theory in the last decade have not yet been incorporated into common ways of thinking about our economic problems, even in contexts more general than the problem of the rural poor. In this section I intend to concentrate on these new contributions, but the discussion is not limited to this theory. Included also is a consideration of some theory that has been with us for some time.

The Accumulation of Resources. Poverty is a characteristic of individuals or households. The incomes that families or individuals receive is largely a function of the quantity of assets or resources that the entity holds and the value or price that society puts on those assets. Neoclassical theory has much to say about the value that society will place on resources. But until recently, at least in its static formulation, neoclassical theory had very little to say about the resources the individual or family had or about resource accumulation over time. That is because for all practical purposes it takes the distribution of assets as given. Macrodynamic theories, especially those that are Keynesian in tradition, have dealt with the resource accumulation problem at the macro level, largely through an investment function. But the micro underpinnings of this theory have been rather weak.

Dynamic extensions of the micro theory, on the other hand, have provided some insights into this problem. The farm management literature, especially by Heady (22) and Glenn Johnson (11), has been particularly useful in dealing with the problem of credit and capital rationing. I would like to focus first on this body of theory.

Farmers and households tend to operate with both their own assets and borrowed assets or credit. Willingness or ability to borrow resources is an important means of obtaining output and income growth and may influence the rate at which new production technology is adopted, the rate at which the stock of owned resources grows, the mobility of the family unit, and in turn its ability to take advantage of alternative income opportunities.

In a static framework a farm or family unit would borrow resources up to the point where the marginal value product (MVP) of the last unit is just equal to its marginal acquisition cost. However, we know that in the presence of risk and uncertainty, farm family units do not in general do this. Rather, they impose credit rationing on themselves as a hedge against risk and uncertainty and as a means of remaining flexible to take advantage of new income alternatives. In addition, banks and other lenders impose external credit rationing on farm units as a means of protecting themselves against the same risk and uncertainty associated with the farming unit.

Control over a larger quantity of resources is clearly an important source of growth or income for a farm family. If the unit lacks owned resources, credit becomes an important alternative. And strictly from an efficiency standpoint, credit should be extended and utilized to the point where its MVP is equal to the marginal factor cost (MFC). To the extent that credit is not extended or utilized to this point, both the family unit and the economy sacrifice potential growth.

Such credit rationing can be an important cause of poverty or at least an explanation of why a family or an individual does not move out of poverty. Unfortunately, all too often banks and other lending institutions make their lending decisions on the basis of the assets the individual has already accumulated rather than on his capability to use his resources efficiently. In the United States, specialized public lending institutions have been established to help overcome this problem.

The capital rationing theory does not address itself to the question of the particular investment decision. But the theory of human capital does, and provides important insights into the causes of poverty. The formal elaboration of the theory of human capital owes much to Schultz (44, 46) and Becker (5, 6), but traces its antecedents to Frank Knight's theory of capital, and before him to Alfred Marshall and Adam Smith.

The theory of human capital rests on a division of the total stock of capital in a society into physical capital on the one hand and human capital on the other. Human capital includes the knowledge expressed in the culture of a society and embedded in the minds of its population, the skills that its population has, and the status of its health. Physical capital, of course, refers to the machinery and equipment that we use, tools, roads, and other physical infrastructure.

The distinction between these two types of capital rests in part on the peculiar social institutions that western civilization has evolved. Slavery is not permitted, so one person cannot take possession of another. This tends to lead to underinvestments in the human agent if only free market forces are allowed to come into play, because the market for human capital will be imperfect. Similar market imperfections affect investments in the production of new knowledge. Although of great value to society, it is difficult for private firms to capture the benefits of some new knowledge. Hence, with a free market organization, society will tend to underinvest in the knowledge industry.

Education has been found to be an important determinant of cross-sectional earnings profiles and is thus justifiably treated as a capital good. Similarly, the production and distribution of new knowledge has been found to be an important source of output growth, both in agriculture and in other sectors.

Because of the market imperfections associated with human capital and the related tendency of societies to underinvest in this form of capital, the social rate of return to such investments is often quite high. For this reason such investments are often viewed as high payoff investments when growth and development are the goals. Undertaking such investments at the appropriate level is a key to the problem of absolute poverty, although it is easy to forget that the proportion between physical and human capital can be an important determinant of the rate of return.

In the context of relative poverty, the problem is threefold. First, the market imperfections may be more serious for some groups than for others. Second, since some components of both education and research tend to be socialized in order to obtain the optimum level of investment, all groups in society may not have equal access to the system. This, of course, has been one of the problems for blacks. And finally, not all individuals have the same innate talent to benefit from the particular training programs that society provides, or their particular talents may not be valued highly by society.

The New Household Economics. Recent extensions of economic theory enable us to deal with, and in fact stress the importance of, problems of human capital, the allocation of time, and nonmarket household behavior. These contributions to the theory enable us to deal systematically with conventional economic variables such as income, consumption, saving, and labor force behavior within a unified choice-theoretic framework. In addition, they enable us to deal with such nonconventional (at least to economics) aspects of behavior as fertility, marriage, divorce, birth control, child rearing practices, schooling, and health. Both the conventional and the nonconventional variables specified here are important to understanding the problem of poverty. Moreover, they are critical to understanding longer-term problems of growth, the trajectory of such growth, and the limits to growth. (As an example of the limits to growth, Schultz has recently argued [45] that the basic constraint that determines the upper limits of modernization, or economic growth, is the increasing scarcity of human time for consumption.)

The new contributions to the theory give us basically an economic theory of the family or, as it has been called, a theory of family economics. The theory has three essential ingredients that distinguish it from previous ways that economists have viewed economic activity. In the first place, it views the household essentially as a firm or factory, with the result that our powerful theory of the firm enables us to understand what takes place in the household. (This is in contrast to earlier consumer theory which attempted to explain the activities of *individuals,* with all of the obvious economic activities of the household left essentially unexplained by economic theory.) Second, the important variable *time* is brought within the scope of economic analysis, largely by recognizing that individuals seldom consume only a consumption good or service, but rather consume some combination of that consumption good or service and some parcel of the rigidly limited time available. And finally, the theory attempts to help explain nonmarket activities that have to do with schooling, investments in health, marriage, birth control, child rearing activities, and so forth (31, 36).

In this theory the family is treated as a complex social institution in which the interdependent and overlapping life-cycle behavior of family members and the family unit as a whole is determined by the interaction of the preferences and capacities of its members with the social and economic environment they face currently and expect to face in the future. The theory has not yet been fully elaborated to provide a full explanation of life-cycle behavior. However, the theory as presently developed is particularly rich in insightful hypotheses, and there is a growing body of empirical work designed to test it and to extend it on the basis of those empirical results.

Becker's contribution (7), in a sense a special case of Lancaster's more general theory (25), was to introduce the element of time into this revised formulation of the household. His concern was that economic development has led to a large secular decline in the work week that today involves less than a third of the total time available. Consequently, the allocation and efficiency of *nonworking* time may now be more important to economic welfare than that of working time.

Becker notes that one of the first recognitions of the importance of time came from economists who viewed the time of students as an important input into the educational process and viewed earnings foregone by the students as one of the important costs of education. He notes more generally, however, that the cost of a service like the theater or of a good like meat involves more than their market prices since the consumption of both takes time that could have been used productively. Therefore, the full cost of these activities equals the sum of market prices and the foregone value of the time used up. In other words, indirect costs should be treated on the same basis in discussions of all nonwork uses of time as such costs are treated in discussions of schooling.

Becker attempts to develop a general treatment of the allocation of time in nonwork activities. This theoretical analysis of choice includes the cost of time on the same basis as the cost of market goods.

Becker devotes part of his article to the application of this theory to a number of problems—some of which are quite important to the poverty problem. One is the hours of work question, or the short-run labor supply issue. A second is the productivity of time, which is the source of the familiar increase in earnings that has characterized the economics of the advanced countries, and which is due to the accumulation of human and physical capital, technological progress, and other factors. One conclusion that evolves from this analysis is the importance of the productivity of consumption time, or the level of production technology used in the household and what it implies for labor supply. A third problem is the need to reestimate demand elasticities in such a way as to take account of differing time intensities. For example, some analysts believe the large increases in demand for beef in the advanced countries in recent years are due to the low time intensity of beef compared to that of other animal protein sources; the demand increases as the opportunity cost of time rises and as women participate to a greater extent in the labor market. The division of labor within families can also be understood with this framework.

Becker also explains why Americans appear to be so wasteful of material goods and overly concerned about and economical with immaterial time, while people in low income countries are "wasteful" and somewhat unconscious of time, but quite economical with respect to material goods. The theory suggests that this is not due to a basic difference in tastes or temperament, but is rather a response to a difference in relative costs.

The combination of the Lancaster and Becker model and the theory of human capital has recently been applied to a wide range of new "household" problems. Among these are fertility (36), population growth (35), marriage (8, 9), and division of labor within the household and earnings (30, 33). T. W. Schultz (45) has carried it out to the extreme in hypothesizing a limit-to-growth model that is based on the increased value of time, in contrast to scarcity of material resources.

Empirical work is based very much on determining the shadow price or opportunity costs of time within the household. Because much of the empirical work to date has been based on secondary macro data, various proxies for this variable have been used. One important finding is the value of the education of the wife, which determines her opportunity costs to the household. Since children are time-intensive goods, the opportunity cost of the woman's time is an important factor determining whether families increase the flow of services from children by increasing the quality of a smaller number of children or by increasing the number. The implications in terms of fertility, demographic variables, and participation of family members in the labor force are obvious.

Production Technology. Schultz has helped us view new production technology as a source of income streams (47). In this context the failure to produce and distribute new production technology can be a source of poverty. In countries such as Brazil generalized poverty exists in the agricultural sector mainly because such new technology has not been produced.

In the United States the problem is somewhat different. Particular groups may be bypassed by technical change. Researchers may have been unable to make breakthroughs on particular crops, for example, because a new technology has not been adaptable to particular farm size groups or enterprise combinations, or because the factor markets are not efficient for particular groups, with the result that new production technology is not adopted even when it is available.

Generally, however, technical change plays a complex role in the economy, and affects the distribution of income in multiple ways. For example, it can be strongly resource-saving for a factor that has only limited employment alternatives. The classic case of this is technological unemployment. Although perhaps overrated as a cause of unemployment and low incomes in the industrial sector, the production and distribution of new technology has undoubtedly been a major source of low relative incomes in U.S. agriculture. This is because, as noted earlier, the labor force has been forced to bear a major share of the adjustment costs to new technology, with an important share of the incentive to adjustment reflected in the product market through general equilibrium effects.

New production technology can also have an influence on the functional distribution of income, depending on the relative elasticities of substitution in production and consumption, and the demand and supply conditions for the product. If technological progress occurs in a product whose production area is geographically circumscribed, for example, and the demand for the product should be relatively elastic (as when the product is exportable), then the value of the income flow generated by the new production technology will tend to be capitalized into land values. This process can shift the functional distribution away from labor. More generally, technological progress that raises the productivity of a given resource can shift the functional distribution of income in favor of that factor if the elasticity of substitution between it and other resources is less than the elasticity of substitution in consumption between the product in which the factor is used and other products.

In addition to sectoral and functional income problems, new production technology can also cause regional income problems. These problems are usually most severe when a region with highly specific resources is disadvantaged. If the region has only limited production alternatives, asset values will be written down on immobile resources, and mobile resources will eventually be adjusted out of the region. But in the interim incomes will decline as a result of technological progress elsewhere. (Probably some element of this phenomenon contributes to the well-publicized problem of rural poverty in the Northeast of Brazil.)

Lest one conclude that new production technology is only a creator of income distribution problems, it should be noted that under conditions that are quite general (but by no means universal), the production and distribution of new production technology in agriculture can be a powerful force for redistributing income in a progressive fashion. Low income families tend to spend a larger fraction of their budgets on food than do high income families. To the extent that the increased output made possible by technological progress results in a decline in the price of the product, low income groups will benefit proportionately more than higher income groups. This role of technical change in lowering the price of wage goods is often ignored, as is its role in providing a stimulus to economic development. Not only does it keep wage pressures from growing in the industrial sector, but the release of purchasing power with decline of the price of a product with an inelastic demand is a powerful source of demand for the goods and services from the nonfarm sector.

This positive aspect of technical change has largely been ignored in the rather misguided discussion of the so-called second- and third-generation problems of the Green Revolution (15, 28). The emphasis has focused primarily on what was believed to be a serious displacement of labor (on which considerable doubt has been cast by recent studies) and the fact that the value of the new technology was capitalized into higher land values. Little recognition has been given to the fact that many people would probably have died from starvation in countries like India and Pakistan were it not for the increased output that resulted from the technological breakthrough, or that the lot of large numbers of the poor was made somewhat better because food was lower in price and more plentiful as a result of the increased output.

Even in the United States there may be a growing appreciation for the contribution that technical change in agriculture has made to improving the income distribution. The high food prices of the last two years have led to a large increase in the food bill—again a result of the price-inelastic demand for food in the aggregate. Transfer payments have burgeoned, and the cost of the food stamp program in particular has increased rapidly. Although it is not yet generally recognized by policymakers, much could have been spent on research and development in agriculture—with demonstrably high social rates of return (38)—to obtain further technical change in agriculture and to help bring food costs down. In addition to making a more progressive distribution of income, this would release income for the purchase of output from the nonfarm sector. The increase in the aggregate food bill in the last two years has been one of the factors behind our current economic difficulties.

Imperfect Competition. Economists often consider monopoly and monopsony exploitation to be a source of rural poverty. Perhaps its most popular expression is the complaint against the middleman who, it is widely believed, can purchase monopsonistically from the farmer-producer and sell monopolistically to the consumer. Middlemen are very popular scapegoats in developing countries, but even recent U.S. experience shows that we are not exempt from the same afflictions. And prior to the recent upsurge in food prices in the United States, some elements of the monopsony-monopoly exploitation hypothesis were behind the cooperative movement and behind the emphasis in the last decade on attempting to improve the bargaining power of farmers.

Empirical studies which have attempted to identify and measure such exploitation have tended to find them much overrated. Historical analyses of marketing margins have found them to be consistent with competitive behavior (1). Gordon Smith, in an insightful analysis of the Brazilian frontier (48), found that even in these fortuitous circumstances monopoly exploitation prevailed only for a few years before the entrance of additional firms competed the excess profits away.

A circumstance that may have been of historical importance in the United States, and that is still important in some regions of countries such as Brazil, arises from the feudal or near-feudal economic organization that can prevail under certain conditions. If the economic organization in a community is largely controlled by one person, family, or company, and resource mobility is limited by virtue of geographic isolation and/or lack of employment alternatives, considerable exploitation can take place. The company town is a classic example, as is landlord domination of agricultural communities. In such circumstances, the dominant family or company may own most or all of the land—effectively ruling out access to the worker—and so may be able to hire the labor monopsonistically, while "selling" credit and consumer goods monopolistically.

Such phenomena are probably of little current empirical importance in the United States, if for no other reason than the high mobility of our labor force. However, in certain parts of developing countries (northeast Brazil, for example), such economic domination may still play a role in explaining rural poverty. However, the mobility of the labor force is often underrated in these circumstances. Recent studies have shown that even in rural communities in developing countries the labor force has many more employment alternatives than was commonly believed, and there is much more shifting from one employer to another.

Unemployment. During certain periods of our history unemployment has been an important source of poverty, with the last great episode of unemployment-induced poverty being the Great Depression of the 1930s. Since World War II we have had reasonable success in maintaining a high level of employment, and cyclical recessions have been relatively mild by historical standards. Moreover, unemployment compensation has been extended quite broadly in the economy so that many of the income losses that would result from unemployment are largely offset, and retraining programs are generally available to help reduce frictional unemployment. Hence, unemployment as a direct source of poverty has declined in the post–World War II period (for a more detailed discussion see 14, Chapter 3).

But declines in employment due to slack in economic activity still contribute to rural poverty in two interrelated ways. First, the level of unemployment has been an important factor affecting the level of outmigration from agriculture (21, 41). When unemployment increases, outmigration slows and labor is dammed up in agriculture, with the result that relative agricultural incomes decline. An important aspect of this phenomenon is that wage rates in agriculture are more flexible, with the result that overt unemployment does not appear.

The persistent and relatively high levels of unemployment during the 1950s aggravated a serious adjustment problem in U.S. agriculture. For this reason farm incomes tended to lag behind those in the nonfarm sector.

The agricultural labor market appears to be nearing an equilibrium after a long period of adjustment (14, Chapter 6). The rate of outmigration has slowed markedly since 1970, and incomes of farm people have advanced substantially relative to incomes of nonfarm people. In fact, average incomes of the rural population were above those of the nonfarm population in 1973—perhaps for the first time in our history—although median incomes were below.

This emerging equilibrium in the labor market suggests that even in this indirect way unemployment may be declining as a source of poverty. But it should be noted that although the agricultural labor market may be reaching adjustment in the aggregate, regional problems still exist, especially in the Southeast and New England. For the rural people in these regions the level of unemployment will still be an important source of both absolute and rural poverty.

This brings us to the second aspect of unemployment as a source of poverty. Blacks and certain other minority groups in society are affected differentially by unemployment (for recent data see 14, Chapter 3). Typically they suffer higher levels of unemployment than the general population, and when economic activity slackens they tend to be the first to lose their jobs. Given that there is a preponderance of blacks in the agriculture of the Southeast, declines in general economic activity tend to have serious regional effects, with outmigration slowing relatively more in the very region where there is still a relative income problem.

Explanations for unemployment can be found in neoclassical theory. The most common explanation is that it results from downward wage rigidity. Such wage rigidity may be due to strong labor unions, oligopsonistic concentration in the industrial sector, or labor supply curves that are relatively elastic to particular industries.

If the unemployment is of a frictional kind, then it is due to lack of resource mobility. This in turn may be due to high costs of moving, either in pecuniary or nonpecuniary terms, or due to the lack of skills to obtain alternative employment. The latter, of course, traces to lack of training or appropriate schooling.

Nonpecuniary Considerations. Nonpecuniary considerations arise in the discussion of the income problem in agriculture in two rather different contexts. The first has to do with the taste for employment, and elicits quite different judgments about the direction of its influence. Some have argued that farmers have a taste for farming and therefore would accept lower pecuniary income in order to work at an activity they like. Others argue that farming is an unpleasant activity, and that in equilibrium farmers would have to receive a higher pecuniary income, other things being equal, to compensate them for the unpleasantness of this activity.

To the best of my knowledge there has been very little research on this question. In my early work on the agricultural labor market (41), however, I formulated the labor supply model for hired agricultural labor with both a relative wage variable and an income variable. The idea was that the income variable would indicate whether members of the labor force would view work activity in agriculture as being "commodius" or "discommodious" (these terms were suggested to me at the time by H. Gregg Lewis). If the income variable had a negative coefficient this was to be interpreted as indicating that workers found the work activity to be discommodious, and hence for a given relative wage supplied less labor to agriculture as per capita income rose. The interpretation would be just the opposite if the coefficient on the income variable were positive.

Unfortunately, the statistical results for this model were not good, partly because a problem of collinearity arose between the income variable and other variables in the model, and partly because it was difficult to define and measure the variables with any degree of precision. However, this approach to the labor markets would appear to offer much promise, especially as per capita incomes rise and workers take a larger share of their income in nonpecuniary forms. In using the model it is important to focus attention on the *distribution* of tastes and work conditions (19). Tastes do differ among individuals, and it is the relative supply of these tastes compared to the relative demand that is important. Undoubtedly, some people would pay a price to work in a coal mine. But coal miners receive a compensating differential in wages—if they do— largely because there are not very many who would prefer to work in the coal mines.

Nonpecuniarities also affect rural poverty through their role in racial discrimination. (The persistently low relative income problem in the South [rural and urban] is explained in good part by the concentration of blacks in that region.) The modern theory on racial discrimination probably starts with Becker (4), although Arrow (2, 3) has presented the most complete statement of the theory.* I would like to focus on the Becker formulation, however, since it is somewhat more concise and perhaps communicates a bit more easily.

According to Becker, "If an individual has a 'taste for discrimination,' he must act *as if* he were willing to pay something, either directly or in the form of reduced income, to be associated with some persons instead of others" (4, p. 14). He defines a coefficient of discrimination to

* The theory of racial discrimination has recently been surveyed by Ray Marshall (32). I have borrowed heavily from Marshall in the following exposition.

measure this "taste for discrimination" in money terms and assumes that it can apply to different factors of production, to consumers, and to employers. If an employer faces a money wage rate of W for workers, the $W(1 + d_i)$ defines a *net wage* rate, where d_i is the discrimination coefficient against this factor. If the employer has a preference for this factor, d_i will be positive; if he has a taste for discrimination against it, d_i will be negative.

If participants in the labor market behave as postulated, a wage differential will appear in the market. The *market* discrimination coefficient (MDC) is then defined as

$$MDC = (W_w - W_b)/W_b$$

where W_w is the equilibrium wage rate of W workers and W_b is the equilibrium wage rate of B workers. An employee offered a wage of W_j for working with the factor discriminated against acts as if the net wage rate were $W_j(1 - d_j)$, where d_j is his discrimination coefficient against this factor. Similarly, a consumer, faced with a money price of P for the commodity produced by this factor, acts as if the net price were $P(1 + d_k)$, where d_k is the discrimination coefficient against this factor.

The implication of the discrimination coefficient is that the employer is willing to pay the favored workers $(W + d_i)$ and the ones discriminated against $(W - d_i)$, so that if W_w is the wage of white workers and W_b the wage of black workers and the employer prefers W's to B's, $W_w > W_b$. Becker then uses an international trade model to illustrate the effects of discrimination on trade between sectors W and B. An important assumption in this analysis is that blacks are relatively more well endowed with labor and whites are relatively more well endowed with capital.

Before trade, then, it follows that the $MPL_b < MPL_w$ and $MPC_w < MPC_b$ where MPL_b and MPL_w are the marginal productivities of labor in B and W sectors, respectively, and MPC_w and MPC_b are the marginal productivities of capital in W and B, respectively. Thus, before trade, W capitalists could get a higher return in B, and B laborers could get a higher return in W. In the absence of discrimination, whites would therefore export capital to that point where the usual equilibrium conditions would be fulfilled—in other words, to the point where the total returns per unit of labor and capital in both sectors would be equal and maximized so that gains could not be made by additional exports of capital.

The introduction of discrimination into the analysis implies that W capitalists suffer psychic cost whenever their capital is used in B. Therefore, their net return is $MPC_b (1 + d)$, where d is a negative fraction representing the money value of the psychic costs. The result is to reduce the capital exports from the W sector to something less than the equilibrium level of exports in a nondiscriminatory world. Compared with the competitive equilibrium in the nondiscriminatory world, the marginal productivity of B labor will decrease, the marginal productivity of B capital will increase, the marginal productivity of W capital will decrease, and the marginal productivity of W capital will increase.

Obviously, by the usual neoclassical criteria, production is no longer efficient. Hence, the country suffers a loss in pecuniary income when W capitalists discriminate. Similarly, B workers and W capitalists suffer losses in pecuniary income, while W workers and B capitalists gain. Since it can be shown that the gains of the B capitalists are less than the losses suffered by the B workers, the B community as a whole loses from discrimination. In effect, the discrimination coefficient acts like a tariff and causes lower wages, less employment, or both, depending upon the elasticities of labor supplies.

This same model can be used to analyze other forms of discrimination, such as that against women. In the context of rural poverty, however, discrimination against women is probably of less empirical significance than discrimination against blacks.

The Personal Distribution of Income. One of the persistent puzzles in income data is that the personal distributions of income (and wealth) are usually skewed to the right, or positively skewed. (This means that they include relatively few extremely large values.) Yet many basic human attributes and abilities are apparently distributed normally.

Critics of the status quo have argued that the skewness reflects the cumulative consequences of economic institutions such as the inheritance of wealth and nepotism. A number of "natural" or "statistical" explanations have been advanced, however, such as transition probabilities and a Markoff process, or that income depends on the *product* (as contrasted to the sum) of a number of normally distributed independent abilities, which leads to a log normal distribution. (Other "statistical" explanations have been summarized by Hans Staehle [49] and Stanley Lebergott [27].)

A number of economic explanations have also been advanced. Friedman, for example, suggests that the skewed distribution may result from different attitudes in the population toward uncertainty-bearing (18). If a large number of people prefer security, and their incomes are normally distributed, and a smaller number are gamblers, and their incomes are normally distributed but with a somewhat higher mean and a much higher standard deviation, the vertical summation of the two distributions will give a new distribution that is clearly skewed to the right.

A similar result will follow if one focuses on investment in human capital. Becker and his associates have interpreted the inequality in the income distribution in terms of the inequality in schooling and the rate of return to investment in education (5, 10). In states where education is unequally distributed the rate of return to additional schooling will be high, as will the inequality in income. Mincer (34) probably goes the furthest in this direction and relates the skewness of the income distribution to differences in expenditures on human capital formation, primarily education. His results are similar to Friedman's, with investment in education treated as a "taste for uncertainty."

POLICY IMPLICATIONS. My comments on policy will be brief, setting forth some major implications of neoclassical economic theory.

A first point I would like to make is that nothing in neoclassical theory implies a complete laissez faire attitude or lack of government interventions to correct or alleviate problems of poverty. Rather, the theory implies particular ways in which governments should intervene. These have to do primarily with helping to make markets work more efficiently so that in themselves they do not become a source of inequality. If changes in the income distribution are required that are greater than is implied by market disequilibria, with the requirement coming from the political process, the theory can still be a useful guide to policymakers.

In considering the problem of sectoral imbalances, perhaps the primary focus should be on helping the labor market perform more efficiently. This will involve giving workers more information about where better employment opportunities exist and what is required to obtain them. A case can be made for public subsidization of the migration process, especially if part of the imbalance is due to publicly supported programs, such as research and development. Particular groups in society should not be forced to bear all the costs of adjustment to a phenomenon that is ultimately in the public good.

The subsidies might take two forms. Support might be provided for dislocation costs, since the rural worker often has to shift location. Capital markets tend to work rather imperfectly for such purposes, especially for the disadvantaged, so a case can be made for public assistance. (I have been impressed, however, with the extent to which a private "relocation" industry has developed in Brazil designed to recruit, transport, and provide interim maintenance to workers in moving from the Northeast of Brazil to the South and Central West.) In the United States the transportation costs themselves tend to be relatively unimportant in such cases, but costs incurred in moving are generally more than transportation. The worker may be without employment while he engages in job search and will need some form of subsistence.

A second form of subsidy to mobility can be provided through schooling and retraining programs. Gisser (20) has shown that schooling affects the rate of outmigration from agriculture and that it can be an important means of removing sectoral disequilibria between the farm and nonfarm sectors. The case for a public subsidy to schooling, at least at lower levels, has been well made and is generally recognized. The case for retraining programs is less clear. Private companies can and do provide large amounts of such training. But public assistance for particular groups under particular circumstances can probably still be justified.

The maintenance of full employment is also an important policy measure for alleviating the relative income problem in agriculture. Even though the farm-nonfarm labor market in the aggregate appears to be nearing equilibrium, regional disequilibria still exist. Migration out of these regions will be facilitated by the maintenance of full employment.

Policies to deal with the problem of spatial lag in farm incomes will depend on which body of theory or which interpretation is relevant. Policies that have evolved from this body of literature have stressed two kinds of measures, however, both of which are independent of which interpretation applies. The first is to decentralize the industrialization process on a geographic basis. This need not result in a loss in aggregate efficiency; to the contrary, there is growing evidence that negative externalities begin to arise with large concentrations of economic activities.

The second measure is to link local community development efforts to the larger metropolitan areas. In addition to providing a market orientation for the nascent industrialization efforts, such linkages provide a means of tapping larger capital markets and larger pools of skilled workers and technological assistance.

A key to the poverty problem probably lies with solving the resource acquisition problem, especially when the attempt is made to deal with the problem of absolute poverty. Providing the means of acquiring the appropriate human capital is important in this context. But human capital should not be viewed as the only solution to the problem, nor should education be viewed as the only dimension to the human capital problem.

It is interesting that major steps have been taken in the last decade to remove capital market imperfections for education. Unfortunately, less attention has been given to making similar efforts to reduce market imperfections for physical capital. For some individuals additional education may be a low productivity investment. Yet they may experience the same market imperfections in acquiring capital for more conventional uses. Policies to eliminate these inequities are needed.

Similar problems prevail within the domain of human capital. The food stamp program has given us sizable progress in increasing the supply of food available to the poor. But problems of nutrition continue to exist, especially for the children of the poor. The challenge of solving this problem without interfering with individual freedom is great. Education and information are obviously key variables.

Institutions that extend health and medical services to a larger proportion of the population have also grown in recent years. Yet I suspect that we substantially underinvest in certain kinds of medical services, while overinvesting on a large scale in others. One problem in devising a more rational policy to deal with this problem is the current lack of knowledge. Economists have probably underinvested in this important area of research.

Finally, there is the problem of racial and other forms of discrimination. I would question whether economists have contributed their full measure to the literature dealing with this problem. It is my impression that sociologists and educators have pretty much carried the day, with insufficient attention given to discrimination as an economic problem.

To the extent that discrimination is comparable to the monopsony hiring of labor, minimum wage laws may help redress some of the inequities while at the same time increasing employment opportunities for groups experiencing discrimination. But are there not other wage policies or tax schemes that might help reduce the discrimination?

SOME CONCLUDING COMMENTS. It is commonly believed that there is a rather harsh trade-off between growth and equity in most societies. Improvements in the distribution of income—usually assumed to be a more equal distribution of income—are believed to be possible only with a slower rate of growth. This position has been argued on the basis that the upper income groups tend to save relatively more, and that to redistribute income away from them is to lower the saving rate and eventually the investment rate. More generally, it appears to be assumed that income redistribution that is income leveling tends to be at the expense of saving and in favor of consumption.

This assumed trade-off between equity and growth is probably more apparent than real if one brings human capital into the calculus and gives some attention to the form in which income is redistributed. For example, it is widely believed in Brazil that solving the rural poverty problem will result in a lower rate of aggregate growth. Yet both Fishlow (17) and Langoni (26) have shown that rural poverty in Brazil is mainly the result of generalized low productivity of resources. The solution to the problem is not one of increasing transfer payments as we think of them. Rather, the solution is one of investing in new production technology and in rural education. Clearly, such investments will make for a *higher* rate of growth, not a lower rate, and a reduction in *absolute* poverty, even if problems of *relative* poverty may be exacerbated.

Comparable examples are still relatively plentiful in the United States, even though a larger portion of our poverty is found in groups that are marginal to society and the economy than in Brazil. But an important part of the poverty of the blacks is due to underinvestment in human capital, as is an important part of the relative income problems of the rural South. Similarly, fairly large groups have suffered from underinvestment in nutrition and health which could make them more productive.

We have probably been too facile in assuming that the trade-off between economic efficiency and social justice is ever present and for the most part harsh. In the final analysis it depends very much on the means used to improve social justice, and the productivity of those expenditures compared to the productivity of the resources in their alternative use.

Finally, the greatest deficiency of neoclassical theory is its treatment of personal income distribution, particularly its failure to present a theory that handles the resource acquisition problem in a satisfactory way and that enables us to use knowledge about the functional distribution of income in mapping the personal distribution of income. The theory related to functional distribution of income is on a reasonably sound footing, but so far we are relatively limited in translating that knowledge into statements about the personal distribution of income.

The new theory of the household appears to offer much potential for helping fill in the gaps in our knowledge on both these fronts. It provides a basis for understanding how investment decisions are made in the household (involving the full range of human capital decisions) and it also explains the quality of the labor force that is produced. In addition the new theory provides a more unified means of understanding the labor supply phenomenon on a family basis, as well as a means of understanding how time is transformed and allocated between market and leisure activities. In the long run the theory offers much promise as an explanation of the numbers of people that a society will have and the quality of that population.

To date there have been very few attempts to use this body of theory to understand the problems of poverty per se. But it may be one of the most powerful bodies of analytical theory that we have in our arsenal.

Many things have been left unsaid in this chapter or have been treated too briefly. Among these are the problems of economic rents and quasi rents, the very real problems with accepted capital theory, and the problem of externalities that cause a divergence between private and social costs and returns. The list could be extended. But hopefully enough has been said to indicate that we do in fact have a powerful body of analytical theory that can be used to understand the nature of the rural poverty problem and to prescribe some policy solutions for alleviating it.

REFERENCES

(1). Anschel, Kurt R., Russell H. Brannon and Eldon D. Smith, eds., *Agricultural Cooperatives and Markets in Developing Countries,* New York: Praeger, 1969.

(2). Arrow, K. J., "Models of Job Discrimination," in A. H. Pascal, ed., *Racial Discrimination in Economic Life,* Lexington, Mass.: D. C. Heath-Lexington Books, 1971.

(3). ———, "Some Models of Race in the Labor Market," in A. H. Pascal, ed., *Racial Discrimination in Economic Life,* Lexington, Mass.: D. C. Heath-Lexington Books, 1971

(4). Becker, Gary S., *The Economics of Discrimination*, 2nd ed., Chicago: University of Chicago Press, 1971.

(5). ———, *Human Capital*, New York: Columbia University Press, 1964.

(6). ———, "Investment in Human Capital: A Theoretical Analysis," *Investment in Human Beings*, supplement to *Journal of Political Economy* 70: 9–49.

(7). ———, "A Theory of the Allocation of Time," *Economic Journal* 75:493–517.

(8). ———, "A Theory of Marriage (Part 1)," *Journal of Political Economy* 81 (4): 813–46.

(9). ———, "A Theory of Marriage (Part 2)," supplement to *Journal of Political Economy* 82 (2, Part 2): S11–S26.

(10). ——— and Barry R. Chiswick, "Education and the Distribution of Earnings," *American Economic Review* 56 (2): 358–69.

(11). Bradford, Lawrence and Glenn L. Johnson, *Farm Management Analysis*, New York: John Wiley and Sons, 1967.

(12). Bronfenbrenner, Martin, *Income Distribution Theory*, Chicago: Aldine-Atherton, 1971.

(13). Bryant, Keith, "Causes of Inter-Country Variations in Farmers' Earnings," *Journal of Farm Economics* 48:557–77.

(14). *Economic Report of the President*, Washington: USGPO, February 1975.

(15). Falcon, Walter, "The Green Revolution: Generations of Problems," *American Journal of Agricultural Economics* 52 (5): 698–710.

(16). Ferguson, C. E., *The Neoclassical Theory of Production and Distribution*, Cambridge, Eng.: Cambridge University Press, 1969.

(17). Fishlow, Albert, "Brazilian Size Distribution of Income," *American Economic Review* 62 (2): 391–402.

(18). Friedman, Milton, "Choice, Chance, and the Personal Distribution of Income," *Journal of Political Economy* 61:277–90.

(19). ———, *Price Theory, A Provisional Text*, Chicago: Aldine, 1965.

(20). Gisser, Micha, "Schooling and the Farm Problem." *Econometrica* 33: 582–92.

(21). Hathaway, Dale, "Migration from Agriculture: The Historical Record and Its Meaning," *American Economic Review* 50:392–402.

(22). Heady, Earl O., *Economics of Agricultural Production and Resource Use*, Englewood Cliffs, N.J.: Prentice-Hall, 1964.

(23). Johnston, Bruce F., "Agriculture and Structural Transformation in Developing Countries: A Survey of Research," *Journal of Economic Literature* 8 (2): 369–404.

(24). Katzman, Martin T., "The Von Thuenen Paradigm, the Industrial-Urban Hypothesis, and the Spatial Structure of Agriculture," *American Journal of Agricultural Economics* 56 (4): 683–96.

(25). Lancaster, Kelvin J., "A New Approach to Consumer Theory," *Journal of Political Economy* 74 (2): 132–57.

(26). Langoni, Carlos, *Distribuicao da Renda e Desenvolvimento Economico do Brasil*, Rio de Janeiro: Editora Expressao e Cultura, 1973.

(27). Lebergott, Stanley, "The Shape of the Income Distribution," *American Economic Review* 49:328–47.

(28). Lele, Uma J. and J. W. Mellor, "Jobs, Poverty, and the 'Green Revolution,'" International Affairs 48:20–32.

(29). Lewis, H. Gregg, personal communication.

(30). Liebowitz, Arleen, "Home Investments in Children," *Marriage, Family Human Capital, and Fertility*, supplement to *Journal of Political Economy* 82 (2, Part 2): S111–S131.

(31). *Marriage, Family Human Capital, and Fertility*, supplement to *Journal of Political Economy* 82 (2, Part 2).

(32). Marshall, Ray, "The Economics of Racial Discrimination: A Survey," *Journal of Economic Literature* 12 (3): 849–71.

(33). Mincer, Jacob and Solomon Polacheck, "Family Investments in Human Capital: Earnings of Women," *Marriage, Family Human Capital, and Fertility,* supplement to *Journal of Political Economy* 82 (2, part 2): S76–S108.

(34). ———, "Investment in Human Capital and Personal Income Distribution," *Journal of Political Economy* 66:281–302.

(35). Nerlove, Marc, "Household and Economy: Towards a New Theory of Population and Economic Growth," *Marriage, Family Human Capital, and Fertility,* supplement to *Journal of Political Economy,* 82 (2, part 2): S200–S218.

(36). *New Approaches to Fertility,* supplement to *Journal of Political Economy* 81 (2, part 2).

(37). Nicholls, William H., "The Transformation of Agriculture in a Semi-Industrialized Country: The Case of Brazil," in Erik Thorbecke, ed., *The Role of Agriculture in Economic Development,* New York: National Bureau of Economic Research, 1970.

(38). Peterson, Willis, "Organization and Productivity of the Federal-State Research Systems in the United States," paper, Conference on Resource Allocation and Productivity in International Agricultural Research, Airlie House, Virginia, January 26–29, 1975 (mimeo.).

(39). Ruttan, Vernon W., "The Human Resource Problem in American Agriculture," Supplementary Paper No. 15, in *Farming, Farmers, and Markets for Farm Goods,* Committee for Economic Development, November 1962.

(40). Schuh, G. Edward, "Comment on Nicholls" in Erik Thorbecke, ed., *The Role of Agriculture in Economic Development,* New York: National Bureau of Economic Research, 1970.

(41). ———, "An Econometric Investigation of the Market for Hired Agricultural Labor," *Journal of Farm Economics* 44 (2): 307–21.

(42). ———, "The Income Problem in Brazilian Agriculture," EAPA/SUPLAN, Ministry of Agriculture, and Department of Agricultural Economics, Purdue University, 1974 (mimeo.).

(43). Schultz, Theodore W., *Economic Organization of Agriculture,* New York: McGraw-Hill, 1953.

(44). ———, *The Economic Value of Education,* New York: Columbia University Press, 1963.

(45). ———, "The High Value of Human Time: Population Equilibrium," *Marriage, Family Human Capital, and Fertility,* supplement to *Journal of Political Economy* 82 (2, part 2): S2–S10.

(46). ———, *Investment in Human Capital,* New York: Free Press, 1971.

(47). ———, *Transforming Traditional Agriculture,* New Haven: Yale University Press, 1964.

(48). Smith, Gordon, "Agricultural Marketing and Economic Development: A Brazilian Case Study," Ph.D. thesis, Harvard University, 1965.

(49). Staehle, Hans, "Ability, Wages, and Income," *Review of Economics and Statistics* 25:77–87.

Discussion

ROBERT D. EMERSON

P R O F E S S O R Schuh has provided a thorough and useful discussion of the elements of neoclassical theory applicable to the problems of rural poverty. My comments will be organized under the major headings used by Professor Schuh: assumptions of neoclassical theory, sectoral explanations, and micro theories.

ASSUMPTIONS OF NEOCLASSICAL DISTRIBUTION THEORY.
I would first like to raise a definitional point. The chapter begins with the economist's standard definition of the neoclassical theory of income distribution, essentially that it approaches the question of the *functional* distribution of income rather than the *personal* distribution of income. The theory centers around the production function and the derived demand for factors of production. Although I have no quarrel with this, the chapter quickly shifts to questions more directly related to personal distribution while still under the aegis of the neoclassical theory of income distribution. For example, the question of why per capita incomes in agriculture are less than those of their urban counterparts is a personal income issue.

The significant departure from the neoclassical theory of income distribution occurs in the major section of the paper devoted to micro theories. Although the theories are in the neoclassical tradition, they are not for the most part related to questions of functional income distribution, but rather to personal income distribution. Let me hasten to add that this in no way detracts from the approaches; rather, I would argue they are much more viable as a result of this focus on personal income distribution, given the problems at hand. I would simply emphasize that the distinction between functional and personal income distribution should not be overlooked in applying neoclassical economic theory to rural poverty problems. This distinction is suggested in Schuh's concluding section, but it deserves somewhat closer scrutiny when alternative theories are being considered. I would conjecture that the neoclassical theory's inapplicability in general to problems of personal distribution has resulted in many agricultural economists rejecting the theory in total for such problems. As Schuh has argued, there are indeed several attractive approaches in the neoclassical tradition which can offer considerable insight to problems of personal income distribution and the rural poverty problem.

SECTORAL EXPLANATIONS OF RURAL POVERTY. Admittedly sectoral explanations of rural poverty have played an important role in explaining income differences in our society throughout the first half of the twentieth century. They are certainly applicable to similar questions in underdeveloped countries. However, I do not find this approach particularly insightful for the present problems of rural poverty. Most importantly, the question of rural poverty in the United States today cannot be as directly associated with one industry—agriculture—as it has been in the past. In addition, Schuh notes that incomes of the farm population have been approaching those of the nonfarm population. Given both of these conditions (an increasing proportion of nonfarm rural people and converging incomes of farm and nonfarm rural people), sectoral analyses have considerably less appeal for the analysis of rural poverty than in earlier periods.

Schuh suggests that one factor that aggravates the problem of sectoral differences in income is the higher reproduction rate of the farm population. Again, although this has been historically true in the United States and is the case in developing countries, rural and urban fertility rates in the United States appear to be converging (1, p. 599).

MICRO THEORIES. The major section of the chapter is devoted to micro theories related to distribution questions. I quite agree with the emphasis given to the micro theories over the sectoral explanations in relation to rural poverty questions. As Schuh has noted, this is an area in which additional empirical research may be quite enlightening. As yet, very few empirical applications of some of the more recent developments in these theories have been devoted to questions of rural poverty.

Among the several different topics treated in this section of the chapter, the three given most emphasis are the new household economics, the potential contribution of production technology, and the accumulation of resources. This emphasis is appropriately placed, and, in particular, if one approach were to be selected as offering the most promise for an array of rural poverty problems, it would be the new household economics. Correspondingly, the role of imperfect competition as an explanation of the existence of rural poverty has appropriately been portrayed as rather minor.

An interesting treatment of production technology's potential contribution to improvement of the income distribution is given; it is one that has often been ignored. Schuh observes that in an inelastic product market, technological advances reduce the product price and so add to the purchasing power of low income persons for nonagricultural products. The more commonly acknowledged result is the release of labor from agriculture with a subsequent increase in rural incomes. Although the latter case is likely to occur in less developed countries, an extensive resource shift out of agriculture is not likely in the United States.

Schuh notes that increased unemployment of the labor force as a whole reduces migration out of agriculture and rural areas. While I agree with this observation about the effect of general unemployment, the seasonal unemployment characteristic of agriculture is not treated. By the nature of the industry, much employment is of a seasonal nature leaving the worker with the choice of remaining unemployed during an off-season or locating other work during an off-season. To the extent that seasonal workers remain in the same region, this presumably places downward pressure on the equilibrium wages for other nonseasonal employment. Although this effect is important at the local level, it is glossed over by emphasis on state or regional unemployment data.

SUMMARY. In summary, I would like to note that the chapter provides a good background for persons interested in doing empirical work on rural poverty questions. The case for the contribution that neoclassical economic theory can make to the analysis of rural poverty has been well focused.

REFERENCE
(1). Gardner, Bruce, "Economics of the Size of North Carolina Rural Families," *New Economic Approaches to Fertility*, supplement to *Journal of Political Economy* 81 (2, Part 2): S99–S122.

Radical political economics, poverty, and income distribution

J O S E P H   P E R S K Y

P R O F E S S O R Koopmans in his book of three essays on economic theory has made an interesting statement concerning the nature of neoclassical theory. In discussing the Arrow-Debreu model of competitive equilibrium, Koopmans notes that it is "best suited for describing a society of self-sufficient farmers who do a little trading on the side" (7, p. 62). To the extent that the distribution of marketable resources in modern society is far less egalitarian than this rustic picture, Koopmans recognizes that there may indeed be a problem of what he euphemistically labels "consumer survival." In other words there may be people who come to the marketplace with too few resources to eke out an adequate existence. This simple statement alone raises significant moral questions concerning a market approach to providing goods and services. Nevertheless it is this type of thinking that lies behind most of the policy oriented research on the economics of poverty. In general the question has been posed as one of increasing the marketable resources of those who have lost out in the marketplace.

Koopmans' formulation has a certain plausibility. It clearly points out one facet of market transactions grasped by neoclassical theory: "them that have are them that get." And as the song goes: "how you get something when you got nothing is still a mystery to me." Taking this as the starting point leaves little debate between left and right concerning the immediate correlates of poverty. Ample evidence exists concerning the income prospects of a young person with neither human nor physical capital. The root question is why some people enter the market in such a poor position. If in the entertaining game of Monopoly some players were endowed at the beginning with the bulk of the assets and some were granted only a small portion, there is little doubt who would emerge as financial titans. All of us recognize such a starting alignment as unfair, and the original distribution of wealth in that game is designed accordingly. If it were not, few of us would agree to play. But in the real world the luxury of rejecting one's initial position is denied us. Most of us play out of necessity and take what we can get.

In general most economists do not show a great interest in the historical origins of the current property distribution. Rather they sidestep this question and proceed directly to the "common interest" in stabilizing the economic relations of society. Hence that closet libertarian, Milton Friedman, has written that "however attractive anarchy may be as a philosophy it is not feasible in a world of imperfect men. Men's freedoms can conflict, and when they do, one man's freedom must be limited to preserve another's" (5, pp. 25–26). The answer is of course government. What modest function does this necessary evil serve? Merely to provide for "the maintenance of law and order to prevent coercion of one individual by another, the enforcement of contracts voluntarily entered into, the definition of the meaning of property rights, the interpretation and enforcement of such rights and the provision of a monetary framework" (5, p. 27).

In this one stroke we find economic orthodoxy admitting the indeterminacy of the market and the need for a broader conception of political economy, for the system can only be closed by this grant of governmental power. Indeed that institution is charged with ratifying the initial position of all the players in the game as well as establishing the rules by which they will play. Despite the coyness of the economics profession in pretending not to recognize the central role of government, few of us are so naive as to doubt the significance of these governmental "functions" for determining the outcome of the game.

Having paid passing recognition to the existence if not the importance of state power, the majority of economists promptly drop the question of collective action. The state in their world is a mystic union divorced from the mundane world, capable of Olympian disinterest. Even more shocking is the assertion that while people can conceive and operationalize this most abstract of collective goods, narrow avarice prevents these same people from more limited action in the interest of a more closely defined collectivity. It is this gaping hole in economic theory that puts it at odds with the dynamics of economic history; for it is at the level of class that the major struggles over the nature of property and the rewards to be obtained from the division of labor have been waged. To understand the actual game we are playing, it is imperative that we acknowledge the possibility and importance of group cohesiveness in general and class consciousness in particular. Where the orthodox economist finds no middle ground between the nuclear family and the state, we must see the richness of economic history as it is played out in class conflict. This realization is the basic distinguishing characteristic of political economy as opposed to economics.

CAPITALISM AS A MODE OF PRODUCTION. In any actual society we are presented with two closely related economic questions. The first is to explain the origin and meaning of the major rules of the economy and the second is to explain the distribution of initial positions. In capitalist societies the major rule is that of the marketplace or, as Friedman would call it, the freedom of contract. In the standard treatment of capitalism the market is simply an extremely convenient institution to facilitate trades of mutual advantage. As such it would seem difficult to question this cornerstone of Western economies. However, this is a purely historic view of the market as it exists only in the world of rarefied economic theory. The radical and, I would argue, the appropriate view of the market must concentrate not on the distribution of goods, but rather on the historic meaning of the market for those who enter with nothing but labor power. To the extent that such a class exists (and without its existence there can be no capitalism) the market creates a mechanism through which its members can and must gain a livelihood. To the extent that labor is separated from the means of production, it must turn to the market for subsistence. In the market, as opposed to the feudal manor or the colonial plantation, the laborer must "voluntarily" enter into a contract with capital. While the contractual form of the labor market denies the exploitative relation between employer and employee, it legitimizes in its abstract coolness the ability of those who have to get more. It is important to note that while traditional economists have generally identified the market with vigorous competition, that institution has been a relatively inefficient regulator of intra-bourgeois conflict. Only in the complaints of the petite bourgeoisie has the need for antimonopoly policies been linked to the market as a necessary adjunct. Guaranteeing pure competition is beyond the capacity of the market. Indeed, by their very nature capitalist markets have generally produced concentration and the emergence of monopoly.

In this view, then, the market as a rule of economic life is most significant as an obfuscation of primary property relations. Too much of the liberal critique of capitalism has been concerned with market failure. Increasing returns to scale, externalities, and public goods are important, but certainly not the central problems of capitalist economies. Rather, radical political economy would argue that the very existence of the market is predicated on a specific class structure in which the bulk of the population comes empty-handed to the trading place. It is in this sense that the rules of the game are not independent of the distribution of initial positions. Thus the specification of "market rules" is part of the rise of the bourgeoisie to a privileged initial position. While neoclassical theory may emphasize the allocative functions of the market, it completely ignores this important distributive function with respect to initial positions. In the long struggles over the enclosure movement we see the labor market emerge in its capitalist sense. In its effort to set initial positions and to establish the rules of the game, labor finds itself as the possessor of only one commodity, labor power. For all the elegance of the neoclassical analysis of the trade-off between labor and leisure, this basic fact belies the claims of "neutrality" that are so often voiced in favor of the market.

Thus the significant, indeed the central, point of the radical critique of capitalism is the objective reality that as the bourgeoisie champions the spread of market rules into noncapitalist modes of production, it has facilitated the separation of a large proportion of the population from their admittedly meager means of production. By achieving this division in what may appear as a "fair" and even reasonable application of market principles to noncapitalist structures, the bourgeoisie inevitably creates a mass of labor, a mass that must work not for the use value or even the exchange value of its product, but for the exchange value of its labor power.

None of this should be taken as a glorification of precapitalist modes of production. There can be little doubt that in most actual societies before the advent of capitalism the share of total product controlled by the mass of people was relatively small. By the same token capitalist economies have proven themselves to be relatively good at accumulating useful capital and encouraging technological development. Even Marx was willing to pay the devil his due. The point is that capitalist societies have been able to achieve these positive accomplishments only by constantly keeping the largest proportion of the population in a state of great insecurity, constantly disciplined by the threat of unemployment. Rather than an internal discipline based on future interest, the worker in capitalist society is faced with an apparently external force as represented by the labor market and the reserve army of the unemployed. Regardless whether this structure actually produces some commiseration with the working classes, the fact remains that it can only function through a denial of the very slogans the bourgeoisie used to universalize their cause. It is incapable of fulfilling the promises made.

Another important observation is the extent to which the rising capitalist class struggles to shape government and the rules of the game in their interest. That they will have great power to do so can hardly be questioned. At the same time it would be simplistic and mechanistic to assume that they act without constraint. In particular, radical theory recognizes the working class and the labor movement as major checks on the ability of the bourgeoisie to define completely initial positions. Thus the state's recognition of the right to organize is a major change in the "birthright" of a worker. While this struggle of the labor movement continually runs the risk of co-optation, to underestimate its importance would be a gross error.

NINETEENTH CENTURY STRUGGLES IN THE UNITED STATES. Up to this point I have reviewed the major points of radical analysis: the historical origins of the market, the importance of the state, the central role of class struggle and the specific character of two major classes, the bourgeoisie and the proletariat. Of course the discussion so far represents a gross oversimplication of a theory that continues to acquire a rich literature concerning the complexities of the capitalist system. This is hardly the place to go into more detail concerning the whole of that theory. Rather, I will consider now the relevance of radical political economics to one often neglected aspect of modern capitalism in the United States: the fate of the rural classes which have their origins in noncapitalist modes of production.

At first this may appear a rather strange manner in which to pose the problem of rural poverty in the United States, since our country emerged on the periphery of the Western European world already transformed by the industrial revolution. The United States was never an area populated by serfs and lords. The rise of a bourgeoisie in this country was not accomplished against the backdrop of a declining feudal nobility. Rather, it was achieved in struggle with two major rivals for political hegemony: the farmers of the West and the border South and the slave plantation owners of the deep South. To what extent did these agrarian systems represent noncapitalist modes of production?

The plantation system clearly carried out production in a precapitalist form. As Genovese has pointed out, this mode of production represented a major contradiction for the slave South since the plantation was inextricably linked to the emerging capitalist world market. While ideologues such as George Fitzhugh argued for a rationalization of the slave system along autarchic lines, the core motivation for the plantations was always to serve the world market. To destroy that link would have been to destroy the slaveholders' very purpose of being. On the the other hand there was little chance of internal reform of the production system of the slave South. If the slaveholders' purpose was exchange, their mode of being was a primitive exercise of coercion.

In the West and to a lesser extent in the South another major force existed: the operators of small- and intermediate-sized farms. Again this class grew up in a system where provisioning the market was a major consideration. However, as Anne Mayhew has argued, it was not until the frontier was destroyed in each region that the farmer class of that region became perforce a participant in the market (8). While the American farmer was always eager to market a surplus, the necessity to do so was not compelling until the passing of the frontier. But once participation in the market began, the decision became irreversible as the farmer's dependence on credit, fertilizers, and manufactured goods increased. Like the slaveholder, the farmer faced the contradictions inherent in a situation where a noncapitalist mode of production is enmeshed in a capitalist market. As long as the market runs strong there is an air of independence, but when the downturns come, as they ininevitably must in such a system, the weaknesses of these peripheral relics become all too clear.

Neither of these two major agricultural interests waited passively in the face of an encroaching capitalist center. The slaveholder fought a bloody Civil War, while the farmer mounted significant political attacks on the emerging bourgeoisie, first in the Jacksonian era and then in the Populist movement. The interests of the South and West were tied not so much by their agricultural products as by their noncapitalist modes of production. That these two were themselves in conflict allowed the bourgeoisie to divide and conquer.

In approaching these struggles we must be careful to avoid a romantic or idyllic picture of farm life. In particular, it is inappropriate to look at the transformation of agricultural classes into industrial workers as a fall from grace. Moreover, we must acknowledge the simple material fact that if a society is to advance and achieve a basis for satisfying people's more profound needs, it must be able to free a large proportion of its labor from basic agricultural production. There can be little doubt that a productive agricultural sector is a first requirement for meaningful growth.

Thus the issue is not the reduction of labor time devoted to agriculture. This in itself is an accomplishment to be praised. Rather, the focus of our discussion must be the concrete meaning of the agricultural revolution. Here one fact of paramount importance stands out: the bulk of the rural classes were transformed from an essentially noncapitalist status (they were either independent farmers or slaves) into laborers directly dependent on the capitalist. Again it must be emphasized that this does not imply that the rural migrant to urban industry does not earn a higher living or have greater access to consumption goods. That fact seems quite indisputable. Rather, the point is that the movement from country to town represents more than a simple economic adjustment. It signifies the destruction of the rural classes and their political power to shape the society. Though this change can hardly be considered a net loss for the slave, for the heretofore independent farmer the results of the change are much less clear. And even for the black population of the South it is very unclear what exactly the alternative was. By conscious policy these people had been denied the land they had helped to develop. As a class their relation to agricultural means of production had been quite different from that of the western farmer. Like the farmer they were to face the insecurity of the industrial labor force, but their point of reference was the certainty of dependency, not the confidence of independence. That slavery was an unmitigated evil hardly proves that capitalism was the best that people were capable of.

This is the broad picture that must be filled in by careful historical analysis. What is significant in this view is not the decline in agricultural labor time, but the separation of a large class from its control over the means of production. Whether this is accomplished by force or inducement is of only secondary importance. In truth we find examples of both in the record.

All of this may seem quite congenial to the traditional view of off-farm migration. Even the most orthodox of neoclassical economists would agree that the profound change from independent farmer or slave to industrial worker is likely to produce significant psychological, sociological, and political consequences. But these are supposedly beyond the scope of interest. In the neoclassical view all we have to do is look at the potential rewards facing the individual and the choice of off-farm migration will be obvious and irrefutable. Yet in phrasing the question in this way the neoclassicist ignores the possibilities generated not by atomistic economics but by direct class action. Thus the analysis becomes thin in the extreme. It does not explain why things happened, because it cannot include the alternatives available in the analysis.

What were these alternatives? As the agricultural sector was two-fold, so were the major possibilities for a noncapitalist process of industrialization. The first possibility, growing out of southern agricultural slavery, was thoroughly unattractive: it was industrial slavery (see 11). Carried to its logical conclusions, this system might indeed have made a consistent base for the autarchy that Fitzhugh saw as desirable. However unappealing such a solution to the contradictions of the slave South appears to us now, it might have proved workable if armed intervention by the North had not occurred first. The scope of this deviation from what is familiar is so great that it is hard to imagine any serious analysis of the possibilities. In particular I find it difficult to fathom the implications of such a system for the nonslave agricultural population of the region. I cannot see how industrial slavery would have diminished white southern rural poverty, since by definition these people would have been excluded from industrial pursuits. As for the fate of the slaves I will leave it to Messrs Fogel and Engerman to show how attractive and rewarding an industrial slave life might have been (3).

If this discussion of the slave alternative seems pure fantasy, much more relevant to the current topic were the possibilities inherent in the Populist movement of the late nineteenth century. Despite its reactionary tendencies, the Populist movement in its various political manifestations suggested a very different course of events from that which occurred. Essentially this was a program to maintain the agricultural classes in an independent position by guaranteeing to them increasing control over the means of production. While often ignored in discussion of that movement, a major theme was the conflict between concentrated capitalism and the producer, whether farmer or laborer. This movement was not exclusively concerned with high farm prices or cheap money policies, as it is so often characterized. Rather, in an infant form it contained a much more profound image of an industrialization process in which the majority of the population would maintain access to the means of production. In its simplest form this demand was expressed in Populist proposals for taking over the railroad corporations and turning them into public utilities. The Populists also advocated major reforms of the distribution system along cooperative lines to do away with "useless" profits for middlemen. In its most ambitious forms the Populist program advocated the establishment of such cooperative industrial concerns as tanneries, fertilizer factories, and textile mills. Short of this all Populists supported a graduated income tax and vigorous antimonopoly legislation (for a "progressive" interpretation of Populism see 9). Nor was this message misunderstood by the already dominant capitalist classes. Thus Henry Adams, who was himself sympathetic to the Populist position, wrote a simple explanation for the defeat of that spirit:

> A capitalistic system had been adopted, and if it were to to be run at all, it must be run by capital and by capitalistic methods; for nothing could surpass the nonsensity of trying to run so complex and so concentrated a machine by Southern and Western farmers in grotesque alliance with city day-laborers, as had been tried in 1800 and 1828, and had failed even under simple conditions. (1, p. 344)

Ultimately the failure of the Populist movement was ordained not by the power or efficiency of the capitalist. All things considered, these might have been overcome. Rather, it was the internal contradictions in the class that advocated this program that doomed it to failure. The farmer recognized dimly what was necessary: a collective form of control over the means of production. And yet the same farmer's petit bourgeois nature balked at the enormity of the sin proposed as solution. Basically hostile to their potential allies, the southern blacks and the industrial workers of the East, small-scale farmers mismanaged their relations with these groups and tended to isolate themselves, not for lack of knowledge but for lack of will. At the same time, as if ignorant of their own insight into what was necessary, they overemphasized the points of their program that appealed only to their agricultural interests. Ultimately they threw in their lot with Bryan and the silver standard. And with this single issue they lost their spirit.

THE TWENTIETH CENTURY DEMISE OF AGRICULTURE. The chance was lost as it had been before in Adams' "simple conditions." As a result the rural classes were doomed to relative political impotence and gradual erosion as their offspring moved into the capitalist mainstream. This is not to say that along the way there were not important struggles. As Arthur Ford has suggested in his interesting book, *Political Economics of Rural Poverty in the South* (4, pp. 50–55), the issue of exactly what the agricultural sector of the economy would look like was a significant policy problem for the dominant capitalist class in the 1930s. It is to this issue that I turn now. However, I would emphasize that the basic scenario was already set by the beginning of the twentieth century. With the defeat of Populism there was little chance that the continuing industrialization of the nation would guarantee a healthy rural economy.

Having decided the issue of whether agricultural classes would dominate both the government and the process of capital accumulation, the capitalist classes had essentially guaranteed the flow of labor out of agriculture and into the labor pool. The question that remained was only the extent of the vindictiveness with which this policy would be carried out. The not surprising answer was to have little mercy. Thus Arthur Ford has convincingly argued that the government has followed a conscious policy of encouraging agricultural concentration to the detriment of the small-scale and poor farmers (4). This outcome was largely the result of an alliance between the Farm Bureau (representing operators of large successful farms and the residual political power of the rural states) and the dominant capitalist classes. In exchange for agricultural programs that favored their own position, the Farm Bureau actively opposed legislation that would put those on smaller farms in a position to compete more actively. Thus Ford points to the support of the Farm Bureau for the Agricultural Adjustment Act which favored large-scale farmers and the Bureau's general opposition to the Federal Securities Administration with its emphasis on reorganization of agriculture. Ford also considers other examples from our farm programs, drawing on the work of Bonnen, Herr, Wallace and Hoover, and Schuh (see also 2, 5, 10, 12, 13, 14). These studies seem to indicate the general bias against small-scale farmers and the heavy weight given to programs that further the concentration of agriculture, thus producing significant income problems.

In general I find this work quite convincing. It suggests strongly that government policy has been implemented with the aim of minimizing the size of the independent farm petite bourgeoisie. However, I would not overemphasize the historical importance of these decisions. For example, if all the excessively large-scale agricultural firms were broken up, how many more farmers could obtain a reasonable income? In a very rough calculation I have estimated that perhaps as many as two million new farms could be created on lands controlled currently by less than a million farms. As an argument in equity there is little reason not to encourage policies that would achieve such an objective. However, had the government followed such policies in the past, it is quite doubtful that the problems of rural poverty would look much different today, for the original population pool dwarfs the potential increase in sustainable farms. Making agriculture more feasible for some offers little guarantee that the lower end of the rural income distribution would look much different, only the top end.

In any case such policies were clearly an unlikely tack to take for a government concerned with guaranteeing an ample labor force. Only in periods of severe dislocation such as the Depression were they generally considered. Having decided that the rural population was not to be encouraged, and certainly not encouraged to gain meaningful control over the means of production, it would have been self-defeating to subsidize its continued existence in an independent role.

Thus in the basic struggles at the turn of the century and in the more recent exercise of policy, the dominant classes have provided themselves with a substantial labor force drawn out of agriculture. This pool has fueled the growth of both urban centers and the increasingly important spread of industry to nonmetropolitan areas. Nor is it in the interests of the capitalist class to subsidize too greatly the accumulation of human capital by these classes. If the radical analysis is correct, the labor force must be continually threatened by the existence of a relatively unskilled reserve. It is difficult enough to maintain this reserve under present conditions. The relegating of both blacks and women to the secondary market is clear but also difficult to guarantee under political pressure. The rural population forms a less protesting reserve of relatively unskilled labor for use by the capitalist class. Only if the needs of industry change substantially or the costs of supporting the rural classes through welfare become too great should we expect to see significant programs to better equip them for the market. Many liberals have argued that these conditions already hold and that such programs are already "appropriate." If so we should expect to see an extension of some of the rural poverty programs of the sixties. However, it is far from clear that these conditions are indeed pressing. The explosion of urban higher education in the sixties has probably guaranteed more than enough labor for higher level jobs. Not everyone can have such jobs, so clearly it would be uneconomical to prepare everyone for them. All that is needed is a surplus at each level. Once obtained there is little incentive to go further.

Thus we have the major hypothesis of the radical approach to rural poverty: this situation is not an unfortunate accident but rather functional to the topsy-turvy system of capitalism; it helps to guarantee a surplus labor pool. But why, says the ideologue of pure competition, is this pool not completely absorbed into the economy? The only possibility in the traditional approach is that such labor has somehow priced itself out of the market. Or its marginal product is not substantial enough to justify its wage. This is certainly a possibility, but in light of the great ease with which the military is able to train a skilled labor force or with which labor during the war was able to advance rapidly in skill level, these arguments seem weak. If the army with a modest four year contract finds it economical to train its own craftsmen as opposed to using civilians, it seems dubious that the private market could not work out such simple contractual relations.

Whatever the merits of the reserve-price or social-minimum-wage argument may be, the radical hypothesis is that a fully employed economy is the last thing that the dominant classes want, for there is a fundamental difference between the bargaining power of a worker facing a depressed labor market and that of a worker facing a tight labor market. On this point I would disagree sharply with those who maintain that high aggregate demand cannot begin to touch rural poverty for structural reasons. The question should rather be phrased in terms of the level of demand necessary to begin to break down those structural variables. According to this analysis, the disincentive to reaching such a level is not the costs of training workers, but rather the substantially enhanced bargaining power of the labor force. This is of course an empirical question, but one that obviously should be explored before we commit ourselves to the structuralist position. The problem is that profits are eroded long before full employment is reached. If this is what the neo-classicist means when arguing that labor prices itself out of the market, then I heartily agree. But certainly a more rational way of organizing production must exist than one that disciplines labor by maintaining an artificial poverty in a rich society. If this is the only way that capitalism can work, then perhaps it is not worth the price. If the argument presented here is sound, we should give up on programs that can only patch over this fundamental contradiction and consider with more care strategies that address it directly.

REFERENCES

(1). Adams, Henry, *The Education of Henry Adams*, New York: Modern Library, 1918.
(2). Bonnen, James T., "Distribution of Benefits from Selected Farm Programs," in U.S. President's National Advisory Commission on Rural Poverty, *Rural Poverty in the United States*, Washington: USGPO, 1968.
(3). Fogel, Robert W. and Stanley L. Engerman, *Time on the Cross: The Economics of American Negro Slavery*, Boston: Little, Brown, 1974.
(4). Ford, Arthur M., *Political Economics of Rural Poverty in the South*, Cambridge: Ballinger, 1973.
(5). Friedman, Milton, *Capitalism and Freedom*, Chicago: University of Chicago Press, 1962.
(6). Herr, William, "Credit and Farm Policy," in U.S. President's National Advisory Commission on Rural Poverty, *Rural Poverty in the United States*, Washington: USGPO, 1968.
(7). Koopmans, Tjalling C., *Three Essays on the State of Economic Science*, New York: McGraw-Hill, 1957.
(8). Mayhew, Anne, "A Reappraisal of the Causes of Farm Protest in the U.S., 1870–1900," *Journal of Economic History* 32 (2): 464–75.
(9). Pollack, Norman, *The Populist Response to Industrial America: Midwestern Populist Thought*, Cambridge: Harvard University Press, 1962.
(10). Schuh, G. Edward, "Interrelationship between the Farm Labor Force and Changes in the Total Economy," in U.S. President's National Advisory Commission on Rural Poverty, *Rural Poverty in the United States*, Washington: USGPO, 1968.
(11). Starobin, Robert, *Industrial Slavery in the Old South*, New York: Oxford University Press, 1970.
(12). U.S. Department of Agriculture, Economic Research Service, "Economics of Scale in Farming," *Agricultural Economics Research*, Vol. 107, 1967.

(13). ——, "Our 100,000 Biggest Farms," *Agricultural Economics Research,* Vol. 49, 1964.

(14). Wallace, T. and M. Hoover, "Income Effect of Innovation, The Case of Labor in Agriculture," *Journal of Farm Economics* 48 (2): 325-36.

Discussion

EDNA T. LOEHMAN

A S I read Chapter 7, I tried to see how I fit as an economist in the radical-neoclassical dichotomy. On one hand, I am interested in poverty issues. On the other hand, I use neoclassical theory with its marginal concepts, where the theory applies, to describe economic behavior. My feelings as I read the paper were that one does not need to be a radical economist to do research in income distribution nor does one have to rely completely on neoclassical theory in all situations. All schools of economic thought have something valuable to give to the science of economics. Our responsibility as scientists is to take from each theory that which fits best in any problem situation we are studying.

The radical analysis is correct that economists and traditional economic theory have not taken enough cognizance of income distribution problems. On the other hand, the radical economists have yet to present us with more theory than merely an alternative description of historical events. A radical model of the economic system as complete as neoclassical theory has not yet been developed. It might not be entirely fair, however, to refuse to pay attention to radical economists unless they play our game of model making.

Chapter 7 has the following three components:

A. A critique of neoclassical MVP theory and presentation of the radical economic viewpoint.

B. A radical economic description of the rural poverty situation in terms of class struggle.

C. A brief mention of radical economic policy for the rural poverty problem.

I will discuss what I consider to be important points in these three areas.

RADICAL CRITIQUE OF NEOCLASSICAL THEORY. The radical economic position is that neoclassical economic theory does not adequately explain or consider income distribution problems or the role of political power in the allocation of resources.

I agree that the neoclassical market model as given by Koopmans takes income distribution as given in explaining the efficient allocation of goods and services by the market. This limitation regarding income distribution does not mean that the neoclassical theory is a poor theory in all respects, merely that it is incomplete in the income distribution area. In terms of positive economics, the Koopmans model is a description of how the market works to achieve efficiency, given income distribution. Also as a positive description, marginal value product theory seems a good behavioral rule for business owners since, if more than the marginal value product is paid to labor, owners would not remain in business long.

In terms of the normative aspects, the Koopmans model is not contradictory to income redistribution goals. Many economists believe that redistribution of income through public programs should be accomplished outside the market itself, leaving the market to accomplish efficiency. Thus, if we do not like the existing distribution of income, it can be changed outside the market. The new distribution of income can then be taken as given and the Koopmans model used to describe the resulting market allocation.

It may be possible to include power and income distribution considerations in neoclassical models; for example, the Keynes IS-LM model with sticky wage rates includes the effect of labor unions on the labor supply function. Also, it could be argued that wages depend on both MVP and organization of labor. A group with low MVP will tend to have low wages, but the more power it has, the more of its MVP it will claim as wages. I am not persuaded to throw away neoclassical theory on the basis of its deficiencies in income distribution and political aspects.

RADICAL ECONOMIC THEORY AS AN EXPLANATION OF RURAL POVERTY.

In the radical economic view income distribution can be explained by a model of class struggle and capitalist exploitation of labor. Political power is linked to ownership of capital. Government and capitalists conspire to keep the working classes down and wages low.

Much of Persky's description of historical rural situations could be accepted by everyone if words such as "bourgeoisie, proletariat, class struggle," and the like, were deleted. Persky's description deals with the replacement of production on small farms and plantations by capitalist agricultural farms and vertically integrated agribusiness complexes due to their more efficient means of production. Farmers became more dependent on the capitalist system in two ways: they needed capitalist inputs if they chose to remain competitive in such a system, and they needed alternative work if they left the farm. The political power of small-scale farmers deteriorated with their economic position and declining numbers, compared with those dependent on the capitalist system. The landless agricultural workers, mostly former slaves, never had any political power. On the other hand, the agribusiness complex had a disproportional share of power due to collective political organizations such as the Farm Bureau.

Note that MVP theory is not contradicted by this historical description. A person who owned no capital and had only his own labor had a low MVP and therefore low wages.

The main explanation that Persky gives for the poverty situation is a conspiracy theory. He says that the rural poverty situation is not a historical accident but the result of a conspiracy between government and capitalist to guarantee a large employed labor pool and hence low wages. Conspiracy theories are always hard to prove! The existence of poverty and lack of political influence of poverty groups is not a proof of conspiracy but may be just the unfortunate result of historical and economic forces.

Thus I find the application of radical economics to rural poverty presented by Persky to be merely descriptive; this description does not contradict MVP theory. A model of income distribution including power considerations is needed to formulate and analyze alternative policies to deal with rural poverty. While there may be a need to test MVP theory, by the same token radical theory has not yet even developed testable hypotheses. Besides recognizing the importance of collective action and power, radical economists need to do further work on how to model them. (Some political-economic models that have been developed might offer fruitful lines of exploration.)

PROPOSALS OF POLICY BASED ON RADICAL ECONOMIC THEORY. Some radical economists advocate drastic redistribution of ownership of capital because owners of capital do nothing valuable for society as compared to labor. Persky does not say this. In fact he argues that redistribution of land would not help the rural poor and would be detrimental to food production. Therefore, he does not seem as radical as some radical economists. He does mention the need for rorganization of means of production to eliminate "artificial poverty," but he does not explain what he means by reorganization. Many economists would agree we need some reorganization in terms of making the market system more competitive.

Persky's main policy proposal seems to be in terms of collective political action. This certainly can help, as examples show (milk producers cooperatives and labor unions). It should be noted that capital is not always needed as a basis of political power (for example, the growing influence of environmental groups and Common Cause is not based on capital). Persky also proposes full employment as a requirement for improved labor income. Most nonradical economists would agree with the need for full employment. However, it should be noted that even if full employment is achieved, without retraining programs the relative position of low skilled workers will still be on the bottom of the income distribution scale.

Persky makes no mention of policies related to formation of human capital, health improvements, and income maintenance; do radicals believe these help eliminate the poverty situation? Also, he combines both small-scale farmers and other rural workers as well in his analysis. It seems to me that different policies are needed to help small-scale farmers and rural workers because their problems and backgrounds are different.

SUMMARY. My criticism parallels the criticism of other economists of radical theory. While the theory identifies and emphasizes an important problem area, it is mainly descriptive and not a theoretical model. It may be just as incomplete a description as neoclassical theory. It needs to be formalized into theory and then have hypotheses tested as a framework for policy analysis. In formulating policies, radical economists need to consider more alternatives than just power to deal with poverty, such as formation of human capital.

CHAPTER EIGHT

Institutional processing of human resources: a theory of social marginalization

HARLAND T. PADFIELD
and
JOHN A. YOUNG

SOCIAL science theory and policy research in the last two decades have had two compelling concerns—on the one hand, to offer explanation for and suggest ways to reduce the social isolation of minority groups and balance the mainstream economic systems' unequal distribution of benefits; and on the other hand, to sort out and deal with human performance characteristics of importance to the national production system. It is the central tenet of this chapter that these concerns are aspects of one phenomenon: the institutional processing of human resources. Furthermore, we contend that social science research on human resources has strengthened the social and economic forces working *against* equality.

THE CURRENT STATE OF SOCIAL THEORY AND POLICY RESEARCH

Systematic Biases from the Knowledge Market. Although few scientists would deny that scientific work responds to incentives, many would

Research for this chapter was made possible by Grant Nos. 216-15-98 and 316-15-95 from the Cooperative State Research Service, USDA; Grant No. GA SS 7404 from the Rockefeller Foundation; and supplementary support from the Oregon Agricultural Experiment Station. Some components of the chapter were developed in a paper presented by Padfield at the 1974 meetings of the American Psychological Association. That version appears in *Genetic Destiny: Scientific Controversy and Social Conflict* (edited by Ethel Tobach and Harold M. Proshansky), published for the Society for the Psychological Study of Social Issues, AMS Press, Inc., New York, 1976. The authors express appreciation for critical commentaries from Paul Barkley, Jan Newton, Marianne Padfield, and Joe Stevens. Responsibility for views expressed in this chapter is that of the authors only.

argue that incentives vary with the individual, that biases are variable and counterbalancing, and that gaps in knowledge are random. But

> if scientific knowledge and professional work is increasingly important for defining and solving public problems, it is also true that highly organized centers of power substantially influence what is defined as problematic, that for which knowledge is sought, and acceptable solutions. Although the public has become more and more dependent on science, science has become increasingly dependent on the resources of a few. . . . Knowledge that develops and the problems that are investigated are those of direct concern to the centers of power. One of the most powerful institutions that has influenced scientific work and its content has been the modern industrial corporation. . . . Corporations invest in research primarily for production development. Consequently, conditions such as housing, pollution, and general environmental deterioration receive little attention. Organizational goals become the primary determinant of scientific work rather than public need. (20)

For similar reasons, government exerts a similar power over the development of knowledge. In short, a relatively few nonscientists are in a position to make enormous resource allocations to the conduct of scientific inquiry. The inevitable results have been more stringent and explicit cost-benefit constraints on research and a quantum increase of single purpose, mission oriented research as opposed to curiosity satisfying, diffuse, and comprehensive purpose research. These dynamics derive from the rational decision rules and political imperatives by which industrial corporations and government bureaucracies exist.

In terms of effects on the behavioral or social sciences, systematic pressures dictate concerns about people in certain capacities and not in others. For institutions in the business of using human resources, human characteristics that provide clues to how people will perform in the production process are of direct concern. For complementary institutions whose job is socialization or investment in human resources, the efficient processing of people to match production requirements inevitably becomes rational. The consequence of these dynamics is an enormous convergence of interest in how to capture the benefits of human resource investments already made by other institutions. This interest creates incentives to develop and refine continuously the science of identifying, selecting, and improving people who are already adjusted to and cognitively consonant with the mainstream economic and social system, while it creates disincentives to develop a science of rehabilitating and retraining people, including linguistic and racial minorities, who are maladjusted to and cognitively dissonant with the mainstream system. *Processing* rather than creating or recycling human resources is thus the primary mission of the educational establishment, and the primary purpose to which social science research and knowledge is put.

Systematic Biases from the Professional Systems. Response to pressures created by national economic and political institutions are not the only biases in the social sciences affecting cultural minorities. In a recent review (4) of Robert K. Merton's *The Sociology of Science,* Charles C. Gillispie, a Princeton University history of science professor, notes the main thrust of Merton's analysis: that in the scientific community

two main sets of norms constrain behavior and do so in ways that conflict, the one enjoining selflessness in the advancement of knowledge, and the other ambition for professional reputation, which in science accrues from originality in discovery and from that alone. The analysis exhibits the scientific community to be one wherein the dynamics derive from the competition for honor even as the dynamics of the classical economic community do from the competition for profit . . .

If desire for recognition and honor are indeed the basis of incentives operating in the scientific community, then it is rationally inevitable that the knowledge generated by social science will in the main address isuses of central interest to the discipline professionals, elaborating and extending conventional theoretical constructs rather than challenging them, and making these constructs define problems and solutions that are politically and economically acceptable. Having noted this generally recognized fact, we wish now to address the problem of how the peculiar biases of the social science disciplines have created systematic distortions in our constructs of reality, particularly as they apply to the experiences of subordinate cultural minorities.

Without recapitulating the numerous critiques of the "culture of poverty" tradition in anthropology and the lower class culture theory in sociology (see 12 and 25), we will simply summarize general deficiencies and distortions in these bodies of literature.

Probably the most serious general bias is the a priori assumption that culture as a commonly held set of values and beliefs determines rather than rationalizes behavior.* The anthropologists' tendency to emphasize the unique characteristics and internal dynamics of small societies as opposed to their articulation with larger societies also reinforces a priori assumptions of cultural causation.

Anthropological biases have been further reinforced by those sociological studies of the lower class using theoretical constructs which equate urbanization with social deviancy. Again, theoretical concepts of internal dynamics, supported by observations on the behavior of lower

---

* The work of Oscar Lewis (13) demonstrates the tendency toward cultural determinism, despite his theoretical statements about the possibilities of generalizing his data beyond the specific culture he describes. To Lewis, however, goes the credit for establishing a major focus of interest among anthropologists and for developing the theory of cultural dynamics of the poverty situation.

class subjects made by their caretakers in public agencies, emphasize the determinism of the social subsystem without relating it to the larger social system (for an example, see 15).

The biases of the social sciences derive in large part from the way the disciplines have philosophically defined the behavioral systems in which they specialize. Each discipline and professional community has come to be identified with what each likes to regard as a separate, analytical reality, despite the fact that methodologically all social science must depend upon natural, complex, behavioral systems.

The result of this philosophical discontinuity has been that instead of being limited to its proper analytical domain, each discipline has been allowed to assume professional proprietary rights over a *natural* system. In the process each has come to speak authoritatively concerning the complex whole with which it is dealing. Thus enormous blind spots develop which are inevitably filled by conventional (usually culturally conditioned) assumptions the scientist has about "human nature."

Economics, for example, has generated partial explanations regarding the behavior of industrial firms; but leaving the behavior of such "economic institutions" to the interpretation of economists implies that these institutions do not have major political, social, and even psychological functions. The public is not well served when research used in policymaking ignores these functions. This partitioning also implies that other institutions of little concern to economics, such as the family, the school, and the church, do not have major economic functions. Similarly, psychology in its focus on individual behavior of white middle class Americans tends to be preoccupied with microsituational covariation and to accept larger environmental systems such as political and criminal justice institutions, public education and welfare, private medicine, organized labor, and industry as given. The result is that psychologists may ignore the effects of institutional variation on different ethnic groups.

Compound bias results when social scientists make assumptions and pronouncements about social reality based on the biases of other disciplines. Economists, psychologists, and sociologists, for example, tend to incorporate constructs from anthropology and attribute maladaptive behavior to irrational goals determined by exotic cultural imperatives. Or, if constructs from sociology are used, behavioral explanations are more likely to be based on assumptions about social deprivation of the family. If perspectives derived from psychology are adopted, the problems of cultural minorities are explained primarily in clinical terms (for example, see 16), even though solutions to the problems are more likely to be economic, political, or social in nature. Obviously, minority groups face constraints that are different from the institutional constraints surrounding mainstream industrial and labor institutions; therefore, using constructs of economics based on such institutional constraints to assess the rationality of the economic behavior of minority groups is invalid.

The upshot is that scientific understanding of lower class and minority group behavior, and public policy toward it, has contended with an enormous bias generated by the social science disciplines from the time of their formation. Without taking or joining issue with others who have written on this subject (5, 6), the consequences we wish to summarize at this point are philosophical rather than social. *The complementary sensitivities and insensitivities of the social science disciplines have persistentliy overemphasized variability among ethnic, class, family, and personality systems, while preconceiving uniformity of institutional environment.* This means that in the scientific consultation to social policy, the blind are leading the blind in explaining how our basic economic and public institutions touch upon the lives of their workers, students, cases, clients, patients, inmates, and general outcasts. Thus it comes as no shock to foreign scientific observers of the American system that the "enlightened" social policies of the sixties failed, and that we are now engaged in a compelling reexamination of wholly and partially discredited social scientific tenets.

THE STUDY OF LOWER CLASS BEHAVIOR AS GOAL-DIRECTED AND RATIONAL. It is our contention that the partial failures of the massive, publicly funded social programs of the sixties occurred *not* because they ignored the inherent economic relevance of class and race differences, but because they ignored the differential benefits to class and race inherent in our basic economic institutions. We suggest further that public human resource institutions that administer compensatory social programs help build inequality into the economic system.

Marginalization vs. Assimilation. Milton Gordon's classic study *Assimilation in American Life* (9) defines the "ideal type" of *assimilation* by describing a hypothetical country with the fictitious name of Sylvania. In Sylvania race, religion, and previous national extraction are the same and cultural behavior is relatively uniform *"except for social class divisions"*; groups and institutions are differentiated *"only on a social class basis."* Gordon introduces another hypothetical group called the Mundovians, who immigrate to Sylvania. By the second generation the immigrants are no longer distinguishable racially, culturally, or structurally from the rest of the Sylvanian population. In Gordon's words, becoming assimilated in Sylvanian society means the Mundovians have changed their cultural patterns to those of the Sylvanians; entered fully into their societal network; intermarried and interbred fully with them; developed a Sylvanian ethnicity; no longer encounter discrimination or prejudice; and are not in political conflict with Sylvanians (9, pp. 68–70).

Events have made it all too apparent that Gordon's assimilation model does not hold for a number of minority cultures in the United States. An oversimplified antithesis to Gordon's model that would account for nonassimilation might be the following: several centuries and 10 to 20 generations since the Indians, Africans, and Mexicans encountered the "Sylvanians," a preponderant majority have neither entered the Sylvanian mainstream cultural system nor have they been able to maintain their original cultural system. Thus the simplistic assimilation model $A + B = A$ gives way to the cultural pluralistic model $A + B = AB$, $AB + C = ABC$, etc., as exemplified in Moynihan and Glazer's book, *Beyond the Melting Pot* (8). However, the disquieting persistence of intergenerational poverty among ethnic and class minorities indicates that the cultural pluralistic model distorts reality as well. Therefore, instead of attempting to develop models of assimilation or cultural pluralism we propose a model of social marginalization: $A + B = Ab$, $Ab + C = Abc$, etc., which suggests movement from a geographically separate and culturally distinct position to restricted or marginal participation in the mainstream economic and social system.

Although cultural pluralism may have been a valid model for some groups of immigrants in the past, increasing institutional regulation of ethnic and class minorities suggests that the social marginalization model is more useful for the present. Much of the socialization of such minorities within the structure of public institutions is useless or has negative effects. And at the same time, economic differentiation associated with the socialization process excludes minorities and thus isolates them from the American economic mainstream. As a result, increasing numbers of minority people find themselves in cultural enclaves, living out their lives and socializing their children—neither in their own native culture nor in the mainstream American culture, but in what can more accurately be termed the culture of marginality. (We use this term rather than "the culture of poverty" because sheer material—including dietary—deprivation is less at issue than the deprivation of economic and social status. See 24 by Turnbull for a case study of institutionalized starvation that could be termed "the culture of poverty.")

Effective Economic Environments and the Administration of Benefits.
In a recent demographic study of "Institutions in Modern Society," Octavio Romano concluded that on any given day 40 to 45 percent of California's total population is subject to some form of public institutional regulation (21). Romano refers to four service systems: schools, social welfare, law enforcement, and hospitals. All are involved in socialization, enculturation, or, as economists say, *human resource investment*. Not only do all citizens of modern affluent societies experience publicly administered socialization in the early stages of their lives, most continue to experience it in some form virtually all their lives. Considering public broadcasting, public occupational training, and training provided by industry, our society is saturated with human resource investment.

Why does heavy investment in public education and other public services fail to eliminate systematic economic disparity and social inequality? An answer to this question requires a closer examination of the key institutional systems involved in the investment, processing, and management of human resources. These systems include public education, the labor market, criminal justice, public health, and social welfare. All health, education, and training programs in this country are predicated, at least in part, on the doctrine of a free, competitive human resource market—as opposed to a highly regulated, discriminatory market—and the naive assumption that our social system is subject more to the force of inertia than to the force of change. Repeatedly, educational psychologists and economists alike falsely assume that the educational system operates according to egalitarian principles. Perhaps the educational system *was* egalitarian when the administration of educational benefits occurred as a natural by-product of the welfare-rationing function of other social and economic institutions, i.e., only the wealthier people could afford to educate their children. But after the national educational system became a truly universal institution, its disparate investment function (which it was performing *de facto*) of maintaining class distinctions could be protected only with the development of a human resource *processing* function—testing, grading, and sorting in order to provide certification of human resources for the mainstream economy.

In this conceptual framework the study of educational "problem populations" becomes less important for policy than the study of how the public educational system administers its investment function, and how the evolution of this function interacts with changes in other economic institutions. The theory of social marginalization suggests that schools produce failure systematically. The educational system's investment function is to ration economic opportunity; it fulfills this function by giving some groups short rations.

In the development of manpower policies, emphasis similar to that in the educational system has been placed on altering the behavior and occupational competencies of the unemployed, ostensibly to increase their chances of becoming selected in the labor market. But it is a simplistic notion that labor markets screen the labor pool for the most productive competencies, while ignoring noneconomic factors. The major federal training program which demonstrated conclusively that labor markets do not operate this way was the urban ghetto-oriented NAB/JOBS program (National Alliance of Businessmen/Job Opportunities in the Business Sector) launched amid urban unrest in 1968. The program subsidized direct employment of "unqualified" people in industry, thus effectively altering the discriminatory function of the labor market. Between 300,000 to a half million ghetto unemployed were exposed to industry, with two-thirds becoming converted in the process. (Although it was relatively successful, the program was ended by economic recession and union pressure less than two years after it began [19].) Yet, in spite of this positive response to employment opportunity, most of the research on labor force problems continues to focus on the behavior of the unemployed, instead of focusing on the more central issue of job rationing in industrial labor markets and public regulatory agencies. The latter approach suggests that the economic behavior of the hard core unemployed is in fact a rational, resilient adaptation to an economic environment in which disincentives to personal investment are as profound as the disincentives to business investment in a global depression. Economic studies of lower class occupational performance in terms of incentives/ disincentives, although relatively infrequent, tend generally to support this rational theory of motivation (for examples see 3, 11, 22, 26).

In the private as well as the public sector, the institutional rationing of benefits is increasingly decisive in economic success. The dairy industry, for example, evolved from a community of milk producers competing for profit on the open market to a complex quasi-public association producing milk for a government subsidized market and lobbying for price suports in an effort to benefit from public policy. Thus a contribution by the dairy industry to a political candidate in a position to control the federal regulatory agencies becomes as much an investment as the building of a new creamery.

Clearly a broader understanding of investment is necessary. Investment should be considered as diversion of present income to increase future skills, and to increase access to *administered* benefits. Thus public investments in education and private investments in regulatory agencies both maintain inequality because they support the differential administration of benefits by public institutions.

This broader political-economic framework gives us a new perspective on labor markets and formal educational systems. Labor markets must be seen as complex systems that function as importantly in the rationing of economic benefits as they do in the production process. Rationing mechanisms are operating in the recruitment of labor because industry and other economically organized groups—especially unions and the professional associations—continually invest to maintain or increase their own (as opposed to the public's) economic well-being (see 2, pp. 249–54, for an example in the welfare system). These rationing mechanisms are linked directly with public education, where economically useful credentials are administered more or less consistently with the preferences for cultural and racial characteristics established by the users and organizers of labor. The learning process in school involves the mapping of these preferences and self-selection in response to incentives and disincentives established by school administrators and teachers to correspond to the preferred characteristics (see 7, especially Chapters 1, 3, 7 and 8). Therefore in this, its wider context, *formal education is primarily a system for the development and administration of differential credentials by means of which the labor market rations economic opportunity and social status.*

The Family as an Economic Institution. When economists discuss the woes of a business community, the economic environment in terms of incentives/disincentives is generally recognized as an independent set of variables, and the policies and practices of the industry in question are considered a dependent set. When the health of an economic sector or a major industrial corporation is at stake, restructuring the economic environment is invariably called for. Operating within the deductive framework of economic theory, this analysis assumes the industrial corporation to be a rational system with specific goals and a core technology—including formal organization, behavioral codes, and a corporate rationale—for the achievement of these goals. Given the overwhelming importance of production goals and core technologies, industrial corporations tend to oppose changes that would disrupt the internal organization of the core technology (20). Whether this technology is used to achieve maximum profit in the production of gasoline, automobiles, munitions, opium poppies, or USDA subsidized crops makes little difference to the rational pursuit of the goal.

To see macroeconomic theory for what it is—namely, behavioral theory—it is necessary to recognize public policy as the effective environment, the industrial corporation as the adaptive unit, and core technology as the adaptive strategy. Economists are the consultants to public policy, and macroeconomic policy changes are simply intended to create a system of incentives according to behaviorist principles, otherwise known as "sound business principles." Thus the woes of industry are regarded by policymakers as the result of an "unsound business climate," or a lack of proper incentives in the business environment; for example, the price of gasoline is too low to stimulate greater production and refining of oil.

But when it comes to family units operating in the context of the same economic system, policymakers fall into the trap of attempting to control and cajole, often arbitrarily asking for controls and sacrifices that run counter to rational self-interest. The public is asked to buy this approach on a purely normative as opposed to a pragmatic basis. Those who violate social norms are criticized as being immoral, while the effective environment of incentives and disincentives to economically preferred behavior is ignored. For example, the conventional wisdom supposes that people who use too much gasoline are greedy and that welfare clients are lazy. The fact that families are not considered rational units in the construction of economically effective environments may lead to the exclusion of valuable resources from the productive economy and to feeding the fires of inflationary psychology, as individuals rationally strive to capture a fair share of a diminishing set of benefits. The dual system of remunerative controls for business and normative controls for the family and the individual leads us to ask, Is this any way to run an economy?

The family, whether it be the working middle class, male-dominated nuclear family or the lower class, female-centered family, does have a set of specific goals. One of the most basic, single purpose goals of the family unit is to produce income. Whether this income is in the form of wild animal and plant nutrients; domestic foods; trade items; wages, salaries, inheritance, dole; or a combination of these makes little difference to the rational pursuit of the goal. In the pursuit of such goals, the family unit may be said to have a core technology, including knowledge of its effective environment, a technical language, decision rules, production requirements, role differentiation, and a rationale. Given the overwhelming importance of production goals and core technologies (adaptive strategies), family units, like industrial corporations, tend to oppose changes which would disrupt the internal organization (principles of effective behavior) of the core technology. Whether this technology has been organized to gain the most from a professional career, public assistance, or famine relief makes little difference in terms of resistance to change in the core technology (on the family's adaptation to famine relief, see 24, pp. 280–82).

The deterioration of the family as an economically adapted unit can be said to occur when the rational pursuit of *organizational* goals is replaced by the rational pursuit of *individual* goals. Then the basic economic decision-making unit (other than the individual) becomes a social network.

Attributes that contrast the lower class from the working middle class must be considered adaptive responses to their different *effective economic environments*. Thus high achievement motivation, future time perspective, and internal locus of control—classic middle class indicators of success—are maladaptive in the economic environment of the lower class. Moreover, public policies and programs aimed primarily at transforming "undesirable" traits of lower class people without restructuring their effective environments are spending taxpayers' money to take benefits away from the poor (for empirical evidence, see 10, and 19, pp. 205–53).

Social Marginalization: An Interactive Process. *Social marginalization is the process of interaction between disincentives in the effective economic environment and rational adaptation to that environment. Adaptation to disincentives tends irreversibly to segregate people into an economically peripheral, dependent position, and it tends to result in modes of activity counterproductive to society as a whole.*

The dynamics of social marginalization originate in the labor market, which is the core system for the distribution of economic and social benefits. Socialists like to contrast what they consider to be the central tenet of their system of distribution—"to each according to his need"—with what they say is the central tenet of the capitalist system—"to each according to his ability." Actually, the American system ad-

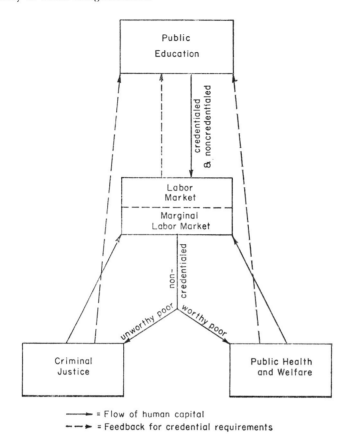

FIG. 8.1. *Human resource processing system.*

heres more to the practice of "to each according to his credentials, and those without credentials will be administered benefits according to their worthiness."

The persistent dilemma of the capitalist model is the moral and political issue of how to dispose of the labor surplus upon which capitalism depends (see Fig. 8.1). Public education starts the general flow of human capital with a set of administered credentials, predetermined and rationed according to the cultural preferences of the taxpaying participants (principal investors) in the labor market system of benefit-rationing. Those not assimilated in the mainstream labor market are not rejected outright, but rather undergo a *process* of rejection involving underemployment, unemployment, exploitation (where returns to the employee are not sufficient to provide human investment capital), and the like. The labor market outflow divides into two streams—one, the worthy poor flowing through the public welfare system; the other, the unworthy poor, whose illegal economic activity sends them through the criminal justice system. The components in the system are also connected by a network of information feedback on what credentials have been accumulated by whom.

In effect there is a dual system for processing human resources in the system at large and most especially in the public school system. (As an aside, it can be stated that in promoting mass education, the educational establishment was sociologically naive to the profound dilemma it would create. Either public education would have to change other human resource institutions, thereby fundamentally changing the entire human resource system, or it would have to develop subtle, infrastructural changes to maintain its integrity with the system at large.)

Institutions within the human resource system cooperate to distribute discriminatory information pertaining to members of marginal groups, who are certified variously as educational failures, work failures, and criminals. Information about marginal cases is not only cumulative but consistent (systematically discriminatory), thereby altering the effective economic and institutional environment for classes of people who will adapt and remove their surplus labor from the mainstream system. In other words, they will respond rationally to a net *disincentive* to develop competencies to exploit the mainstream economic environment, and to a net *incentive* to develop competencies to exploit economic environments marginal to the mainstream system. The long-term effect of such disposal of human resources, for individuals and for groups, is irreversibility in the organization of the core technology—in other words, the longer marginal status continues, the more likely it is to continue.

SOCIAL MARGINALIZATION IN TIME AND SPACE: CONNECTING RURAL AND URBAN PHASES. What we have attempted
to describe to this point is a dynamic system of interaction between an effective economic environment and rationally adapting social units. This analysis implies temporal evolution and spatial connections between rural and urban phases of marginality. The temporal dimension relates to changes in effective economic environment, while the spatial dimension relates to population movement between rural and urban areas within a particular time period.

Rural systems are characterized by underinvestment when compared to urban systems. The relative degree of underinvestment is the dynamic link between the two systems. Rural human resource systems vary with the industry. In agricultural industries developed in the South, Southwest, and plantation Pacific—such as cotton, sugar cane, fruit crops, and vegetables, all based upon labor-intensive technologies—labor markets depend on human capital underinvestment (political and economic subordination). The means of this subordination is race and class discrimination built into the institutions that administer benefits in all key components of the human resource system. These components include the labor market, public education, criminal justice, and welfare (17, 18). In the case of other rural industries such as mining, wood products, cattle, and highly mechanized agriculture, underinvestment in human resources is maintained by specialized socialization limited to the skill and knowledge requirements of a particular industry. The industry tends to protect its labor supply by insisting on specialized socialization even in the face of increased mechanization and diminished raw materials. The result is that human resources that are in surplus of industry demand become trapped in cul-de-sacs of the rural economy.

In cities labor markets offer a greater variety of opportunity. Public schools are of higher quality, and substantially greater benefits are to be gained from urban public health and welfare programs. The net human resource flow from rural to urban areas, therefore, is determined by young people with credentials seeking to enter the urban labor force and young people without credentials seeking to take advantage of marginal labor markets and welfare services (26, p. 379).

To develop a comprehensive rural-urban model, we must address two questions: what roles do rural institutions play in urban human resource deterioration, and under what circumstances, if any, do adaptive social units (families and social networks) in declining rural communities become subject to social marginalization? The emphasis here must be placed on understanding how *institutions* invest in, process, use, and discard human resources, and not on describing how individuals adapt to institutions. The model must also provide for the possibility that these institutions function in significantly different ways in different phases of the social marginalization process.

We have tentatively developed a process model of the marginalization of human resources. The model plots four temporal phases across rural and urban settings (see Fig. 8.2).

1. **The Golden Age or Frontier Phase.** It is probable that every rural and urban community had at least one golden age when its core economy was developing, employment opportunity was expanding, basic social institutions were consonant with economic requirements, and the economic base was adequate to sustain the social system (local industry was able to absorb the normal human capital flow within the mainstream system). In rural areas the boom was created by the development of agriculture and industries concerned with the extraction of natural resources, while in urban areas industrialization characterized the frontier phase.

2. **The Setup or Attenuation Phase.** The dying community is the consequence of a prolonged state of imbalance between locally generated human capital and the demands of the local labor market. In the rural setting, development of the core industry has leveled off or declined to the point where public investments in services and welfare can no longer be maintained at levels sustained during the golden age.

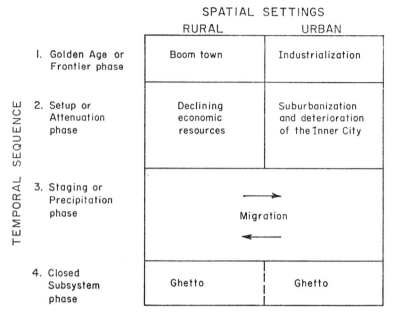

FIG. 8.2. *Connecting rural and urban phases in the process of social marginalization.*

Inner city deterioration in the urban setting occurs when high wage earners are displaced by low wage earners, the underemployed, and the unemployed, and a subsequently diminishing tax base cannot provide services and welfare. (For a recent article viewing inner city decay in a process framework, see 14.)

Some of the universal behavioral tendencies of declining rural and urban communities are:

—fear and distrust of outsiders
—factionalism within the community
—limitation of social expression to extremes—the church/bar syndrome
—development of subtle discriminatory "credentials" for local labor markets
—intensive cultural identification with occupational roles, for example, loggers and hardhats
—higher than average incidence of homicide, suicide, depression, and alcoholism.

These and other characteristics of a declining community reflect the interactive adjustment processes occurring within the human resource system. We are particularly concerned with the long run effects of this adjustment on the social and economic competencies of the people who live in declining communities.

A rural community experiencing attenuation may or may not be suffering a net population loss. Whatever migration there is tends to be age-, sex-, and class-specific, leaving a high proportion of females, the very old, the very young, and others who possess traditional skills and who are exclusively oriented toward the local industry (1).

The emigration of young adults is of central concern to local families and schools seeking to protect the integrity and solidarity of the community. Educating youth for urban labor markets is seen as investing in someone else's community, while educating youth for local labor markets is assumed to be a duty to the community. Ultraconservative solutions to the dilemma of whether to educate broadly or narrowly often emanate from policymakers determined to serve local interests at the expense of the broader human resource system.

> Depending on the time span of development, local institutions will become re-oriented to provide a continuing stream of labor into the extractive industry. This influence pervades both formal (e.g., local government, especially schools) and informal (e.g., intergenerational work patterns) institutions, and is thus highly resistant to change. Moreover, the surplus of labor can be alleviated only slightly by the less dominant sectors of these specialized economies. (23)

Whether local human resources are destined for migration or local utilization, this kind of educational policy is tantamount to creating a *general* set of technical skills juxtaposed with a highly specialized, culture-specific set of social skills designed to protect access to declining local labor markets. The net effect on human capital is compound. Human resource investment declines and institutional capacities to create human capital decline, thus insuring a continuing transfer of human resource deficit to other human resource systems in the national economy. Thus the concept of *setup* is applied to the declining or economically attenuating rural community.

In other respects as well, the concept of setup is appropriate since the consequences of underinvestment in human resources do not tend to be felt in the local setting, perhaps primarily because of the functional and important role the family unit maintains with respect to other local human resource institutions. The family in the setup phase tends to have institutional integrity, its assets are capable relative to local demands, and its wisdom generally valid. Putting it another way, the economic-social setting in rural communities may not constitute the effective environment for social marginalization, but it sets up its young to move into marginal environments.

Where gradual attenuation and selective migration have occurred, the decline in the economic base may be offset by population loss, as has happened in small towns dependent on the wheat industry in eastern Washington. Where attenuation is more severe and has a simultaneous effect on the population, an enclave of marginality may develop, for example, Appalachian coal miners. In the city, attenuation is accompanied by the migration of middle class working people to the suburbs, leaving a potential vacuum in housing and urban labor markets. Rural people have immigrated in great numbers to this city environment, where underinvestment in the human resources of rural communities has produced the most severe consequences.

3. The Staging or Precipitation Phase. The precipitation phase refers to a dramatic change in the effective economic environment of a community previously experiencing attenuation. When this precipitating change occurs, the community's adaptive social units are unable to adjust to it effectively. Such a change does occur when rural people migrate to cities or when they are inundated by urbanites migrating to a rural setting. A rural migrant to the city finds decisions regarding new courses in his life forced upon him. The same problem is faced by a rural person who remains unemployed or underemployed in the local setting while a new industry is established and attracts more qualified outsiders as employees at his expense. In either case obsolescence and inadequacy latent in the old human resource system are abruptly precipitated as people encounter novelty and extensive variation in economic and cultural environments.

A decline in importance of the extended family, perhaps even of the nuclear family, in this staging phase is inevitable—not because urbanization by itself brings family decay, but because economic survival comes to depend less on family cooperation and more on activating social networks attuned to industrial labor markets. Individuals are also affected by a different set of investment institutions as to the kind of labor demand human capital they carry.

Economic environments in the staging phase are characterized by increased exploitation and increased incentives for the individual to develop the counterproductive (in terms of the public good) economic and social skills required for survival. In the modern, regulated environments and controlled labor markets of the twentieth century, unlike the relatively unstructured environments and freely operating labor markets of the nineteenth-century frontier, a majority of noncredentialed people are likely to find their greatest opportunity in marginal markets, dealing in illegal goods and services.

4. The Ghetto or Closed Subsystem Phase. A ghetto is a closed subsystem: a natural community in western industrial societies where residents systematically learn behavior that is antithetical to the main system. That is to say, the competencies necessary to cope with exclusion from the mainstream economic system and to cope with such institutions as welfare and criminal justice compel inappropriate behavior vis-à-vis the mainstream labor market. Moreover, other human resource institutions record experiences with welfare and criminal justice institutions as validation of incompetence, thus reinforcing environmental boundaries of the subsystem.

Economically, the ghetto constitutes a subeconomy in that it has specialized markets for goods and services, the exploitation of which again requires specialized competencies that must be learned in specialized human investment institutions—gangs and other social networks. The problem is that these institutions also socialize their members within an ethical system antithetical in many respects to mainstream society, thereby increasing conflict and frustration when the individual attempts to translate from one system to the other.

IMPLICATIONS FOR RESEARCH AND PUBLIC POLICY. We view economic and social inequality as natural consequences of the way human resource processing institutions structure effective economic environments according to racial, cultural, and class characteristics. This analysis implies that social science research would do well to turn away from the study of client groups as isolated phenomena—welfare cases, criminals, racial and cultural minorities, and school dropouts—and turn toward the study of institutional variation and its effects on the allocation of economic and social credentials. It must be recognized that the human resource processing function of any institution is as important as its production function. Too often the effect of industrial firms and public institutions on human resources has been regarded as a by-product, when it should have been calculated into the cost-benefit equation of the production process.

In the United States in the last few years we have become conscious of the wastefulness of wantonly discarding physical resources not destined to become end products, and of the pollution caused by this waste. It is not generally recognized, however, that discarded human resources are also a form of pollution: waste products in a production process whose only self-conscious goal is to maximize profit and/or commodity output. We contend that the human resource investment function of any private industry or public agency should become a self-conscious aspect of its operation, just as the continuing investment in physical, environmental resources recently has become a self-conscious goal in some private industries. If this argument is accepted, it means that the applied social scientist has a mission to address continually the issue of the costs and benefits of keeping or changing various features in the structure of effective economic environments.

The greatest need in achieving efficiency in the use of human resources is that the costs and benefits accruing to individual institutions be made consonant with the welfare of society as a whole. We suggest that this would be a good place to begin restructuring national goals, following justifiable public disillusionment with the policy of dumping money haphazardly on social problems, and with the counterpolicy of benign neglect while the problems continue to fester.

The arguments we have made in this chapter, at least in part, have been developed from ongoing work at the Western Rural Development Center where we are conducting a cross-cultural, cross-industry study of rural human resource systems in five widely separated communities experiencing economic decline.† As we began this study, we intended to focus on the social marginalization of human resources as a function of adjustments to changes in effective economic environments. Two difficulties arose as soon as data became available: it was not possible with any degree of certainty to identify people who would be most affected by the surrounding circumstances, and all research settings were confined to the attenuation phase of a rural decline, so that precipitating forces leading to easily perceptible changes in effective economic environments were not immediately present. Therefore, we have shifted our emphasis to investigate more closely how the institutional processing system operates in the five communities in evaluating credentials and allocating benefits. We have also determined that understanding of the intermediate (attenuation) phase in the rural setting is essential to the further development of scientific theory and policy, since much past error has been based on false inference from the end state (closed system ghetto phase) back to the process. At the conclusion of the study we hope to demonstrate the usefulness of becoming informed about the effects of human capital institutions on human resources, not only to managers and laborers but to public agencies and policymakers as well.

We contend that the effects of human resource systems on specific communities and populations can be researched and their effects can be explicitly described. We also argue that an understanding of marginalization theory is necessary for realizing what is going wrong with well-intentioned human resource programs. Accordingly, we can offer a suggestion or two about conventional courses of action to be avoided in dealing with human resource problems. Underemployment in an economically declining rural community, for example, might appear to be easily eliminated by locating a new industry in the area. Given a nondiscrim-

† The locations, groups studied, principal investigators, and their universities are as follows: eastern Washington, small businessmen in rural communities, Dr. Paul Barkley, Department of Agricultural Economics, Washington State University; Oregon, wood products industries workers facing layoff, Dr. Joe Stevens, Department of Agricultural Economics, Oregon State University; California, small farm operators in Colusa County, Dr. Jerry Moles, Department of Anthropology, University of California, Davis; Hawaii, sugar and pineapple workers facing layoff due to phasing out of these industries, Dr. Robert Anderson, Department of Agricultural Economics, University of Hawaii; and Arizona, workers facing layoff due to phasing out of copper mining operations, Dr. William Martin, Department of Agricultural Economics, University of Arizona. For more information on this project please write to the authors at the addresses indicated.

inatory labor market or adequately credentialed human resources this might hold true; but in reality the local population, maintained in a disadvantaged position through local underinvestment in human resources, is very likely to be ill-trained for the new jobs, compared to newcomers with more suitable credentials. Hence, instead of rehabilitating the local labor force, a new industry may precipitate development of a rural-urban fringe ghetto. A similar argument can be made about economically declining inner-city areas.

Another axiom suggested by marginalization theory is that compensatory programs for "disadvantaged" people, whether focused explicitly on education, jobs, income, or political effectiveness, will more than likely be of little benefit and may even deprive of benefits the people they are intended to help, so long as they are administered primarily through institutions that function interactively in the human resource system, which is itself the root of the problem. The theory of social marginalization casts doubt on the usefulness of much policy oriented research in the social sciences and on the wisdom of many conventional courses of action. But it leads us also to largely unexplored territory where the solutions to many interrelated problems may be found.

REFERENCES

(1). Bender, Lloyd D., Bernal L. Green, and Rex Campbell, "Rural Poverty Ghettoization," Department of Agricultural Economics and Economics, Montana State University, 1971 (mimeo.).

(2). Carkhuff, Robert R., *The Development of Human Resources: Education, Psychology, and Social Change,* New York: Holt, Rinehart and Winston, 1971.

(3). Gayer, Paul and Robert S. Goldfarb, "Job Search, the Duration of Unemployment, and the Phillips Curve: Comment and Reply," *American Economic Review* 62 (4): 714–19.

(4). Gillispie, Charles C., "Mertonian Theses," book review, *The Sociology of Science, Theoretical and Empirical Investigations,* Robert K. Merton, in *Science* 184 (4137): 656.

(5). Gjessing, Gutorm, "Commentary" and "Book Reviews" sections, *Human Organization* 31 (1): 95–110.

(6). ———, "The Social Responsibility of the Social Scientist," *Current Anthropology* 9 (5): 397–402.

(7). Glasser, William, *Schools Without Failure,* New York: Harper and Row, 1969.

(8). Glazer, Nathan and D. P. Moynihan, *Beyond the Melting Pot: The Negroes, Puerto Ricans, Jews, Italians and Irish of New York City,* Cambridge: M.I.T. Press and Harvard University Press, 1963.

(9). Gordon, Milton M., *Assimilation in American Life: The Role of Race, Religion, and National Origins,* New York: Oxford University Press, 1964.

(10). Graves, Theodore D., "Urban Indian Personality and the 'Culture of Poverty,'" *American Ethnologist* 1 (1): 65–86.

(11). Harrison, Bennett, "Education and Underemployment in the Urban Ghetto," *American Economic Review* 62 (5): 796–812.

(12). Leacock, Eleanor Burke, ed., *The Culture of Poverty: A Critique,* New York: Simon and Schuster, 1971.

(13). Lewis, Oscar, "The Culture of Poverty," *Scientific American* 215 (4): 19–25.

(14). Morrison, Peter, "Urban Growth and Decline: San Jose and St. Louis in the 1960s," *Science* 185 (4153): 757–62.

(15). Moynihan, Daniel Patrick, "The Negro Family: The Case for National Action," in Lee Rainwater and William L. Yancey, eds., *The Moynihan Report and the Politics of Controversy*, Cambridge: M.I.T. Press, 1967.

(16). Ogbu, John U., *The Next Generation: An Ethnography of Education in the Urban Neighborhood*, New York: Academic Press, 1974.

(17). Padfield, Harland, "Agrarian Capitalists and Urban Proletariat—The Policy of Alienation in American Agriculture," in *Food, Fiber and the Arid Lands*, Tucson: University of Arizona Press, 1971.

(18). Padfield, Harland and William E. Martin, *Farmers, Workers and Machines: Technological and Social Change in Farm Industries of Arizona*, Tucson: University of Arizona Press, 1965.

(19). Padfield, Harland and Roy Williams, *Stay Where You Were: A Study Of Unemployables in Industry*, Philadelphia: J. B. Lippincott, 1973.

(20). Rickson, Roy E., "Industry, Science, and Pollution: Some Problems that Industrial Societies Have in Developing a Quality Environment," Department of Sociology, University of Minnesota, 1974 (mimeo.).

(21). Romano-V., Octavio I., "Institutions in Modern Society: Caretakers and Subjects," *Science* 183 (4126): 722–25.

(22). Shlensky, Burt, "Evaluation of Training Programs for the Disadvantaged Through a Psychological Cost-Benefit Model," New York, Hadley C. Ford & Assoc., 1974 (mimeo.).

(23). Stevens, Joe B., "On the Process and Consequences of Job Rationing in Declining Extractive Industries," abstract, Department of Agricultural Economics, Oregon State University, 1974 (mimeo.).

(24). Turnbull, Colin, *The Mountain People*, New York: Simon and Schuster, 1972.

(25). Valentine, Charles A., *Culture and Poverty*, Chicago: University of Chicago Press, 1968.

(26). Weiss, Leonard and Jeffry G. Williamson, "Black Education, Earnings, and Inter-regional Migration: Some New Evidence," *American Economic Review* 62 (3): 372–83.

Discussion

B E N J A M I N   L .   G O R M A N

P A D F I E L D and Young offered a brief but effective review of the situational versus the cultural perspective on poverty and came down hard in favor of the situational. They then proceeded to offer a model for stages of the societal marginalization process, and they showed how marginalization produces impoverished population groups.

I find the basic argument persuasive—perhaps because I have long held a similar view. The proposed model is innovative and potentially productive. Beyond this general approval I see room for substantive exploration in three directions. First, I take issue with Padfield and Young by suggesting some further implications of adopting the situational perspective; I ask that social science, education, and society itself be judged by the standards applied to the poor. Second, I suggest that the stages-of-marginalization model needs explication regarding its range and focus: is the model primarily an analysis of individuals, institutions, or subcultures? Third, I offer some queries concerning where we go from here with the proposed model.

The basic thrust of the situational interpretation of poverty is to grant to poor individuals or families the same rationality as is usually attributed to business firms or other complex organizations. The poor, then, do not "fail" through perversity, immorality, or incompetence—but because their environmental constraints admit no alternative. Their behaviors are best understood as efforts to optimize personal satisfactions in the context of the situation they face. They behave differently than middle class people do because they have different problems, not because they have different goals.

This analysis makes sense. And it makes equal sense to grant to other institutions and social systems the same rational response to the effective economic environment. Padfield and Young accuse social science of having failed in its diagnosis and treatment of social ills. Rather, a situational perspective and the assumption of rational behavior would suggest that social scientists have developed theoretical constructs and policy prescriptions consistent with the incentives or disincentives offered by the mainline economic system. In short, they have prescribed the medication the patients were willing to take. In so doing, social scientists have built up their "practice" among well-to-do clients; the social sciences have survived and grown in support and respect. Given this point of view, it makes little sense to blame the course of social science on the myths and assumptions of the disciplines; such interpretation is simply a variation of the culturological perspective.

As with the interpretation of the situation, so with the solution. If society desires different answers or actions from its scientific institutions, it must restructure the incentive system in and to science. Padfield and Young offer instead an urging to moral rededication: "You could do better if you really tried." Such an analysis is reminiscent of blaming the poor for their problem. The fault, then, and the remedies rest in the powerful institutions of society, and no more in its scientific than in its impoverished sectors.

The same argument can be offered with regard to the educational institution. Without covering all the ground again in detail, surely it is more sensible to see the educational leadership of recent decades as a calculating and efficient one which has produced the class-segregated

and labeled generation that its paying clients in the political and economic spheres desired.

When the authors' perspective on poverty is applied to the remainder of society, it forces different questions than the ones their interpretations suggest. Why does society encourage its educational systems
to process and certify young people so as to produce marginalization?
Why does it structure the working context of social scientists so that
they sanction and facilitate the process? And why does it devise its welfare and criminal justice systems for the "cooling out" of the marginal-
ized? Obviously, within this framework, the answer is that having substantial marginal populations is advantageous for society as a whole or
its dominant power groups. This conclusion was reached from quite different perspectives in the chapters by Bould-Van Til and Persky.

It would appear that the labor of the poor is not needed in modern
society, or that their utility as a poor class outweighs their utility as
human resources. Labor may not be a scarce resource, subject to the
same sort of economic analyses as minerals and other nonhuman resources. In this sense the notion of "wasted human resources" may be
spurious. If the so-called "massive" federal programs for the elimination
of poverty are compared to the investment in programs such as space,
defense, and highways, the low societal priority of eliminating poverty
becomes clear. If Padfield and Young would assert the contrary, they
must offer data and analyses not apparent in this paper.

The proposed model of marginalization stages offers real promise
as an analytic device. As with scientific models generally, the ultimate
test of its utility must rest in its capacity to explain variance in the
phenomena under observation. But before turning to the matter of
explained variation, some clearer definition is needed concerning exactly what level of phenomenon the model describes. Is this work to
be informed primarily from the foundation of cultural anthropology,
political economics, or social psychology? Correspondingly, is the basic
consequence to be found in community ideology, the institutional structure, or individual socialization? Which is cause, which effect, so that
strategic points can be designated for breaking loose from the apparent
inevitability of this evolutionary sequence? These implications carry
over to my next point.

I turn now from a critique of the chapter to some suggestions concerning work which might follow from the chapter. Perhaps the most
crucial and effective documentation of the value of this model would
follow from being able to show that the frontier, setup, staging, and
closed phases of the authors' Figure 8.2 differed in cost profiles for the
cells of Table 8.1. Other supporting documentation would compare
communities of the different phases with regard to kind of treatment,
clients acted upon, intended result, and human and social consequences.

Another line of analysis would be a comparison of the four stages
of marginalization as hosts for social science. What is the place of so-

TABLE 8.1. Dollar costs of human processing by institution, class of persons, and the result of processing.[a]

	Class of Persons Processed			
	Core people and their children Process		Marginal people and their children Process	
Institutional Locus of Process	Centralization	Marginalization	Centralization	Marginalization
Education				
Welfare				
Criminal Justice				

[a] To be completed separately for communities of the four phases of Figure 8.2.

cial science in each stage? How is it supported? What are its mandates? How much leverage does social science have for effecting social change? Where can this leverage be applied?

One more detailed example of the sort of analysis which this model encourages focuses on the marginalization process in school systems at each stage.

Some school systems, both urban and rural, are ghettoized. These systems have middle class schools to train and certify the children of middle class parents, and ghetto schools to provide disincentives and stigma to the marginal. Under these circumstances, comparing resource, policy, and structural differences between the two types of schools should be revealing.

Other schools, due to ecological accident or such legal strictures as busing, serve a heterogeneous student population. There, the marginalization process must be carried on by recognizing and channeling individuals into appropriate tracks. Key issues would include the mechanisms by which this channeling is managed and how, meanwhile, the appearance of equality and universalism is maintained.

These examples may help to show that the Padfield and Young model leads to the formulation of sensible and crucial questions. In this it meets the first test. The second, more important, and as yet unassayed test is whether research into those questions yields powerful and useful answers.

Policy implications of alternative theoretical frameworks for viewing rural poverty and income distribution

B O B B Y   R .   E D D L E M A N

T H I S book focuses on two groups of underprivileged persons who are found in disproportionately large numbers in rural areas—the unemployable rural poor who cannot work because of age, disability, or responsibility to care for young children or invalid family members; and the underemployed (including unemployed) rural poor who are able to work and who do work but whose earnings are below those of other persons in society with similar age, sex, education, occupational, and other general qualifications.

I distinguish between the two groups because different policy measures are required for dealing with each group. In the first case the policy measures must almost entirely deal with income maintenance programs, education programs, and general "public welfare" services. In the second case, in addition to income maintenance and education programs, policy measures may concentrate on increasing employment participation, incomes, and jobs for the persons included in this group. I recognize at the outset that certain policy measures will not deal exclusively, or independently, with one group or the other. For example, a negative income tax program could provide a minimum income maintenance level and be an incentive as well for a greater participation in the labor market to increase family earnings of the employable rural poor. Similarly, programs to aid small-scale, low income farm operators and their families can serve as a part of income maintenance as well as employment and income enhancement, especially when coupled with off-farm employment programs.

A second reason for making this distinction is that the bulk of the three previous chapters on alternative theoretical frameworks for viewing rural poverty is directed to this second group—the underemployed rural poor. In line with this concern, I shall deal with income maintenance programs in a minimal way and focus most of this discussion on policies to increase access to higher incomes and jobs by the underemployed rural poor. I shall conclude by discussing the role that technological change has played in our society—and the place it should have in our national priorities and goals.

POLICY IMPLICATIONS FOR THE UNEMPLOYABLE RURAL POOR.

Income transfer programs are often proposed as the most compelling and obvious solution to poverty. Simply give the poor enough money, it is argued, and poverty will disappear. Transfers of sufficient size can eliminate poverty by bringing all the poor over the poverty line. The apparent simplicity of income transfer solutions to poverty is deceptive and can create significant problems. Persons just above the poverty line could have an economic incentive to abandon other sources of support and join the ranks of the poor. In doing so, they could gain much more leisure at little private individual cost. Similarly, persons already counted as poor could have an incentive to substitute public transfers for whatever employment income they already possess. However, no other alternatives exist for those rural (and urban) poor who cannot enter the productive economy—the unemployable (or unsalvageable) rural poor. This point cannot be overstressed. If we do not want poverty, we must be prepared to support some of our fellow members of society at a living level that is commonly believed to be nonpoor.

If we accept this premise, then income maintenance programs or payment-in-kind welfare programs are necessary for the unemployable rural poor. The major question then becomes whether transfers-in-kind, transfer in cash, or combinations of both will accomplish the goal of eliminating or at least reducing poverty among the unemployable rural poor at minimum total public dollar outlay.

Among the public assistance programs involving cash payments to the poor, most are directed to specific population groups. Old Age Assistance (OAS) provides income transfers only for the aged poor; Aid to the Blind (AB) for the blind poor; Aid to the Permanently and Totally Disabled (APTD) to the disabled poor; Aid to Families with Dependent Children (AFDC) to poor female-headed families with dependent children. A fifth program, General Assistance (GA), aids those of the poor who do not fit one of the other categories. The blind, disabled, and aged poor are clearly handicapped in the labor market and society feels a greater obligation for their support. Mothers of young children under the AFDC program are not so clearly unemployable, however, and public assistance is rendered to them with comparative reluctance and in smaller amounts per recipient, even though total funding going to the AFDC program is much larger than for any of the other categories.

Among the major welfare reform programs to aid the unemployable poor as well as the employable and working poor, who abound in rural areas, are four major income maintenance proposals: the Family Assistance Program (FAP), a substitute for AFDC (see 5), which would provide every needy family with a uniform federal minimum payment, regardless of location, with incentives for both adult males and females to find and secure employment by allowing recipients to retain some part of what they earn (6); the demogrant plan, which would provide a continuing grant to every person, scaled as deemed appropriate for age and place in the family (7); the negative income tax (5 and 6), which would provide a guarantee of some minimum amount to a family of a given size, with a set proportion deducted from that guarantee for each dollar earned by the family up to a break-even level of earnings; and a wage or earnings supplement (4) which would pay some proportion of the difference between a target wage per hour and the actual wage per hour. Tweeten and Walker in Chapter 4, and others (2, 3) have indicated from their studies that the costs of a comprehensive income maintenance program, as measured by reduced output of goods and services, are small—something on the order of 1 to 2 percent of national income.

A number of welfare programs currently involve or can involve transfers of goods and services rather than cash. Among these programs are food assistance (Food Stamp Program and School Lunch Program); medical care (including Medicare, Medicaid type programs, and national family health insurance programs); housing assistance (through tax deductions, mortgage guarantees, and public housing programs); legal aid (woefully trivial in amount); education for the poor (principally through Title I of the Elementary and Secondary Education Act, Neighborhood Youth Corps, Headstart Program, and Upward Bound); and manpower training (through the Manpower Development and Training Act, JOB-Optional component of MDTA, Work Incentive Program, and Public Service Employment), to name just a few. Many of these programs involving transfers-in-kind are directed specifically at reducing absolute poverty. Some—particularly in education, housing, health, and worker training—can, if revamped and expanded, aid in reducing relative poverty by reducing inequality.

Critics of payment-in-kind welfare programs stress that most have low target efficiency with only a small proportion of the funds spent on them actually going to the poor. Furthermore, critics argue that even those with much higher target efficiency, for example, Food Stamps and Public Housing, can be replaced by an increase in cash income maintenance payments with the net result that a given amount of real income can be provided to the poor at less cost to the public through cash assistance. I tend to favor the idea that cash transfers are generally preferable to transfers-in-kind, with the possible exceptions of education, health, and some aspects of worker training if they are expanded and geared to reducing inequality. Such transfers-in-kind appear most useful when they provide what the market would not bring forth even if the recipients received an increase in cash income.

POLICY IMPLICATIONS FOR THE UNDEREMPLOYED RURAL

POOR. In addition to provisions of income through direct transfer programs to the employable rural poor, two other basic approaches to reducing rural poverty are provision of jobs, either in the existing geographical area or in other localities, and elimination of barriers between existing jobs and underemployed individuals. Attendant to the first approach is a whole host of policy measures, including direct public subsidization of the migration process, subsidies for education and retraining to improve mobility, stimulation of aggregate demand to maintain full employment, policies to influence the location of industry, creation of growth centers in areas heavily endowed with underemployed rural people, and equalization of social costs and benefits from industrialization in urban areas with private costs and benefits.

Measures to stimulate migration of the underemployed rural labor force may take many forms. Subsidies for education and retraining can improve mobility through their influence on the quality of the labor force, and they are often consistent with economic efficiency. Individuals may underinvest in their own education and training because of ignorance, imperfections in the capital market, and divergence between private and social rates of return. Furthermore, it is now well documented that poorer rural areas tend to underinvest in the education of their children because outmigration tends to be selective toward the young, who leave these areas when jobs are not available. (Rural communities are reluctant to invest in human capital that they will have to export just when the returns are due to begin.) However, there is a difference between accepting the justification for intervention in education and retraining, on the one hand, and deciding the level of subsidy to be provided, on the other. Calculation of the social rate of return on retraining underemployed rural workers who may be employed elsewhere depends upon a comparison of total social benefits with total social costs, a difficult procedure, especially since some of the benefits may be nonquantifiable.

Policymakers may also intervene with direct financial assistance to potential migrants. Such assistance may include travel and removal expenses, initial subsistence allowances to cover the period of job hunting and to help with temporary accommodations, housing subsidies, and allowances to defray other resettlement costs. Because the costs of retraining and moving, along with the uncertainties of finding suitable employment, may wipe out expected income gains, subsidies of this kind may be necessary even though intersectoral, interregional wage differentials provide an incentive to migrate.

A policy to influence the location of industry probably has a much wider measure of acceptance than policies to subsidize migration. The two approaches are not inconsistent with each other, and in certain situations the optimal solution for a particular area heavily endowed with an underemployed rural labor force might be a modest amount of subsidized outmigration and a subsidized inflow of capital and industry.

Reluctance to invest in those rural areas characterized by high levels of underemployment may reflect subjective judgments about high risks and uncertainties rather than the fact of lower returns to capital. There is a widespread impression, though only partially tested in studies such as the one by Tweeten (7), that the technical changes of the last few decades have reduced the importance of location costs in the overall cost structure, because in many industries plants of optimum size can operate in a wide spread of city sizes with only minimal differences in production costs and profit rates. Thus cost minimization and profit rates depend far more on the way in which a plant is operated (in other words, on managerial efficiency) than on where it is located, but most firms still associate metropolitan location with private economic efficiency. Tweeten (7) has pointed out that such economic efficiency involves the equating of private marginal costs and returns. However, in many urban locations these do not correspond to social costs and benefits, because the firms do not have to pay the full costs of crime, air pollution, and transportation congestion; in these cases social real income is not maximized. Thus there is justification for intervention to change the structure and incentives to firms to decentralize their location to raise social efficiency.

Another justification, perhaps a much stronger one, for intervening in firm location is the social benefit derived from using underemployed (perhaps wasted) labor resources in the form of nonparticipants in the labor force who might wish to work if employment opoprtunities were present. Large subsidies to migrate may still fail to induce many unemployed workers in rural areas to move. Assuming that forced movement of labor is not permissible in a free society, the only way of employing these truly immobile workers is to create jobs for them where they are. Since their employment will raise national output, the justification for locating industry in their area is economic, not social. The provision of jobs is consistent with efficiency, provided that the capital for job creation is not diverted from a much higher productive use elsewhere. If the scale of capital inflow is large enough, the necessity for migration will be reduced. Thus such a policy could satisfy the locational preferences of individuals to a much greater extent than other alternatives. This is a social justification. If the objective is to increase the net satisfaction of the immobile, underemployed rural poor, it may be quite rational to follow such a policy even though losses to national efficiency result.

Apart from measures to aid migration and reliance on improvements in the market mechanism, a wide range of policy instruments is directed to the attraction of capital and industry into rural areas with high rates of underemployment. These include publicity and provision of information about the area and its labor supply; increasing the supply of basic industrial services, infrastructure, and social amenities in potential growth centers; investment in education and retraining targeted to the poor clientele; direct inducements to firms such as grants, loans, federal tax write-offs, or investment incentives favoring capital, wage, or price subsidies and contingent upon employing a given proportion of the underemployed; emphasis on the awarding of government contracts and the construction of new government establishments in depressed areas; economic incentives to industry to move their facilities from urban centers to nearby rural towns and cities; selection of and stimulus to area growth centers; and regionalization of health services as well as other public services to improve the quality and accessibility of these services to the rural poor.

Policies to aid migration and influence the location of industry are mostly aimed at improving the functioning of the labor and capital markets. The second approach, that of eliminating barriers between existing jobs and underemployed rural individuals, can also influence the efficiency of labor and capital markets. Two of the most widespread barriers confronted by underemployed rural people are racial and class discrimination both in education and in the labor market. Much of this discrimination is traceable directly to the institutional structure of educational services, and to institutionalized patterns in recruitment procedures and hiring practices of firms.

In Chapter 8, Padfield and Young provide a broad, dynamic perspective on this aspect of rural poverty by focusing on the relationship of underemployed rural people to the labor market, educational programs, and other rural institutions. Their thrust is away from the more popular demographic analyses of rural poverty, which focus on the personal characteristics of those who are poor, toward a study of how rural institutions affect various groups of people.

Persky in Chapter 7 suggests that the capitalistic system, working through markets for both products and resources, consciously and overtly through collective behavior keeps the economy at less than full employment. The system thus guarantees a surplus labor pool which weakens the bargaining power of workers facing a depressed labor market. An antipoverty policy, then, should focus on full employment so that, in the aggregate, jobs are available. Of course, the way in which aggregate demand for labor is stimulated will have a significant impact on the economy. Every fiscal or monetary action affects the distribution of output, as well as its volume, and particular aggregate demand policies will have different impacts on employment and price levels. Some actions can provide more jobs for the poor, with little effect on prices, while others can do just the reverse. Therefore policymakers must not only decide to expand the demand for labor; they must also strive to have maximum impact on the poor at some level of social cost. The demand for labor provided by the poor must be kept at high levels if the poor are to gain financial independence.

CONCLUDING COMMENTS. My views parallel very closely those expressed recently by Bishop (1) and may be summarized as follows. The many problems we face today regarding poverty, environmental degradation, and pollution in our cities as well as in the countryside are secondary effects from the rapid technological advances in production over the past 3 to 4 decades. These effects were not planned or promoted by anyone; they simply were not anticipated because of our emphasis on the development of technological knowledge and because our approaches to developing and integrating technological knowledge into society were too specialized. We have not attempted to develop technology consistent with any particular pattern of social and economic organization. Rather we have emphasized the development of technology to provide the most efficient production of commodities and have left the pattern of social and economic organization to be determined by market forces as they adjust to that technology.

The concern today over urban and rural development, resource conservation, environmental quality, income distribution, and the general quality of life derive mainly from the social costs of technological development that have mostly been ignored in the past. They reflect continuing questions with respect to how various groups of people fare under conditions of national economic growth.

Technological change will continue to have a major impact upon the location of employment and population and the distribution of the proceeds from economic growth; but it should not be the overly dominant factor that it has been in the past. We must have a broader frame of reference through which we concern ourselves with fundamental questions about the organization of society. Such organization of society, both spatially and structurally, is dependent upon setting national priorities and goals. We must ask whether this organization is consistent with reasonably efficient production of goods and services and with equity in the distribution of income. If not, we must determine what kinds of trade-offs appear possible and desirable.

Such an effort will be required to reduce or eliminate poverty. The intent of such a policy strategy is to prevent or minimize poverty in future generations. It involves effort not merely to alter the income distribution, but also to change the probability of certain groups being at the bottom in future generations. In the interim the other policies that have been discussed will be necessary. These include income maintenance programs for the unemployable poor as well as some of the employable and working poor; policies to promote full employment so that jobs are available; training and other human capital endowments targeted to the poor, together with necessary supportive services; improvements in the functioning of labor markets through removal of racial barriers to employment, provisions for providing retrained persons with jobs, migration assistance, and improved information on job vacancies; and policies to influence the location of industry in areas heavily endowed with underemployed rural poor.

REFERENCES

(1). Bishop, C. E., "The University's Role in Rural Development," Proceedings, Rural Community Development Education Conference-Workshop, Raleigh, N.C., March 27–28, 1974.

(2). Elesh, David, et al., "After 15 Months: Preliminary Results from the Urban Negative Income Tax Experiment," Institute for Research on Poverty, University of Wisconsin at Madison, 1971. (Mono.)

(3). Greenburg, David H. and Marvin Kosters, "The Impact of Income Maintenance Programs on Hours of Work and Income of the Working Poor," Santa Monica: Rand Corporation, 1970.

(4). Haveman, Robert A., "Work Conditioned Subsidies as an Income Maintenance Strategy: Issues of Program Structure and Integration," discussion paper, Institute for Research on Poverty, University of Wisconsin at Madison, 1972. (Mono.)

(5). Schiller, Bradley R., The Economics of Poverty and Discrimination, Englewood Cliffs, N.J.: Prentice-Hall, 1973.

(6). Stein, Bruno, On Relief: The Economics of Poverty and Public Welfare, New York: Basic Books, 1971.

(7). Tweeten, Luther, "Emerging Issues for Sparsely Populated Areas and Regions Under a National Growth Policy," American Journal of Agricultural Economics 55:840–50.

Institutional role and responsibilities on poverty policies and issues

Survey of poverty issues and programs: can we improve the performance?

E M I E L   W .   O W E N S

T H I S chapter examines rural poverty development from two perspectives. First, we are interested in the scope and magnitude of rural poverty, and some effects of poverty upon rural individuals and families. We consider a selected sample of rural black low income households, focusing particularly on some causes of their poverty. We also discuss some problems associated with formulating policy for dealing with low income rural households.

Second, we are interested in reviewing trends in federal income support programs, in particular how changes in federal budgetary emphasis have affected income maintenance programs, and how they have affected the low income population in general. Expenditures on income maintenance programs have risen rapidly in recent years, as existing programs have expanded and newer ones have been inaugurated. For example, the 1973 federal expenditure represents almost a fourfold increase since 1960, and a 55 percent increase since 1970 (3). This increase in outlay reflects a major shift in the composition of the federal budget and hence a shift in the primary focus of federal activities.

THE MAGNITUDE OF RURAL POVERTY. The growing awareness of the pervasiveness of rural poverty and its dehumanizing effects has called forth new public and private interest. One result of this new initiative has been a 70 percent reduction in the number of poor persons living on farms, from 4.4 million in 1964 to 1.3 million in 1972 (2). (Some of the decrease was the result of rural-to-urban migration. For example, between 1960 and 1970 a net annual average of 694,000 persons, or 5.6 percent of the farm population, migrated from the farm [1]. Although such a change decreased the number of farm

TABLE 10.1.   Farm residents below poverty level by family status and race, U.S., 1972.

Family Status	All Races			White			Black		
	Total	Below poverty level		Total	Below poverty level		Total	Below poverty level	
	(thous)	*(thous)*	*(%)*	*(thous)*	*(thous)*	*(%)*	*(thous)*		*(%)*
All Persons	9,337	1,392	14.9	8,699	1,102	12.7	560	271	48.3
In Families	8,912	1,258	14.1	8,319	993	11.9	524	246	47.0
Unrelated Individuals	425	134	31.5	380	109	28.7	36	25	69.0
Female Heads	617	205	33.2	470	109	23.4	142	95	67.2
Unrelated Females	212	79	37.2	195	68	35.0	12	11	92.0

Source: (17).

poor, it did not necessarily decrease the total number of poor.) These data show that through access to migration or raised income, the gross flow of rural households across the poverty line during this period was substantial. But it is also true that the problem of low income still persisted among subgroups within the rural population. This fact suggests that aggregate demand exerts an uneven influence over time across various demographic groups. For example, Table 10.1 shows that 15 percent of the farm population was poor in 1972, but these statistics represented 13 percent of white farm residents, on the one hand, and 48 percent of black farm residents, on the other. The most dramatic variation in the incidence of poverty in 1972 occurred in rural households headed by females: 33 percent of white female household heads were poor, compared to 67 percent of black female household heads. The forgotten poor might be the rural black females who lived outside family households; some 92 percent of these women were poor.

Rural poverty status differed also by regions. In spite of some economic gains in the South, the 11 states that formed the Civil War Confederacy had 25 percent of the nation's population but 38 percent of the nation's poor in 1970 (17). The margin was even wider for children, with the South having 25 percent of the nation's under-18 population living at home but 41 percent of that category's poor. In 39 states outside the South the proportion of persons in poverty was 11 percent in 1970, but it was almost twice that, 21 percent, in the 11 southern states. Almost half of southern farm laborers and about one-fourth of southern farm owners were in the poverty class (17). However, for rural blacks, the poverty rate of farm owners was nearly as high as for farm laborers, 58 percent and 65 percent, respectively (17). The magnitude of poverty among rural black farm families and the unrelated rural poor has forced us to look for some possible causes of the plight of these Americans.

RURAL BLACK POOR. A University of Houston research team surveyed some 429 rural black low income household heads in 12 central Texas counties. The object was to determine some causes of low income in the population and the level of participation of these families in government sponsored income maintenance programs. The first obvious finding was that economic activities and income maintenance programs had been relatively ineffective in reducing the poverty of these rural black families. The work experience of family heads in the sample population showed they were unable to change substantially their economic plight with their own efforts. Seventy-two percent of the sampled rural poverty family heads worked full time or at least 40 weeks during the year. Nineteen and one-half weeks represented the work year for 24 percent of the sampled heads. In spite of these work schedules by the household heads, the annual family cash income of some 46 percent of the sampled families was less than $2,000—the average American family earning for 12 weeks. On a national basis, of the 3.3 million poor family heads who worked, approximately 60 percent worked 40 weeks or more during the year and yet remained in poverty (10).

It is appropriate to ask here what rural low income families have in common and what keeps them in poverty. Perhaps surprisingly, the barren life style of the rural poor is not primarily the result of ignorance or indifference. True, the experience of marginality and the opportunity for value conflict are increased by the tendency of many of the poor to "drift" within levels of poverty and nonpoverty. But being poor is often the by-product of community and working conditions over which the individual has little control. The rural poor, then, find themselves trapped, both within themselves and by external circumstances that grip them. Since we now know that increased farm production through better farm practices would not eliminate conditions associated with rural poverty, we are forced to examine other possible causes.

Income Level Regression Model. Many factors in a person's life contribute to his level of income. Factors known to be related to economic deprivation include being in a female household with no adult male present; having heavy family responsibilities, such as the care of a large number of dependent children; being an agricultural laborer or operator of a very small farm; or being black in a society that affords more support to those who are white.

If a regression equation is estimated using income of head of household as dependent variable in a simple linear form, we get the following results:

$$Y_H = 150.75 + 39.42(X_4) - 580.19(X_5) + 31.70(X_6)$$
$$(2.88)^* \quad (137.01)^* \quad (16.29)^*$$
$$+ 57.28(X_7) + 5.33(X_8) + 17.60(X_9)$$
$$(13.84) \quad (1.98)^* \quad (3.16)^*$$

$$R^2 = .56 \quad DF = 469 \quad F \text{ Value} = 99.79$$

Where
the numbers in parentheses are the standard errors of the coefficients;
an asterisk indicates the parameter is significant at a 1 percent probability level; and

Y_H = annual income of household head
X_4 = weeks worked last year
X_5 = sex of household head
X_6 = family size
X_7 = education—head of household
X_8 = hours worked past week
X_9 = distance traveled to work

The poverty regressions indicate that most of the explained variance
in the income levels of poverty households can be explained with approximately six of the nine available variables. The above equation with
a computed F value of 99.79 and a R^2 of .56 was the best predictive
model available from the sample.

All the coefficients in the model had signs that had been expected
theoretically. For each percentage point alteration that local, state, or
federal government programs can make in the independent variables,
the model suggests that rural black income would be enhanced by the
following percentages, based on calculated elasticity coefficients between
income and selected significant variables: number of weeks worked, .451;
hours worked the past week, .226; education, .213; and distance traveled
to work, .095. These elasticity coefficients suggest that making jobs
available, thus increasing labor force participation, is the most important step to be taken in eliminating rural poverty among the sampled
families. Education plays a secondary role to weeks worked as a predictor
of income.

DISCUSSION. If the coefficient of the number of weeks worked by the
household head in the poverty model is correct, improvement in
labor force participation is one of the most effective ways of mitigating
rural black poverty. The correlation coefficient between household income and weeks worked, holding the other four significant variables
constant, was .54—a significant relationship. But many of those living
in rural poverty were not unemployed, but rather underemployed (or
not in the labor force). Seventy-two percent of the sampled family
heads in this study worked full time or at least 40 weeks during the year
and still remained in poverty.

The poverty model further suggests that household heads with a
high work-week year will not have as high an income as the normalized
regression coefficient predicts. For household heads with a high work-
week year, this could mean that other economic constraints such as a
minimum wage would have to be imposed and a reduction in discrimination would be necessary to raise black rural household income. For

those household heads with a very low work-week year, the model indicates a threshold effect. Family heads below this minimum work-week simply have no chance of raising their income above the poverty threshold.

Results show a negative correlation coefficient (—.43) between family income and sex of head of household. The regression coefficient in the rural poverty model suggests that income of female-headed families is some $580 (about 26 percent) less per year than the median rural family income. If this prediction is true, it implies that an increasing proportion of rural households will be poor in coming years, because of the trend toward an increasing proportion of rural black households being headed by women. Traditionally, as family income levels rise, the proportion of families with a female head tends to decrease. Few researchers have observed the disparity in the black sex ratios and how they significantly affect the marital and family pattern among black females. For example, 1970 census data show that if no adjustment is made for age, there are some 1.6 million black women in the United States without available monogamous mates. These omissions have tended to victimize the black female and have prevented the development of social reforms necessary to improve the lives of a portion of the black female population (10).

The coefficient of education in our poverty model indicates that the education variable is a good predictor of income, and that improvement in education is one of the most effective ways of eliminating rural poverty. But we know also that the marginal value of education is less at higher levels of school for blacks, because labor market discrimination limits most of them to relatively low level jobs. The paradox of the whole education function is that discrimination hurts the better educated blacks more than the less educated.

The number of hours worked by up to four household members is the variable inserted in the model to measure the degree of unemployment in the sample population. Since the percentage of full-time workers takes into account the number of part-time workers and the labor force participation rate, as well as the number of unemployed workers, it is a broader measure of the employment characteristic than hours worked by the household head alone. As full-time work increases, the hours of work per week of part-time workers and the number of secondary workers rise. The result is less rural poverty among families where part-time work plays an important role in family income. The beta coefficient for hours worked in the regression model was small.

The positive regression coefficient for distance traveled indicates that potential income level increases as the distance traveled to work increases. This finding suggests that programs and investment by local, state, and federal governments that are designed to improve mobility among the rural black poor are preferable to those that subsidize immobility.

Rural Household Indebtedness. Families differ in their organization patterns, including management of resources and decision making. They differ in psychological aspects, including family communication networks, feelings, and ideas that bear on goal achievement. Families differ in ideological factors, such as beliefs and attitudes that bind individuals together and identify them with one of the several subcultures in our society. Additionally, they differ in the amount and quality of resources available to them, and in their opportunity and ability to use resources in the manner desired.

The rural poor heads of the families sampled had an extremely low level of living. Millions of Americans have never known what it is to lack proper lavatory facilities, running hot and cold water, telephones, kitchen sinks, and transportation. Yet, millions of rural Americans are beset by the absence of these and other basic necessities. Among the poverty families sampled in this study (11) one family out of three had no means of public or private transportation, one out of two had no running water, and three out of four had no hot water. On the other hand, seven out of eight families did have television sets and four out of five had radios. These priorities are indicative of values of the poor, including the significance they attach to customs of the average American and their incentive to emulate him.

These data document the fact that low income rural families usually live at subsistence level, and that most of their disposable income is spent on bare necessities such as food, clothes, and shelter. The critical question is how much the rural poor participate in the credit market to purchase desired consumer durables. Installment debt traditionally has appeared to be a middle class phenomenon and has not been associated with poor people. On the other hand, among those who are in debt the percentage of income allocated to installment payments diminishes as income rises. Variables that affect debt probability include income stability, liquid asset holding, and family life cycle. For the average consumer, income stability and liquid asset holding appear to be negatively related to debt; in other words, the more stable a family's income, the less likely the consumer is to have installment debt. On the other hand, spending units with small liquid asset holdings are more likely to purchase goods on installment than are those with large holdings.

Do the rural poor fit into this traditional model of spending, or does indebtedness resulting from purchases beyond current income compound the burden of low income rural consumers? Results of our study show that those families with few or no liquid assets purchased consumer durables on installment more frequently than those with larger holdings (see Table 10.2). Here we see that 9 out of 11 families in "deep trouble" had liquid assets of less than $125, substantially less than the required "transactions balance" of $200. (The ability to support installment payments requires a "rainy day" fund to cover periods when earned income fails or falters. Table 10.2 shows that many of the low income rural families had inadequate liquidity for this purpose and

TABLE 10.2. Liquid assets and level of indebtedness.

Lower Bounds of Intervals of Variable 6	Lower Bounds of Intervals of Debt Ratio		
	0	.2	
Liquid Assets			Total
$ 0	134	9	143
125	4	2	6
375	1	0	1
500	1	0	1
Total	140	11	151
Chi sq = 10.61; DF = .8			

Source: Computation from research data.

thus tended to fall into the category of "deep trouble," composed of families with an annual income of less than $3,000 and a debt-payment-to-income ratio of greater than 20 percent. Those families with a ratio of less than 20 percent but greater than 10 percent were considered in "some trouble," and those with a ratio of less than 10 percent in "no trouble." These classifications assume three things: (1) the greater the debt-payment-to-income ratio, the greater the probability of default; (2) if a family's liquid assets minus a "transactions balance" of $200 exceed outstanding installment debt, installment debt owing will pose no problem; (3) the higher the family's income, *ceteris paribus*, the greater the debt-payment-to-income ratio it can sustain without encountering problems.) Those not using consumer credit at all, on the other hand, frequently struggle along at an even lower standard of living than those in "deep trouble." Thus we see the double dilemma of the rural poor (8).

DEBT RATIO REGRESSION MODEL. When a regression equation was estimated using the debt-payment-to-income ratio (or debt ratio) as dependent variable and using as independent variables the number of months credit allowed on recent purchases, the amount still owed on recent purchases, and total family income from all sources, the following results were obtained:

$$D_r = .205 - .0032(X_1) + .0000915(X_2) - .0000154(X_3) + U$$
$$ (.057) \quad (.0082) \quad\quad (.0000275) \quad\quad (.0000090)$$

Where
the numbers in parentheses are the standard errors of the coefficients, and
D_r = debt ratio
X_1 = number of months credit allowed on recent purchases
X_2 = amount still owed on recent purchases
X_3 = total family income from all sources
U = error term

The signs of the coefficients may be interpreted as follows:

1. The basic family debt ratio of .205 places a family in the category of "deep trouble."
2. The debt ratio increases for larger total indebtedness.
3. The debt ratio is lower when longer terms (more months to repay) are allowed, or when total family income increases.

ABSOLUTE DEBT REGRESSION MODEL. In addition to the regression model using the debt ratio as the dependent variable, we have also constructed a model that attempts to describe the influence of eight socioeconomic variables on the absolute amount of debt owed. These variables include earned income of family head (X_1); family expenses for the past year (X_2); method of payment of debt (X_3); tenure of indebtedness (X_4); the amount of down payment on consumer durables (X_5); the sex of the household head (X_6); the amount paid on all debt last year (X_7); and occupation of the family head (X_8).

To test the relationship between the dependent variable—the actual amount of debt owed (Y)—and the independent variables listed above, a stepwise regression model was used.

The results of this model are as follows:

$$Y_{Do} = 46.4 + .035(X_1) - 450(X_2) - 120(X_3) - 7.08(X_4) + .77(X_5)$$
$$\phantom{Y_{Do} = 46.4 + } (.019)** \quad (112)* \quad (62.4)** \quad (2.69)* \quad (.04)*$$

$$R^2 = .43 \quad DF = 519 \quad F \text{ Value} = 79.3$$

Where
the numbers in parentheses are the standard errors of the coefficients, with one asterisk indicating the parameter is significant at 1 percent probability level and two asterisks indicating significance at the .07 level.

Discussion. As the equation shows, only the variables of income of family head (X_1); family expense for past year (X^2); method of payment (X_3); and the amount paid on debt last year (X_5) are significant in explaining the dependent variable (Y_{Do}).

The indebtedness regression indicates that 43 percent of the variance in the amount of debt owed by household heads in the sample population was associated with five of the eight available variables. The absolute debt regression model equation with a computed F value of 79.3 and a R^2 of 0.43 was the best predictive indebtedness model available from the sample.

The regression coefficient of X_1 indicates that among those who are in debt, the percent of income allocated to installment payments increases as income rises; for example, a $100 increase in household income is associated with an approximately 4 percent increase in family indebtedness.

No satisfactory explanation could be found for the negative coefficient for X_2. Perhaps higher family expenses are associated with higher incomes, and hence the income variable masks the impact of X_2. This interpretation, however, is certainly not wholly satisfactory. The negative and significant value of X_3 (method of payment of debt) is expected, because as the level of poverty moves further below a set poverty threshold, more purchases are made for cash as credit sources dwindle, and cash purchases do not reduce debts. In addition, a family's ability to borrow increases with its income, but after income reaches a certain level, the relative need for credit decreases. The negative and significant value for X_4 (the number of months' credit) indicates that people owing the most owe it the soonest; in other words, those who can get extensions are the ones who already have longer installment payouts. For each month of extended credit to the rural poor, the debt-payment-to-income ratio is reduced by approximately 7 percentage points; the positive coefficient for X_5 (the amount paid on all debt last year) indicates the higher the indebtedness, the higher the payment on that debt each year. In other words, .77 indicates that only 77¢ of each dollar owed in a year is paid off in that year. Thus, with new debt being incurred each succeeding year, families in financial trouble are likely to become more deeply committed unless a substantial increase in family income occurs (8).

Critique. A variety of findings in this study suggest that rural poverty is often permanent. Data on earnings by heads of families point to chronically low earnings. Low incomes, financial disasters, and inability to provide for the future often leave the rural poor with meager assets. For example, some 46 percent of the sampled rural population had an annual income of less than $2,000; less than 4 percent of family heads had health insurance; and only 1.28 percent had any type of pension rights. The lack of planning or finances with which to plan suggest that the rural poor will continue to be burdened by financial difficulties, since they have little protection against poor health, inadequate income, and involuntary retirement.

Clearly there is a rural poverty problem. The focus in the rest of this chapter is on income maintenance programs directed toward alleviating that problem. Emphasis will be placed on the shift of the federal budget to income support, the problem of income distribution, and some suggested welfare reforms. In the following discussion, the terms income support, income transfers, income maintenance, and income supplement are used interchangeably to refer to federal public programs that maintain or supplement personal living standards through assistance in cash or kind.

SOME INCOME MAINTENANCE PROGRAMS AND ISSUES

Shift in Budget to Income Support. The tenth anniversary of the government's declaration of "war on poverty" came in 1974. Federal

TABLE 10.3.　Growth in federal income support programs, U.S., 1960-73.

Program	1960	1970	1973
	(bil dol)		
Old Cash Transfer Programs, Total[a]	21.4	49.3	75.6
OASDHI (Social Security)	10.8	29.7	44.7
Aid to Aged, Blind and Disabled	1.4	1.9	2.8
Aid to Families with Dependent Children	0.7	2.2	4.7
Veterans' Benefits	3.4	5.2	6.4
Unemployment Compensation	2.6	3.1	5.9
Railroad, Military, and Civil Service Retirement	2.5	7.2	11.1
New In-kind Transfer Programs, Total[b]	9.2	11.3	19.0
Medicare	. . .	7.1	10.4
Medicaid	. . .	2.7	3.8
Food Stamps	*	0.6	2.3
Other nutrition	0.1	0.4	0.7
Housing subsidies	0.1	0.5	1.8
Other, Total	3.7	5.1	7.1
Farm price supports	3.3	3.8	3.7
Student aid	0.4	1.3	3.4
Total Benefits	25.5	65.7	101.7
	% federal expenditures		
Total Benefits	27.7	33.8	39.4
Cash benefits	27.2	28.0	32.0
In-kind benefits	0.4	5.8	7.4

Source: (12, Table 6.1, p. 176).

[a] Old cash transfer programs refer to programs that were legislated primarily during the 1930s as part of New Deal Reforms.

[b] New in-kind transfer programs refer to programs that were legislated primarily during the 1960s as part of Great Society reforms.

* Less than $50 million.

support for this war on poverty has been channeled through several programs, such as Social Security (that part of it reaching the poor or near-poor and programs for human resource development, education, health, welfare, vocational rehabilitation, and housing. The federal government spent an estimated $102 billion in 1973 on programs that provide families and individuals with income support (3). The share of federal resources going to nonmilitary programs rose from 47 percent in 1963 to 66 percent in 1973, and some of the largest increases in expenditure for these programs were in the income support area (Table 10.3). In 1973 federal spending on income support accounted for 60 percent of the nonmilitary expenditures and 39 percent of the total budget. Cash income maintenance programs and programs to help people buy essentials accounted for about 43 percent of federal outlays in fiscal year 1975 (2). This increase in outlays reflects a major shift in the composition of the federal budget and hence a shift in the primary focus of federal activities. These income support measures have become the main government weapon against poverty in recent years, particularly in view of the declining impact of aid for social programs (3). Although more income support for the needy has alleviated poverty, it has also compounded the difficulties of reforming and simplifying the nation's welfare system.

TABLE 10.4. Percentage share of aggregate money income received by each fifth of families and unrelated individuals, U.S., selected years, 1950–71.[a]

Income Rank	1950	1960	1970	1971
		(%)		
Families				
Lowest fifth	4.5	4.9	5.5	5.5
Second fifth	12.0	12.0	12.0	11.9
Third fifth	17.4	17.6	17.4	17.4
Fourth fifth	23.5	23.6	23.5	23.7
Highest fifth	42.6	42.0	41.6	41.6
Top five percent	17.0	16.8	14.4	(NA)[b]
Unrelated Individuals				
Lowest fifth	2.3	2.6	3.3	3.4
Second fifth	7.0	7.1	7.9	8.1
Third fifth	13.8	13.6	13.8	13.9
Fourth fifth	26.5	25.7	24.5	24.2
Highest fifth	50.4	50.9	50.5	50.4
Top five percent	19.3	20.0	20.5	20.6

Source: (17).

[a] Money income includes earnings, transfer payments, and income from property, but excludes income from the sale of capital assets.

[b] (NA) = Not Available

The Problem of Income Distribution. The problem of the rural poor reflects the national problem of unequal income distribution. Table 10.4 shows that in 1971 the 20 percent of families at the top of the income scale received about 42 percent of all family income while the bottom 20 percent received less than 6 percent (17). The distribution of income among unrelated individuals was still more uneven. The richest 20 percent received half the income and the other 80 percent shared the remaining half. These percentages have remained virtually unchanged since World War II. The share of before-tax money income received by the top 5 percent of families declined slightly, from 17 to 14 percent, between 1950 and 1970, but the share at the bottom 20 percent increased only from 4.5 to 5.5 percent during the same period.

We have little information about the distribution of wealth. Lampman (7) states that the top 2 percent of American families hold 39 percent of personal equity; Goldsmith (7) reports that 40 percent of net worth is held by the top 10 percent of households. Among families with incomes of less than $3,000, net assets amounted to only $2,760 at the end of 1962 (7). The stability of individual positions in the income distribution and the shape of the distribution are important in determining preference about the desired distribution. At the low end of the income distribution curve, individual positions are relatively stable. Of those families escaping poverty, for example (income > $3,600 poverty threshold), one-fourth remained within $500 of the poverty line. Those families falling into poverty fell relatively deeper— over 55 percent fell more than $500 below the poverty threshold (9).

Data on unrealized capital gains are practically nonexistent. The limited data available on realized capital gains indicate that they primarily affect high incomes. Realized capital gains account for less than 2 percent of incomes below $10,000, but they account for more than 60 percent of incomes between $500,000 and one million dollars. Unrealized capital gains may be more important at low income ranges, but low income families lack large assets to produce capital gains. One of the continuing functions of government is to alter the market structure of income distribution to that desired by society. Great disparity in incomes tends to rigidify the social structure.

Present Income Maintenance Programs. The present federal income maintenance system is composed of two parts, social insurance and public assistance. Social insurance programs are designed to prevent a complete collapse of family or individual income upon retirement or in the event of unemployment. Public assistance programs supplement social insurance programs by providing income grants to certain categories of the poor, including the aged, the blind, the disabled, and mothers with dependent children. States also maintain general assistance programs.

This categorical approach to income maintenance has been increasingly questioned in recent years; consequently, a few of the newer programs determine eligibility on the basis of need alone, without regard to category. However, the newer programs do not offer cash payments to the poor but rather benefits in kind such as food stamps, subsidized housing, and medical care. Our present system, based on the distinction between those who can work and those who cannot or should not, is inherently inequitable and ineffective (13). The staff of the Joint Economic Committee, subcommittee on fiscal policy, estimates that about 119 million separate benefits were paid in 1972, but this figure represents only about 60 million different recipients (13).

The federal income maintenance system also provides vastly different levels of benefits depending upon geographic location and family structure. This is true even if family size,, income levels, and work efforts do not vary. For example, rural Americans do not share proportionately in federally funded income maintenance programs (13). Federal spending on human resources development programs such as education, health, welfare, vocational rehabilitation, worker training, and development disproportionately favors metropolitan areas over nonmetropolitan areas. A USDA report entitled "Economic and Social Conditions of Rural America in the 1970s" shows that the per capita federal outlays for health services are four times greater in metropolitan counties than in nonmetropolitan ones, that welfare payments are also four times greater, and that worker training and development expenditures are three times greater (13).

The Griffith Committee report also showed wide variation in the distribution of welfare benefits between rural and urban population (18).

For example, 71 percent of the sampled urban households received in-kind benefits, compared to 34 percent in rural counties. Twenty percent of urban families received housing subsidies compared to 1 percent in rural counties; nonmetropolitan counties accounted for 66 percent of all substandard housing units but received only 16 percent of all federal housing assistance (18). Sixty-six percent of urban households with children received free school lunch in 1970, compared to 13 percent for rural areas. (These differences probably reflect both availability and acceptability of this type of subsidy as well as households' perceived need for it.) Nonmetropolitan counties accounted for 50 percent of all children between the ages of 6 and 17 in poverty level families, but they received only 20 percent of all federal child welfare service funds, 26 percent of federal Headstart and follow-through assistance, and 41 percent of federal expenditures on elementary and secondary education programs for disadvantaged children in low income areas. Free medical care was financed by the Medicaid Program for as few as 11 percent of households in rural counties, compared to 27 percent average in urban centers. These proportions were consistent with the proportions of households receiving public assistance, which confers automatic eligibility for Medicaid. Fifteen percent of urban households participated in worker development programs compared to less than 5 percent in rural counties. (It appears that these programs were not generally available in rural counties. It may be that the rural public perceives less value in training as a means to employment than the urban public does. And it may be that wage levels and employment available without additional training are better in rural areas than they are in cities.)

The conclusion that may be drawn from these surveys is that masses of the eligible poverty population in both urban and rural settings receive no benefits from the present income maintenance system. In fact, six out of 10 sampled households received 1 or more benefits for some part of the year, but 40 percent did not receive any benefits (18). If rural revitalization is to be achieved, a comprehensive federal policy must be established and implemented to insure that an equitable share of federal outlays are made available to distressed nonmetropolitan areas.

Some Proposals for Welfare Reforms. In 1974, in spite of the growth in income support over the past five years, reform of the transfer system still ranks high on the agenda of many economists, the Administration, and other social scientists. There are three primary reasons for believing that a thorough reform of the income support system is needed (2).

First, after a decade of sharp increases in outlays for transfers under federal and state auspices, poverty has not been eliminated. In addition, the overall distribution of income has not changed substantially. In 1963 there were 36 million people with incomes of less than half the median income in the nation; by 1971, even though the poverty count was lower, 36 million people still had incomes less than half the median national income. Since transfer programs are a major public instrument for bringing about a narrowing of income gaps, many have concluded that these programs have to be radically revised if they are to perform the function of redistributing income.

Second, the income support system has become so complex, uncoordinated, and costly that many problems of inefficiency and inequity have arisen. For example, food stamps have narrowed the gap between groups of poor people, but poor mothers with dependent children can still qualify for substantial cash assistance, while poor families of the same size and income status but with employed male heads cannot.

Third, recent research has made the prospect of moving to a universal cash assistance program seem less risky than in the past. Most major overhauls of the income support system involve a plan whereby the federal government guarantees a minimum level of income to people with no earnings and then reduces the grant by a fraction of each dollar earned. Some suggested reforms are described below.

UNIVERSAL DEMOGRANTS. Portions of this study (2) have documented the fact that the well-being of many rural poor Americans can be improved only by some system of transfer payments. The simplest suggested proposal to put a floor under low income is a demogrant plan, fully integrated with the income tax system. Demogrant is simply a conversion of existing personal exemptions of the federal income tax into higher level tax credits—with the added provision that the taxpayer is allowed to convert tax credits that exceed tax liabilities into cash (2). Demogrants have the advantage of simplicity and are effective as redistributors of income. The universal demogrant is also a manipulatable measure: different degrees of redistribution could be achieved for special groups, such as the aged, blind, and the disabled by varying the amount of demogrants.

UNIVERSAL NEGATIVE INCOME TAX. The negative income tax is a relatively new proposal that has received a great deal of attention in recent months. It was first proposed by Milton Friedman in his 1962 book *Capitalism and Freedom* (6). Friedman states that if society is really serious about helping the poor and wants to help them in the most efficient way possible, the government should supplement their incomes by a so-called negative tax—a payment from the government to the poor.

Like a demogrant, the universal negative income tax covers all categories of people, specifying a guaranteed level of support when there is zero income. The amount of support money varies with family size and phases out as income rises. The negative income tax is designed to confine cash allowances to the lower end of the income distribution, thus greatly reducing costs. The basic advantage of a universal negative income tax over the present system is that it will eliminate the unequal treatment of poor families who fall into different demographic categories (17). Up to now, American social policy has assumed that people in these categories should work for their income and that cash assistance was either unnecessary or a tempting alternative to work. Those that advocate an income strategy rather than social services for the poor argue that taxes, transfer, and subsidized employment can change the income distribution directly and quickly, while investment in work productivity may or may not be a productive means to this end (5). They also stress their belief that as a solution to the problem of poverty, the principal need of the poor is an increase in general purchasing power (5). A major stumbling block to the introduction of such a plan has been the fear that a guaranteed minimum level of income would have a disincentive effect on the recipients, causing greatly reduced work efforts or withdrawals from the labor force. Planners of this negative income tax proposal are resting part of their defense on two relatively recent studies which they contend demolish many of the old notions about poverty. The first study was the New Jersey graduated work incentive experiment, which tested the effect of a negative income tax on labor supply in families with a male head—the major group not now covered under cash assistance programs. Families cooperating in the experiment were guaranteed a minimum income ranging from 50 percent to 125 percent of the poverty level. Tax rates on earnings varied from 30 percent to 70 percent. After three years of experimentation, analysis of data showed that there was virtually no difference in the labor force participation between the experimental and the control group families (18). White husbands in the experiment worked, on the average, only two hours less per week than husbands in the control group, while black husbands did not reduce their work efforts at all. Although there was a reduction in the labor force participation of wives in the experimental group, its impact on family income was negligible. The data analysis did not indicate any relation between changes in labor supply and the various tax rates and guarantee levels. Hence, the evidence seems to indicate that for husband-wife families, no substantial withdrawal from work would accompany a negative income tax program. Thus, design of a universal negative income tax plan, guarantee levels, and tax rates can be determined mainly by social and broad economic considerations; fear of inducing a permanent welfare class by the design of the program seems less germane. Automatic doles for the needy do not encourage shiftlessness.

The second study, conducted by the University of Michigan's Institute of Social Research, was a panel study of 5,000 families over a 5-year period. The findings showed that poverty is a fluid condition—over a short period of time many families drop in and out of poverty and the hard core of perpetually impoverished families is relatively small. The study showed that 9 percent of the 5,000 families were in the bottom fifth of the income distribution in each of the 5 years and that 45 percent of Americans had at one time or another become eligible for some form of welfare assistance in the last 6 years (5).

Beneficiaries of Income Supplement Plan. The real beneficiaries of a public assistance plan with a guaranteed annual income clause would be the breadwinners who work regularly and still live in poverty. By definition, they are the domestic workers, the unskilled laborers, and particularly the farm workers; collectively, they are about half of the working age population that is officially in poverty in this country, and yet they fall through the cracks of that erratic structure, the present American welfare system (5).

If the benefits of the proposed negative income tax proposal of 1971 (Family Assistance Plan) could be interpolated into the proposed Public Assistance Plan contemplated by the Ford Administration, welfare benefits would increase substantially, with major shares of this increase going to poor rural residents (13). Benefits under the Family Assistance Plan would increase by $3.18 billion, or 26 percent over benefits under current programs. Forty-six percent of the increase in U.S. welfare benefits would be received by rural people, compared with 54 percent accruing to the urban poor, assuming 100 percent participation of eligible rural and urban families (13). Income supplement increases would be greatest in southern regions, especially the rural South (13). State differences in welfare benefit levels would be reduced under the Public Assistance Plan. Work incentives would probably be affected most in the South, where the benefits would increase substantially, and where earning potential is low because of low skills and educational attainment.

Critique. The rural poverty models presented in this chapter indicate that low income among the rural black poor cannot be explained solely in terms of any deficiency that can be removed by pure economic measures. Increasing education and training are necessary, but these investments alone are not adequate. The regression model suggests that the variable of number of weeks worked last year, with an elasticity coefficient of .451, is the best predictor of household income. In predictive importance, this variable is followed by the variables of hours worked last week (coefficient .2264); education (coefficient .2129); and distance traveled to work (coefficient .0948). More jobs with better pay in the rural nonfarm sector are the first prerequisite for mitigating poverty among the rural black population. A minimum wage higher than the present one should also be imposed and enforced, as 78 percent of the poor family heads in the sample worked full time or at least forty weeks during the year without escaping poverty. The elasticity coefficient for income and education showed that as the education level increased for sample family heads, the marginal value of education decreased. The economic and social characteristics of the rural black poor, as identified in the sample of 549 households described in this study, do not fit the requirements of our consumer credit system. In all probability, many of the problems confronting the rural black poor are experienced by other poor rural residents as well. This system of consumer credit was designed for the urban wage-earner with stable, predictable, and rising income, and possessed of considerable skill in shopping for the best alternatives. The foregoing analysis supports the conclusion that the needs of the rural black poor (and most probably the rural poor in general) require a special and imaginative approach to the matter of financing the family life cycle.

If past history is any guide, the current categorical approach to income maintenance (categories of aided and unaided people, and a mixture of state and federal programs) will not bring about any substantial narrowing of income differences. The inequity will be compounded if state and federal assistance programs continue to favor metropolitan areas over rural areas.

POLICY IMPLICATIONS. Future gains on the rural poverty front will have to be sought through both structural and distributive measure: measures to raise productivity through education, training, and on-the-job experience, measures to reduce labor market and racial discrimination, and measures to put a floor under income transfers. The well-being of many of today's economically deprived rural households can be improved only through some system of transfer payments. Greater efforts must be made not only to train the rural poor but to increase their access to jobs through provision of moderately priced housing, elimination of various types of discrimination in housing, and improvement of public transportation. Measures that improve mobility are preferable to those that subsidize immobility. It may be necessary to intervene in the poverty cycle and offer solutions to one or more poverty related variables, thus breaking the cycle and allowing the individual to develop solutions himself to other related deprivation problems. For example, training a person who lacks salable skills will not break the poverty cycle if no job requiring his skill is available to him, or if his health prevents his holding the job, or if he lacks transportation to the job site. Implementation of combined investment and acceptance measures would constitute a major step toward increasing investments in human resources and also toward increasing full acceptance of all citizens as Americans. Social rate of return on human capital investments is greater than private return; therefore, it is in the nation's self-interest to eliminate factors causing poverty in America.

REFERENCES
 (1). Beale, Calvin L., "Migration Patterns of Minorities in the United States," *American Journal of Agricultural Economics* 55 (5): 938–46.
 (2). Blechman, B. M. et al., *Setting National Priorities, The 1975 Budget,* Washington: The Brookings Institution, 1974.

(3). Boland, Barbara, "Evaluating Federal Income Support Programs," *Review of Public Data,* Vol. 2, January 1974.

(4). Brimmer, Andrew, "Economic Situation of Blacks in the United States," *Review of Black Political Economy* 2 (4): 34–56.

(5). Chapman, William, "Working Poor Benefit Most Under Minimum Income Plan," *Houston Chronicle,* November 24, 1974, p. 1.

(6). Friedman, Milton, *Capitalism and Freedom,* Chicago: University of Chicago Press, 1962.

(7). Lampman, Robert, "Transfer and Redistribution As Social Process," Discussion Paper No. 25, Institute for Research on Poverty, University of Wisconsin at Madison, 1970.

(8). Owens, E. W., C. Moyer, and F. Yeager, "Dept Probability and the Rural Poor," American Institute of Decision Science, Western Region, University of Oregon, Spring 1975.

(9). Owens, Emiel W., "Income Maintenance Programs in the 1960s: A Survey," *American Journal of Agricultural Economics* 54 (2): 342–55.

(10). ———, "Correlates of Rural Black Poverty," article submitted to *Review of Black Political Economy,* 1975.

(11). Owens, Emiel W., Stubb A. Lace, and Nelson Barden, *The Rural Poor,* Texas Agricultural Experiment Station (in production).

(12). Schultze, Charles L., Edward R. Fried, Alice M. Rivlin, and Nancy H. Teeters, *Setting National Priorities: The 1973 Budget,* Washington: © 1972 by The Brookings Institution.

(13). U.S. Department of Agriculture, Economic Research Service, *Welfare Reforms Benefits and Incentives in Rural Areas,* ERS 470, June 1971.

(14). U.S. Department of Agriculture, Economic Research Service, Part 3 of *The Economic and Social Condition of Rural America in the 1970s,* December 1971.

(15). U.S. Department of Agriculture, Rural Development Service, *Rural Development Goals,* First Annual Report of the Secretary of Agriculture to Congress, January 1974.

(16). ———, *Rural Development,* Fourth Annual Report of the President to Congress on Government Services to Rural America, 1974.

(17). U.S. Department of Commerce, Social and Economics Statistics Administration, "Money Income in 1971 of Families and Persons in the United States," Table 14, in *Current Population Reports: Consumer Income,* Bureau of the Census, Series P–60, No. 85, 1972.

(18). U.S. Government Printing Office, *Studies in Public Welfare,* Paper Nos. 1, 6, and 14, Joint Subcommittee on Fiscal Policy, U.S. Congress, April 1972. (No. 1, "Public Income Transfer Programs: The Incidence of Multiple Benefits and the Issues Raised by Their Receipt" by James R. Storey, April 1972; No. 6, "How Public Welfare Benefits Are Distributed in Low Income Areas." A Staff Study, March 1973; No. 14, "Public Welfare and Work Incentives: Theory and Practice," A Staff Study, April 1974.)

Discussion

L Y N N   M .   D A F T

I N addressing this subject the author had an opportunity to go in any one of several directions in some depth or, alternatively, to treat several dimensions in lesser depth. Owens chose the latter course. I sympathize with his reluctance to limit attention to only one dimension of the topic. I would have been tempted to do much the same. But his approach makes it impossible to give the full array of issues that surface the scrutiny they require. Thus I believe the author might better have narrowed the field of his inquiry.

About half the chapter describes the nature of rural poverty, with special emphasis on indebtedness among the rural black poor. This discussion is followed by a brief glimpse of trends in federal outlays for income maintenance and some of the major proposals for welfare reform. The chief contribution of the paper, in my opinion, is its treatment of indebtedness among the poor. I only regret there was too little time to develop the evidence more fully. The importance of the capital market in overcoming poverty is treated in Chapter 6 as well. Taken in combination, the ideas expressed in these chapters seem to me to offer a promising basis for further inquiry.

Considering specific issues raised in the chapter, several points come to mind regarding the regression analyses. Though I found the results a useful explanation of past behavioral relationships, I would be more cautious than the author in using the results as a basis for policy prescription. For instance, finding that annual household income increases as labor force participation increases within the sampled population helps us better understand why some households have low income: they lack an income stream associated with gainful employment. It does not necessarily follow, however, that "making jobs available . . . is the most important step to be taken in eliminating rural poverty among the sampled families." Some households (due to age of members, disability, and the like) lack employable labor. Others contain employable household members, but their productivity is very low, perhaps too low to cap-

The views expressed are those of the author and do not necessarily reflect the position of the Congressional Budget Office.

ture the jobs that might be made available. The literature is replete with cases of more highly skilled labor migrating or commuting to newly created jobs, leaving the less skilled indigenous population largely unaffected. Furthermore, as the author notes at another point in the chapter, employment alone is clearly not the solution for many of the poor inasmuch as 78 percent of all poor family heads in the sample worked full-time or at least 40 weeks during the year without escaping poverty. Thus the solution is considerably more complicated than just making more jobs available.

As already noted, I would have preferred to have had the indebtedness topic explored in greater depth. The use of short-term debt for the purchase of nondurables is a potential avenue of inquiry. It might also be useful to assess some of the institutional parameters. For example, what are the sources of credit? Cost of the credit? What specifically is the borrowed capital used for? Are there policy implications vis-à-vis the functioning of the credit market among the poor?

Owens' discussion of the absolute debt regression model equation needs to be extended. The specification of some of the variables (for example, method of payment of debt and tenure of indebtedness) requires clarification. As the author observes, the negative coefficient for the family expense variable is unexpected. The possible influence of intercorrelation should be considered.

In response to the high incidence of working poor within the poverty population, the author recommends a higher minimum wage. Though I concur in the need for a higher level of well-being for the working poor, I have strong reservations about this approach. To the extent that the present wage approximates the marginal value product of this labor, a higher wage will reduce its demand. This places an increased burden of responsibility on public services aimed at raising labor productivity and at alleviating the work force adjustment problem that is likely to follow.

Toward the end of the chapter Owens refers to national goals of a "substantial narrowing of income differences" and "rural revitalization." I would advise caution in using such goals to gauge program performance, at least the performance of past programs. I say this because I do not believe these goals, as stated, have been of controlling importance in national policy. Why? The first because it is too drastic, the latter because it is too vague.

Let me turn now to suggestions for extending analysis of the topic. I would like to see three aspects treated at greater length.

THE PERFORMANCE OF EXISTING PROGRAMS. Though the chapter refers to some inadequacies of existing programs, I would have preferred a more exhaustive treatment. Discussing this maze of programs in detail is a complicated, messy, perhaps even pedestrian undertaking. Unfortunately, though, I believe it is also necessary if one is to come to grips with anything more than a general and somewhat hazy outline of the problem at hand. Thanks to the work of such groups as the Commission on Income Maintenance, the University of Wisconsin's Poverty Institute, and the Joint Economic Committee, we have a respectable body of knowledge on which to base a detailed assessment of the principal income maintenance programs. This assessment would require attention to such dimensions as adequacy of the level of income support, work incentive effects, horizontal equity, recipient rights, and the like.

Once you move beyond the more traditional income maintenance programs, the level of information about income transfer effects drops precipitously. Here I am referring to those programs that fall under such labels as manpower development, community organization and development, industrial development, and even rural development. Beyond the absence of reliable information concerning the effects of these programs, one must contend with their multipurpose nature. This factor alone complicates their treatment enormously and, incidentally, is no doubt one reason economic analysts are attracted to the more straightforward income maintenance program aspect of income transfers.

A fringe benefit of dwelling at greater length on the accomplishments and failures of our present programs—beyond the value of detailing some of their absurdities—is that it leads rather naturally into consideration of specific program objectives and the trade-offs between objectives. For example, how much work incentive effect is one willing to trade for how high an upper bound on income coverage? How much budget impact is to be traded for adequacy of support level? And, moving to a broader frame of reference, how much income maintenance is to be traded for how much housing assistance? For how much transportation subsidy? For how much national defense?

THE ISSUES. There are several important program issues that deserve mention. Some were treated in the chapter; some were not. I believe it would serve a useful purpose to isolate these issues and subject them to closer scrutiny. Among such issues I would include these:

1. Should we programmatically distinguish between *rural* poverty and *urban* poverty? If so, why? And how?

2. Should we attempt a wholesale change in our public policy approach to poverty (such as through adoption of a negative income tax), or do we concentrate on incremental improvements in existing programs?

3. Cash assistance *versus* in-kind assistance *versus* a combination of the two?

4. Centrally administered or decentralized?
5. Do we establish our objectives in terms of absolute poverty or relative poverty?
6. If relative poverty, how far do we go toward equality? And at what cost?

WILL WE ACT? I found the most intriguing part of the chapter title to be the question *Can* we improve the performance? If by "can" we mean having the capacity or ability to bring about improvement or, alternatively, if we mean is there room for improvement, then I have no doubt the correct response is in the affirmative. But if the question is, *Will* we improve the performance? well, that is another question and a more complicated one.

I find grounds for both pessimism and optimism. On the pessimistic side, many of us have been urging changes in poverty programs for several years now, with results that have been something less than gratifying. For example, a great deal of effort was expended over the past 6 years in attempting to win passage of a comprehensive welfare reform package. And, at times, the prospect of passage seemed good. But, alas, it never came about. I thought it might be instructive to consider how one of the chief architects of that effort, Daniel Moynihan, interpreted the experience and what it might suggest for the future. As I read him, Moynihan attributes failure to win passage of the Family Assistance Plan to two factors: (1) The competitive outbidding of supporters of welfare reform, who converted a comparatively ambitious proposal (given the heavy economic drain of Vietnam and the conservatism of the Administration in power) into one, as Moynihan says, "verging on the fantasized." Extravagance of this order effectively sealed its political doom. (2) The inaccessibility of both the Congress and the public at large to informed, objective analysis of the issue. After one and one-half years of often intense Congressional debate, it is Moynihan's judgment that not more than 12 Senators fully understood the proposal (1, Chapter 8). These explanations are not, of course, mutually exclusive. Neither are they the only ones. But they are instructive.

On a more optimistic note, and I must caution that I am an optimist by nature, there are several encouraging signs vis-à-vis the question, Can we improve the performance? First, improvements *have* been made in some programs in recent years. Though it is true much remains to be done and it is well not to slip into complacency over marginal improvement, neither must we allow paranoia to distort our view. Second, over the past six years or so we have made some important basic investments in expanding our knowledge of the issue. The negative income tax experiments, the research and training of Wisconsin's Poverty Institute, the Income Maintenance Commission study, the research of the Office of Economic Opportunity, and the study by Congresswoman Griffith's subcommittee are examples. The returns to such investments are always difficult to trace through to final result. But I think they are beginning to influence public decision making. The recent negative income tax proposal advanced by HEW is an important case in point. The architects of that proposal and, perhaps more importantly, its principal advocates among key decisionmakers, are products of this investment process. Finally, lest we forget, the last major proposal for reform came close to acceptance, twice passing a more conservative House of Representatives than we now have.

Owens' good and thoughtful work gives us much to ponder. As he writes in his closing comments, we have miles to go.

REFERENCE
(1). Moynihan, Daniel P., *The Politics of a Guaranteed Income,* New York: Random House, 1973.

CHAPTER ELEVEN

Future poverty programs: political prospects and implications for the rural poor

D. LEE BAWDEN

T H I S chapter focuses on two major poverty programs currently under consideration in Washington—a universal cash transfer program and national health insurance. Both programs are income conditioned and both would have a major impact on the poor.

The chapter is organized as follows: I consider each prospective program in turn, first by describing existing programs in that area, then by discussing the elements of the proposed program, then by assessing its impact on the rural poor, and finally by speculating on its political prospects. (The last subject properly belongs in this discussion; however, I must note that is not my area of special expertise, and my speculation should be appropriately discounted.)

A UNIVERSAL CASH TRANSFER PROGRAM. Fifteen months ago there were five Public Assistance cash transfer programs: (1) Old Age Assistance, (2) Aid to the Blind, (3) Aid to the Permanently and Totally Disabled, (4) Aid to Families with Dependent Children (AFDC) for one-parent families, and (5) AFDC-Unemployed Parents (AFDC-UP) for certain low income two-parent families. In January 1974 the aged, blind, and disabled programs were replaced by SSI, which stands for Supplemental Security Income. So there are now three Public Assistance cash programs—SSI, AFDC, and, in about half the states, AFDC-UP. These programs are categorical, meaning that a family cannot qualify on the basis of low income alone but must meet other eligibility requirements. Among the poor, the least adequately covered by these three programs are the so-called working poor—two-parent families in which the head is able-bodied and of working age. About half the nation's poor live in such families, yet less than 10 percent of those families receive any public assistance (2, p. 180). Nor does Unemployment Insurance (UI) do much to fill this gap. Almost half the male heads of these families work full-time the entire year. Many others receive no UI benefits because they are not covered, they have been unemployed too long, or they have had short but frequent spells of joblessness. Counting all transfers, including food stamps, less than a fifth of the pretransfer poor families in this group are raised above the poverty level by the transfers (1, p. 26, Table 5).

For these and other reasons, serious demands for reform of the present cash transfer system were made as early as 1966. In 1969 Richard Nixon became the first president to propose a universal cash transfer program, meaning that eligibility would be based solely on family income and all poor families (but not single individuals) would therefore be eligible for assistance. Despite this being labeled by Nixon as his number one domestic program, it was never enacted into law. It passed the House Ways and Means Committee twice, only to be stopped by Senator Long and a majority of his colleagues on the Senate Finance Committee.

In early 1973 then-President Nixon asked the Department of Health, Education and Welfare (HEW) once again to come up with a universal cash transfer program to solve the so-called "welfare mess." A task force was formed in HEW in August of that year, and over the next 12 months the members developed a program that was first presented to Nixon prior to his resignation and has since been presented to President Ford. The basic elements of that program are: (1) an income floor for all families, scaled to family size and age, with $3,600 provided to a non-elderly, zero-income family of four; (2) a negative tax rate of 50 percent, meaning that for each dollar of family income, benefits would be reduced by 50 cents; (3) a declining scale of cash transfers, therefore, diminishing to zero as a family of four reaches an income of $7,200 per year; and (4) a work requirement stipulating that nonelderly able-bodied males must register for employment and accept a "suitable" job offer in order to remain eligible for the cash payments. The proposed program would replace all existing public assistance cash transfer programs—SSI, AFDC, and AFDC-UP—as well as the Food Stamp program. The net cost would be between $3 and $5 billion, depending on how the positive tax system would be changed.

While initially receptive to the idea, President Ford decided to keep the proposal under wraps for at least another year. Welfare reform fell prey to the larger policy of halting recession; it was a victim of the President's policy of "fiscal restraint."

How would such a program affect the rural poor? In 1970, only 26.6 percent of the U.S. population lived in rural areas (on farms and in towns of 2,500 or less), but 35.5 percent of the total U.S. poverty population were rural residents. To the extent that the administration's Income Supplement Plan (ISP) would benefit all poor people, then rural areas stand to gain more than urban areas because rural areas have more than their share of poor people. But the impact of a universal income maintenance program like ISP is more complex than this; to trace out its consequences, one must look at rural-urban differences in the composition of the poor, for some groups will gain more than others.

The major difference between a universal income maintenance program like ISP and the current set of welfare programs is that all poor, nonelderly, male-headed households would be eligible for cash assistance. About half the poor people in the U.S. live in such families and, at present, only a handful receive payments under the AFDC-UP program. It is this feature of the program, more than any other, which would cause a proportionately larger share of ISP monies to flow to rural areas. This is because nearly two-thirds of the rural poor are in nonelderly, male-headed households whereas only half the urban poor are in such households.

Secondly, in most states female-headed families would receive no higher payments from ISP than from the current AFDC program. However, in approximately 16 states, female-headed families would be treated more generously, and most of these states are in the South. Since 28 percent of female-headed families with children under age 18 in the South were in rural areas in 1970, compared with only 13 percent in rural areas outside the South (where payments will stay the same), this feature of the program also tends to benefit the rural poor proportionately more than the urban poor.

A third factor is that ISP would also replace the Food Stamp Program. Currently, participation in the Food Stamp Program is much higher among the urban than among the rural poor: the rural poor make up over a third of the total U.S. poverty population, but they represent less than a fifth of the food stamp recipients. So, relatively speaking, the rural poor would "lose" less by the elimination of this program.

In summary, then, rural areas would benefit relatively more than urban areas by the adoption of a universal income maintenance program. Since we do not yet have accurate figures on Food Stamp benefits by income and residence, precise calculations cannot be made of the reduction in the number of poor families under an ISP-type program. Some approximate calculations, however, show that the adoption of ISP would reduce the number of rural poor families by about 55 percent, while the reduction in urban poor families would be about 40 percent. (Estimates are from the Transfer Income Model of the Urban Institute.)

These figures, of course, understate the impact of a universal cash transfer program like ISP because they merely count the number of families moved across the poverty line. More significantly, such a program would set an income *floor* below which family income could not drop.

For a family of four this would be $3,600. And while this is an inadequate amount of income to live on for any length of time, it would still substantially raise the economic status of the poorest of the poor.

What, then, are the prospects for adoption of such a program? It is my judgment that the welfare system will be reformed; the problem is too large to be ignored and the arguments for reform are too persuasive to be denied. The questions are: (1) how soon, and (2) will the reform occur incrementally or all at once.

In the past year, national health insurance has surpassed income maintenance as the number one issue in the area of social reform. In my opinion, therefore, a major welfare reform bill has no chance of being passed this fiscal year. Nor will it have any chance of passage next fiscal year unless a national health insurance program is passed this year, since it is most unlikely that two such expensive programs will be passed in the same year. The fate of both programs obviously depends in part on the state of the economy. Given the predicted sluggishness of upturn in the present economic situation, I would give no more than a 50/50 chance to a major welfare reform bill being passed during the next three-year period.

If HEW planners concur in this assessment, they may adopt the strategy of changing the walfare system *incrementally* over time until the economic and political situation is more favorable for a major over-haul of the system. They have many options for incremental change; some would have more impact than others on the rural poor. One option would be to require states to pay at least some established minimum AFDC payment, paralleling the maximum tax rate on earnings (66⅔ percent) established in the 1967 AFDC amendment. This option would principally affect the poor in southern states and would therefore improve the status of the rural poor relative to the urban poor.

A second option would be to mandate states to establish an AFDC-UP program, which would have some impact on two-parent poor families in the 23 states which currently have no program. Depending on the degree of relaxation, this could have a major impact on the number of poor families. And such a step would benefit the rural poor relatively more than the urban poor.

In summary, the prospect for a major change in the welfare system is not bright in the near future. Without such a change, the rural poor will continue to receive less than their proportionate share of income conditioned cash transfers.

A NATIONAL HEALTH INSURANCE PROGRAM

Current Government Programs. We currently have two major government-sponsored health programs—Medicare and Medicaid (see 3, 4, and 5). Medicare is a federal program for all elderly persons and those who have been disabled for two or more years. Under Medicare, all elderly persons covered by Social Security automatically qualify for hospital insurance, and for $6.30 per month they may also sign up for Supplementary Medical Insurance (SMI), which covers physician services. Neither the hospital nor physician expenses are fully paid by the government, however. Beneficiaries must pay the first $84 of hospital care and must pay a coinsurance of $21 per day after 60 days in the hospital, $42 per day after 90 days, and the full cost after 150 days in the hospital. Under SMI they must also pay for the first $60 of physician charges and 20 percent of all remaining charges.

Medicare covers most of the elderly, but the several hundred thousand not covered—those not eligible for Social Security—are found proportionately more in rural than in urban areas (since 1972 these people have been able to buy into Medicare at full cost, approximately $400 per person per year). Also, for those participating, there are rural-urban differences in the *benefits* received from Medicare. In 1969 central city recipients received 40 percent more benefits than those in nonmetropolitan counties.

The other major government health program, Medicaid, is an optional program to the state, with federal-state sharing of cost. All states but one (Arizona) have a Medicaid program, though the coverage and benefits provided differ markedly across states. In half of them Medicaid is available only to those on Public Assistance. In the other half—mostly the industrial states—eligibility is extended to the "medically needy." On the average, about one-third of the poor do not receive Medicaid benefits, and most of these are two-parent families or nonelderly single individuals. But in the southern and north central states, in which most of the rural poor reside, roughly two-thirds of the poor population receive no Medicaid benefits. In the South, which contains half the rural poor, only 20 percent of the poor nonelderly people receive Medicaid benefits, and the figure is even lower for the *rural* poor population in the South. Moreover, of those who do receive Medicaid benefits, rural residents receive a substantially smaller amount per recipient than urban residents do. This difference in expenditures per recipient, coupled with the differences in coverage, results in vast discrepancies in benefits between the urban and rural population. For example, in 1970 the average Medicaid expenditure *per poor child* in rural areas was less than $5 per year, in contrast to an expenditure of $76 in the central cities.

In summary, then, the two current major health programs dispense a disproportionately small portion of their total benefits to rural residents; the rural bias is fairly small under Medicare and quite large under Medicaid. This is important background for assessing the impact of a national health insurance program on the rural poor. We turn now to the issue of national health insurance.

Proposed National Health Insurance Programs. In the last session of Congress, more than a dozen different national health insurance bills were introduced. They differed in coverage, in payment formulas, in the degree to which premiums, deductibles, and coinsurance provisions were conditioned on income, and in the method of administration. Last year the House Ways and Means Committee took up the issue of a national health insurance program. With many members already seemingly committed to some plan and with this support badly fragmented, no consensus could be reached, and the Committee did not report out a bill. The Committee will surely consider the matter again this year, and while President Ford has declined to resubmit the Administration's bill, last year's version will be one of the most prominent proposals to receive consideration.

The Administration's proposal of last year, called the Comprehensive Health Insurance Plan, has three components: a plan for nonpoor employed persons, a restructured Medicare program for the elderly, and a plan for low income and high risk individuals and families. This last component is called AHIP, the Assisted Health Care Insurance Plan, and it is the program that would be the principal replacement for Medicaid. But it would be much broader than Medicaid, both in coverage of the poor and in coverage of benefits. In terms of benefits, it would cover hospital services, physician services, prescription drugs, limited mental health services, eye, ear, and dental care for children up to age 13, and a variety of other services. These benefits would be extended at no *premium* cost to *all* families with less than $5,000 in annual income and to all single individuals with less than $3,500 in income. "Thus the program would drastically improve coverage for the many poor individuals and families not currently covered under Medicaid. An additional $4 billion would be spent on services rendered to the poor alone. The plan would eliminate current discrimination against single individuals, childless couples, and male-headed families and those inequities inherent in state control over eligibility criteria" (5, p. 103). However, the plan does have coinsurance and deductible features, so medical services would not be free to the poor. The poorest of the poor (individuals below $1,750 and families below $2,500) would have no deductibles, but would pay 10 percent of all medical costs up to a maximum of 6 percent of their income. This coinsurance feature then increases with income, up to 25 percent (with a maximum liability of $1,500) at $10,000 incomes for families and $7,000 for individuals. Deductibles would begin for families with $2,500 in income, and premiums would begin for families with $5,000 in income. The program would, therefore, be scaled to family income, but the most important feature is that it would be extended to *all* the poor, not just those eligible for current Public Assistance. And it is this feature that would result in a relatively larger share of government health expenditures being directed to the rural poor, compared to the present situation. Under the Administration's program, coverage of the poor should be virtually universal. Rural residents would still receive fewer *dollar* benefits than urban residents, partly because medical services are cheaper in rural areas and partly because supply, and therefore utilization, is less. But the *marginal* increase in government paid medical benefits to the rural poor would be far greater than to the urban poor under national health insurance. The reason, of course, is that the rural poor receive relatively few benefits from Medicaid at the present time. The current inequity is partly due to rural-urban differences in the makeup of the poor—a higher proportion of the rural poor are ineligible for Medicaid because there is a higher proportion of nonelderly, two-parent families among the rural poor—and partly because there are proportionately more rural poor in those states which now have low Medicaid benefits. These inequities would be eliminated under the Administration's national health insurance proposal, as well as under most of the relevant alternative proposals under consideration.

The next question, then, is when we might expect passage of a national health insurance program. Despite President Ford's decision not to push for a bill this year, I give it a 50/50 chance this year, and a probability close to 1.0 in the next three years. As I stated before, national health insurance has now surpassed a universal cash transfer program in legislative priority, and I would expect the House, if not the Senate, to pass a bill this year.

Other Proposed Programs. Two other programs deserve brief mention.

One is a national housing allowance. Under this program, all low income families would receive a rent supplement in proportion to family income and rent. Such a program is under experimentation at the present time, but it is my judgment that passage of a bill is not imminent. If and when such a program is adopted, however, it would likely favor the rural poor, because they do not get their fair share under existing housing programs. Such current programs as Public Housing, Model Cities, Urban Renewal, and Rent Supplements are for the urban poor. Of all federal housing assistance in 1970, only 16 percent went to non-metropolitan counties, despite the fact that those counties had 66 percent of all substandard housing units (6). A national housing allowance program would presumably be available to the urban and rural poor alike, and while there is a good deal of uncertainty about how such a program would operate in rural areas, it would probably correct some of the present inequities suffered by the rural poor.

The second program which deserves some mention is public employment. This is not an income conditioned program, but rather an employment conditioned program. Nevertheless, it seems to be the most popular program these days to 'alleviate the inequitable burden of a stagnant economy.'

A $2 billion public employment program under the Comprehensive Employment Training Act (CETA) has already been signed into law. The number employed under this program will, of course, depend on the wages paid. If one assumes an average wage of $2.50 per hour, about 400,000 unemployed will be hired. This represents only about 5 percent of the unemployed people in the U.S. today.

Bills in both the House and Senate would commit another $8 billion to public employment. While expenditures of this size seem unlikely, the Congress may authorize another $3 to $5 billion for this purpose. Added to the present $2 billion, this would make a total of $5 to $7 billion and would probably create between 1.0 and 1.4 million jobs. However, even this effort would provide jobs for only 15 to 20 percent of the unemployed and reduce the unemployment rate by only 1.0 to 1.5 percentage points. Moreover, many of those employed would not be categorized as poor because of secondary workers in the family or because of other income.

Such a program would not have a major impact on the number of people counted as poor in the U.S., and probably it would have even *less* impact on the *rural* poor. Based on admittedly scanty evidence available to date on the public employment programs under the 1971 Emergency Employment Act, rural areas were discriminated against in three ways: (1) funds were allocated on the basis of unemployment rates to the exclusion of consideration for underemployment rates, which are higher in rural than in urban areas; (2) even basing allocations solely on unemployment rates, rural areas received less than their fair allocation of funds; and (3) a higher proportion of the jobs created in rural areas were in terminal public works projects rather than in the expanding area of social services. The result was a lower rate of successful post-program placement in rural areas.

These observations are quite speculative, however, and a thorough study of the impact of past and future public employment programs on the rural poor versus the urban poor would shed a good deal more light on this matter.

CONCLUDING COMMENT. In summary, the two major income conditioned, antipoverty programs currently under consideration—universal cash transfers and national health insurance—would substantially benefit the rural poor, both absolutely and relative to the urban poor. And the relative gains would occur not because these two programs favor the rural poor, but because they would correct inequities in current programs that are biased heavily against the rural poor population in the United States.

REFERENCES

(1). Barth, Michael C., George J. Carcagno, and John L. Palmer, *Toward an Effective Income Support System: Problems, Prospects, and Choices,* Institute for Research on Poverty, University of Wisconsin at Madison, 1974.

(2). Blechman, Barry M., Edward M. Gramlich, and Robert W. Hartman, *Setting National Priorities: The 1975 Budget,* Washington: The Brookings Institution, 1974.

(3). Davis, Karen, *National Health Insurance: Benefits, Costs, and Consequences,* Washington: The Brookings Institution, 1975.

(4). ———, "National Health Insurance," in Barry M. Blechman et al., *Setting National Priorities: The 1975 Budget,* Washington: The Brookings Institution, 1974.

(5). Holahan, John, *Financing Health Care for the Poor: The Medicaid Experience,* Lexington: Lexington Books, 1975.

(6). U.S. Department of Agriculture, Economic Development Division, Economic Research Service, "The Distribution of Federal Outlays Among U.S. Counties," Part 3 of *The Economic and Social Condition of Rural America in the 1970s,* 1971.

Discussion

MELVIN L. UPCHURCH

B A W D E N has provided a thoughtful and informative chapter on some of the thinking about national poverty programs. I congratulate him for his emphasis on direct income transfer programs, for if we are to do anything truly effective in relieving poverty, especially for rural people, we must focus on these. General programs for economic development, rural development, farm price supports, and others have been poor tools for helping the poor.

Moreover, I share Bawden's implied conviction that we must do something to "clean up" present welfare programs. Once welfare of the poor was largely the responsibility of the family. Later, counties assumed part of the burden; rural counties often provided "poor farms" and, unfortunately, they were often "poor." In recent decades state and national governments have become increasingly involved with a hodge-podge of programs that vary widely in effectiveness from state to state. As a people we need no longer tolerate the mess we have now. We must nationalize welfare, especially since the Supreme Court rule that residence is no criterion for eligibility for aid. The nation is too closely integrated for welfare to remain only a state and local problem.

Despite strong reasons for national welfare reform, recent proposals for reform have failed to gain sufficient support at one or more points in the legislative process. Bawden properly summarizes these proposals and their present fate. During the past two years, interest by both the Congress and the Administration in major reforms seems to have waned. The reason is not that the need for reform is less acute now than it was two or three years ago, indeed the need now may be more acute. But Congress and the Administration have become increasingly preoccupied with more urgent matters and they both may feel some futility in striving for major reforms in the present political and economic climate.

Bawden avers he is not a political prognosticator and neither am I. There is little sense in striving to second-guess the Congress. However, since national welfare programs were a major issue in the campaigns of 1976, this item may be high on the agenda for congressional action early in 1977.

Bawden properly points out several directions for reform of income transfer programs. The major goals seem to be coming into focus: iron out disparities among the states; remove the disincentive for earnings now common in welfare programs; establish minimum incomes for all regardless of ability, circumstance, and residence (rural or urban); and encourage occupational and geographic mobility. The proper tools to achieve these goals are subject to prolonged debate. These tools may be forged in pieces and by much trial and error over a long period of time. But, as Bawden says, "the welfare system will be reformed; the problem is too large to be ignored and the arguments for reform are too persuasive to be denied." Precisely how and when remains unanswered.

CHAPTER TWELVE

Role of the university in
rural poverty programs and issues

EMERY N. CASTLE

THIS chapter is divided into three sections. The first part makes explicit certain assumptions concerning the nature of the poverty problem and the university. The second part states some conjectures of the author regarding the university. (Conjectures differ from assumptions in degree of documentation. Given time, it would, I believe, be possible to cite literature in support of each of the assumptions. My conjectures, on the other hand, have not been buttressed either by the collection of primary data or reinterpretation of existing literature.) The third part brings the first two parts into focus in an attempt to make explicit the role of the university relative to the poverty problem. In this attempt I am operating without the benefit of an explicit theory; conceptual models of the university in contemporary society are almost nonexistent, at least for the subject of this chapter (1).

ASSUMPTIONS CONCERNING THE POVERTY
CONDITION AND THE UNIVERSITY

The Poverty Condition. I am not an expert on poverty, except from personal experience as the son of a tenant farmer in Kansas during the drought and depression years of the 1930s, which, of course, does not qualify me to generalize from that particular condition. From the literature I have read, however, I am willing to assume that there is not a perfect symmetry between the social forces leading into poverty and the social conditions which result in a removal of poverty. That is to say, one may trace the reason for the existence of poverty to, for example, certain economic forces or conditions. It does not necessarily follow, however, that the removal of these economic conditions will lead to an elimination of poverty. Thus that degree of understanding necessary for a correction of the social condition of poverty will require the insight of more than one discipline.

The University. It is assumed that one of the functions of the university is to advance understanding by conscious, organized effort called research and, further, that knowledge is capable of being verified by empirical investigation. That is, knowledge is something more than just a consensus of the workers in a particular field. While one may not accept Popper's demanding definition of science (5) and prefer Kuhn's description of the process of science (3), even a follower of Kuhn must recognize the role of anomalies. In other words, there is something that may be called "reality" and that may not conform to the consensus in a field at a particular time (4).

It is also useful to draw a distinction between those intellectual efforts that contribute primarily to an understanding of a social condition and those intellectual efforts designed to change a social condition. Both, I assume, are legitimate functions of university personnel; indeed, the same person may engage in both. Nevertheless, one process is oriented mainly to understanding, and because of this a social problem usually has to be restated in terms capable of being treated or tested within one of the disciplines. The other activity is a process of drawing together, interpreting, and synthesizing existing knowledge. In other words, I still find the positive-normative distinction useful despite some contemporary discussion to the contrary. Of course, one needs to avoid the pitfall of assuming that the person doing research which might be labeled "positive" is motivated only by intellectual curiosity and that choice of research areas or projects is devoid of normative implications.

CONJECTURES REGARDING THE UNIVERSITY

The Decision Framework

THE HISTORICAL LEGACY. The classic, autonomous university was concerned mainly with the preservation of culture, the discovery and transmission of knowledge, and certification of the elite (7). The department subsequently emerged as a useful institutional device for these purposes and has been accorded a large degree of autonomy. This autonomy has resulted in the department being the primary unit for the dispensing of rewards and for the design of incentive systems. Considerable variation has always existed among departments as to how this autonomy is exercised and how internal decisions are made. In some instances, departments are autocratic organizations. In others, faculty participation in decision making is substantial.

Departments have traditionally posed a peculiar problem to deans and presidents. If the motivation of higher administration is to improve the excellence of a department, as defined by disciplinary peer groups, it is necessary to establish the conditions necessary for internal change. This may take the form of naming the department leader or of bringing new thinking into the ranks of the department. When the latter technique is used, skillful higher administration will always try to bring in at least two people who can serve as intellectual pace setters.

RECENT CHANGES. Two interrelated trends that have developed recently have brought considerable pressure on the traditional decision structure of the university. Probably as a result of the student unrest of the late 1960s, and with the emergence of certain tools of operation research, the concept of "accountability" has come into vogue. One result has been a shifting of decision making toward central administration and a decline in the autonomy of the department.

In addition to accountability, there has been a shift toward mission oriented, public service type of activity and away from the autonomous role of the university (for a discussion of the tension created by this changing emphasis, see 2). Those central administrators who now wish to change departmental direction and focus not only must face issues of personnel selection, as these issues are defined within the discipline or subject area; they must also make judgments on appropriate areas for research and public service.

The implications of these trends are being experienced currently, although they may not be appreciated fully by all the participants. Traditional criteria for judging performance have been lacking; new criteria and new processes for judging performance are emerging. Paradoxes are also emerging. On the one hand, one observes the stated need for a flexible university that can address myriad social problems with varying combinations of fundamental research, mission oriented research, and public service. On the other hand, one observes increasingly circumscribed position descriptions and detailed unit plans that tend to reduce flexibility.

Departments are reacting to the new set of pressures in a variety of ways. Some perceive the problem entirely in terms of single discipline versus multidiscipline considerations. They may view the center or institute as a real threat to their future and attempt to bring multiple disciplines into the department for the purpose of addressing mission oriented research. Of course, such a course of action puts immediate pressure on their function of certifying the elite of their discipline through graduate education.

In the short run, of course, the issues relate to the control of budgets, lines of authority, and the dispensing of rewards. In the longer run, I conjecture the issues will be decided by what captures the imagination and interest of the better minds. Should the better minds decide that the work they wish to do cannot be accommodated within the confines of a disciplinary department, the disciplinary department will need to adjust and accommodate that interest or lose intellectual allegiance—regardless of what the budgets may say.

The Schools and Colleges of Agriculture—An Anomaly. The schools and colleges of agriculture do not fit either the classic autonomous or the public service model of the university. Although they have been mission oriented units, the research paradigms have usually been drawn from the disciplines, primarily the biologically oriented fields. The schools and colleges of agriculture have been quite slow to incorporate the social sciences, other than agricultural economics, into their organizations, even though the problems facing agriculture have become more social in nature.

Although agriculture is usually labeled as a professional school or college in the academy, it is not a profession in the sense that law, medicine, engineering, or even business are professions. Very few people with degrees in agriculture refer to themselves as agriculturalists.

Having said all of the above, one must identify a characteristic of these organizations that tends to make them unique in the university structure. This is the tradition of social service that makes it appropriate for university personnel to concern themselves with problems that come to them from the field. While other university personnel may view anything other than classroom teaching and related research as diversionary to their main function, agricultural faculty members view social service as but one part of their total area of responsibility. This difference in attitude should not be forgotten when considering the contribution of the university to the solution of a social problem such as poverty. (In this connection, some private universities seem to have a service tradition more in keeping with the agriculture tradition than do other colleges within the public university. For example, the tradition of Harvard professors serving the federal establishment in a variety of ways is not unlike the role played by many colleges of agriculture.)

The Nature of a Bureaucracy. Even though it is a special kind of bureaucracy, the modern university is still a bureaucracy. I conjecture that very large bureaucracies are usually effective only when they have relatively simple objectives or tasks and reasonably well-defined ways or means of accomplishing these objectives. Examples are finding lawbreakers, collecting revenue, and fighting wars. When multiple objectives or goals exist or when a range of options is available as to the best way of accomplishing a given task, large public organizations are not usually effective organizations. It is beyond the scope of this chapter to argue in detail why I believe this to be so, beyond suggesting that large organizations are possible in the first place because of the development of technology—especially communication and transportation. This type of technology, and the stage of its development, may make control in a line organization possible, but it does not make possible sufficient flexibility to cope with complexity and ambiguity. I conjecture further that the so-called tools of operations research are ordinarily useful only when the output can be standardized. "Student credit hours" is still about the only measure of educational output that operation researchers in education have been able to devise.

A consequence of the observation made above is that a most difficult problem is encountered in bringing together multiple disciplines for a sustained effort on a significant social problem. Further, the closer one gets to application or solution, the more difficult the task becomes. Thus the university that has teaching as a mission must accommodate additional objectives or missions. The complex issues associated with translating a social problem into the framework of different disciplines must be faced if the fundamental research problems are to be addressed. Yet, for a final "solution" or for application of the results, the process must be reversed and the integration of the fragments of knowledge must be accomplished. Thus the performance of universities may be due as much to the behavior of bureaucracies as it is to the behavior of universities. Indirect support for this conjecture may be deduced from the fact that the existence of a variety of research organizations outside the universities has not removed the pressure on universities to become involved in social problem solving, mission oriented types of activities.

THE ROLE OF THE UNIVERSITY

Research. The task that remains is to apply this observation to the university's attempts to help solve the problems of rural poverty. Yet this is not an easy task. One runs the risk of being bland or articulating the obvious if one does not push the assumptions and conjectures to their logical conclusion. But if they are pushed too far, the result is likely to be little but individual speculation. It is apparent that our knowledge in this area is quite "soft" and that we can map from concept to reality with only general approximation (6).

Little controversy exists over the need for understanding the causes of poverty and the conditions that surround it. It is widely considered to be an appropriate subject for research by university personnel from the standpoints of both social need and intellectual satisfaction.

Yet it is doubtful that a laissez faire attitude in the university will result in the best possible environment for such activity. While the research itself may need to occur within the confines of a particular discipline, the motivation for such research and the insights necessary to make such research the most productive will seldom occur within such a setting. At a minimum, there should be opportunity for interaction with other disciplines, and there should be access to those who suffer from the poverty condition. (I have always been impressed when examining

T. W. Schultz's references by the extent to which he goes outside the mainstream of economics for insights and data. His remarkable contributions to the understanding of rural poverty attest to the value of cross-disciplinary work. As for the value of access to people in poverty, the framing and testing of fruitful hypotheses requires original research in a real world setting.) And perhaps most fundamentally, provision needs to be made for stimulating interest in the poverty condition.

Therefore, organizing for effective research on a complex social condition such as rural poverty is a major problem for the university. The trends toward a declining resource base and accountability in a narrow sense may well strengthen the traditional provincialism of the disciplinary department. On the other hand, the university's opportunity to attract additional resources by the study of problems crucial to society would probably be enhanced by some type of multiple discipline involvement.

This involvement can occur within a department, and in fact numerous departments do encompass more than one discipline. Many departments within the schools and colleges of agriculture include several disciplines; departments of animal science, for example, include physiologists, nutritionists, and geneticists. However, agricultural economics is an applied field. Its activity of certifying its elite (educating graduate students) may not be compatible with a multiple discipline department focused on mission oriented research. If the objective is to involve social sciences other than economics in a study of rural poverty, the alternatives will be at least three:

1. Bring social scientists, other than agricultural economists, into departments of agricultural economics.

2. Create centers or institutes for the necessary multidisciplinary involvement. The relationship of the center or institute to the department may vary greatly with respect to prerogative, funding, control, and accountability.

3. Create new departments, perhaps within a school or college of agriculture, on rural poverty or rural studies with a social problem or social condition rather than a disciplinary focus.

It is my observation that universities have opted for alternative two more than any of the other alternatives. Enough experience has now been accumulated on this alternative to permit in-depth evaluation. Someone should undertake such an effort.

Public Service. At the other end of the spectrum, we may speculate regarding the appropriate university framework for public service. At the outset, it is appropriate to reject the model of a simple flow of information from the disciplinary researcher to the extension worker who then translates the results into terms that a person outside the discipline can understand and apply. Reality, especially with an issue such as poverty, does not yield to such a process.

At least three benefits of social science research can be identified. One type of research result has immediate and direct application. For example, the results of research which demonstrates that making a person skilled in the performance of a particular task does not necessarily make that individual employable have immediate practical value.

A second type of research result may add to disciplinary knowledge but have social usefulness only in combination with other knowledge or information. The discovery that those areas having certain climatic and natural resource characteristics are more conducive to the development of rural poverty than are other geographic areas provides an example. Such knowledge alone does nothing to alleviate poverty, but it may be relevant in predicting response to or the consequences of other policies.

A third type of research result seems to benefit mainly those who are doing the research. That is, it adds to the understanding of those who do the research but yields little direct information of value in social problem solving. Such research may have significant social payoff, but this is realized only by the direct involvement of research personnel at some point in their careers in professional work that permits the application of their knowledge.

No one type of organization will accommodate all three types of research results in public service. The first type of result mainly requires communication skill and subject matter knowledge. The integration and application of research results is required for the second. For the third, the contribution of research to education and in turn to policy formation needs to be recognized, and provision needs to be made for the use of knowledgeable people in positions where their expertise can be brought to bear.

It is my opinion that the process by which scientific results are used in policy formation needs systematic development. One can find large bibliographies about research methodology but few studies on the process by which research results are made useful in a policy context. Such a development needs to go far beyond the specification of the policy implications in the presentation of research results. Research is usually conducted utilizing a particular theoretical construct. The knowledge gained is usually partial and fragmented. The policymaker, on the other hand, must integrate and synthesize information generated by different theories. He need not accept the policy implications of a theoretical construct in order to use the knowledge developed by the use of that construct. For example, one may find both the analytical and empirical work of Milton Friedman to be very useful in policy formation even while rejecting the policy proposals advanced by Friedman.

I continue to have great hope concerning the potential of the cooperative extension services. They have demonstrated considerable flexi-

bility in identifying and mounting significant efforts on important social issues. While these efforts have typically lacked depth, they have
often been more responsive to social needs than their research counterparts. Yet if they are to do more than just create awareness of complex
social problems such as rural poverty, they must be willing either to
bring into their organizations greater subject matter depth or to develop
access to and utilize the knowledge of people who do have such depth.
While an organization may survive by moving to whatever problem is
"hot" at the moment at the expense of other problems that are just as
important but do not command as much current interest, this survival
will come at a cost. Questions will continually arise as to why such an
activity needs to be associated with a university. Further, the organization will be bypassed on the more substantive issues.

The University Administrator. Because of the current tendency toward
    centralization of authority within the university, the deans and the
president have additional responsibility and power in regulating mission
oriented, multidisciplinary work. Yet I believe that relatively little has
been done in analyzing the changing problems administrators face at
this level, and that little information is available to assist them in dis-
charging these increased responsibilities.

There seems to be insufficient appreciation of the need for top administrators in higher education to create programs and make decisions
that are *unique* to that administrative level. Frequently, decision making
at the school/college/university level is nothing more than a review of
decisions that are tentatively made on problems defined at the department level. It is not surprising that when departmental decisions are
reversed, misunderstandings arise. The higher level administrator will
usually be subjected to a different set of stimuli and his criteria will be
influenced accordingly. Yet unless there is explicit recognition and acceptance of the criteria used for decision making at each level, the review,
support, or reversal of departmental decisions will be a constant source
of tension and friction. But, more seriously, the result will be program
decision making that is fragmented and piecemeal. Department heads
and chairmen frequently complain, justifiably in my view, that their
superiors can always find time to review the appointment of a minor
employee or a minor salary adjustment but provide little or no opportunity to explain a total departmental program and explore how it fits
into the larger framework of the school, college, or university. The reason probably is that the institution does not have a program that will
permit a decision on such a matter and, more seriously, lacks a decision
framework for bringing about such an integration. Lacking this framework, it is not surprising there is confusion as to the reward or incentive
system that is to apply to individual faculty members. This inconsistency
in attitude is often reflected in department heads or chairmen being ex-
horted by central administration to reward merit with individual faculty

members on the one hand but distribute salary increase money "across the board" among departments on the other. Yet central administration can do little with this problem in the absence of any systematic evaluation of total department programs on the basis of explicit criteria.

This state of affairs arises, in part, because the department typically has an infrastructure for the analysis of decisions pertaining to the selection of personnel, and choice of research has traditionally been an individual responsibility; the centralization of authority has not been accompanied by a comparable infrastructure. The current resentment within departments is not entirely a challenge of the prerogative of central administration; in part, it reflects a lack of faculty confidence in the capacity of central administration to discharge the vast responsibilities the administration has assumed. This reasoning can also be applied to the trend within the USDA-Land Grant complex to centralize the determination of research priorities.

Given the problems of centralized authority in regulating research and selection of personnel, and given my conjectures about the inflexibility of bureaucracies in the face of complex problems, it may be very difficult to establish a multidisciplinary program within a unit such as a college of agriculture. If such a program were responsive to social need and made explicit, it would probably be viewed by departments within the school or college as a threat to traditional clientele groups. Despite the fact that agricultural economists have been remarkably alert to the emergence of social problems in rural areas, they have not universally welcomed other social scientists to the scene. One suspects that some agricultural economists may welcome the position of having near monopoly power with respect to the social sciences and agriculture. (But while they may enjoy applying the principles of imperfect competition in their own interest, they may wish to give some thought to applying the principle of equi-marginal returns in the broader interest of social problem solving. If ten economists are working on a problem, the marginal contribution of a political scientist or anthropologist may be higher than that of an additional economist.) And apart from the political aspects of a comprehensive program for a school or college of agriculture, there is the difficult problem of mounting and maintaining a sustained multidisciplinary attack on complex social problems.

An additional set of issues facing the university administrator who is attempting to be responsive to social problems is the degree of optimism he conveys concerning the prospects for a solution to a particular problem to a potential grantor. One of the real hazards facing social science research is that too much will be promised and expected and that disillusionment will result if results are not forthcoming. The role of the administrator in this process may be crucial.

Public Support for Rural Poverty Work in the Universities. What the universities can do on problems of rural poverty is, of course, related to the resources that are available. If there are no special funds made available for this purpose, the university will probably confine its efforts to incorporating rural poverty conditions and problems in its curriculum and such scholarly activity as the interests and abilities of its faculty will permit.

A sustained multiple discipline approach to rural poverty issues through research and public service will probably require special funding. Conditions at present do not lead one to be optimistic in this respect for the following reasons:

1. The world demand and supply situation for food has directed concern with the rural countryside away from the plight of those people who cannot earn a livelihood from commercial agriculture and toward the output of the commercial farming sector.

2. Political power is with the urban areas. While sober analysis leads to the conclusion that the poverty problem and social blight in rural areas are just as or more severe than in the urban areas, such a conclusion is not likely to be translated into political action. Further, the interrelation of the rural and urban poverty problems has not yet been demonstrated generally.

3. The schools and colleges of agriculture, with their associated organizations of cooperative extension services and agricultural experiment stations, are not in a good position to exert leadership on this problem. On the one hand, they are in the best position to recognize the condition and advance proposals for an appropriate response. Further, their traditional emphasis on public service and problem orientation is a powerful asset. However, their traditional clientele groups outside the university may view an organized effort in this respect as a threat. Further, as noted, internal groups within the schools and colleges of agriculture may not universally welcome such an emphasis.

4. The complex nature of rural poverty does not lend itself to large-scale effort. More concrete objectives such as increasing agricultural production or conserving agricultural land is more likely to command public support and be amenable to treatment by a large bureaucracy such as the USDA-Land Grant complex.

In view of the above, I conjecture that public support for university efforts in this connection is likely to continue at a relatively modest level. Under such circumstances, the most effective effort is likely to be forthcoming from substantial specialization in a few centers of excellence such as the Poverty Institute at the University of Wisconsin. Not only can such units attract a critical mass of expertise, they can also afford the overhead effort necessary to seek out specialized funding sources. Additionally, such centers can serve as a source of stimulus for those workers at other universities who must work in relatively greater isolation from other academic people concerned with problems of rural poverty.

CONCLUDING COMMENTS. No attempt has been made in this chapter to appraise the adequacy of the university in responding to social needs and problems, but perhaps a closing comment in this connection is appropriate. It is desirable, I believe, that there are varying degrees of mission orientation among universities across the land. This not only permits specialization, but it also constitutes a form of experimentation that may be instructive. Of course, the universities need to be somewhat cautious in the response to numerous demands for "relevance." Their long-run capacity to serve society may be significantly diminished by short-run response with numerous mission oriented programs. With respect to rural area poverty programs, I do not fear overemphasis on mission orientation so much as I do a failure to recognize that a successful mission orientation will require fundamental investigations within the social and behavioral sciences. I also fear that the special interest groups both outside and within the universities will warp the effort so that the significant issues will be neglected and significant problems will not be investigated.

REFERENCES

(1). Castle, Emery N., "Priorities in Agricultural Economics for the 1970s," *American Journal of Agricultural Economics* 52:831–40.
(2). ———, "The University in Contemporary Society," *American Journal of Agricultural Economics* 53:551–56.
(3). Kuhn, Thomas S., *The Structure of Scientific Revolutions,* 2nd edition, Chicago: University of Chicago Press, 1970.
(4). Lakatos, Imre and Alan Musgrave, eds., *Criticism and the Growth of Knowledge,* Cambridge, Eng.: Cambridge University Press, Iowa.
(5). Popper, Karl R., *The Logic of Scientific Discovery,* New York: Basic Books, 1961.
(6). Roberts, Marc J., "On the Nature and Condition of Social Science," *Daedalus* 103:47–64.
(7). Trow, Martin, "Reflection on the Transition from Mass to Universal Higher Education," *Daedalus* 99:1–42.

Discussion

W . W . M c P H E R S O N

A L F R E D Marshall in his "Three Lectures on Progress and Poverty" proposed a program that sets the stage for a discussion of the role of the university.

The people might agree to the following rules and principles of action. First, no stranger, or at least none who are weak morally, mentally, or physically, to be allowed to enter the district. No person to be allowed to marry till he was earning enough to bring up a family properly. A first-rate education, general and technical, to be given to every child. Severe treatment to be given to laziness and drunkenness, the most abundant tenderness and charity to misfortune. There would then be no pauperism, and even no poverty. . . . A century ago Scotchmen were a long way behind us in wage-earning power: now they are ahead of us; though Scotland has had a bad enemy in whisky. (2, pp. 195–97)

Dr. Castle discussed the role, organization, and administration of universities with respect to poverty. However, he raised more issues than he resolved. Since I do not know the answers either, most of my effort is devoted to making additions to his list of problems.

ROLES OF THE UNIVERSITY. The appropriate roles for the university are to provide a first-rate education, general and technical, by way of resident instruction and continuing education (extension), and to conduct research to support the educational programs as well as to support action and regulatory programs that should be administered by agencies outside the university. I believe these roles are consistent with those suggested by Castle. I suggest that the education and research should be action or decision oriented but that the administration of action and regulatory programs should remain outside the university program.

If our education and research programs are action oriented, the university can, I believe, play a major role in breaking the barriers that surround poverty groups. There is no reason why this role should be left entirely to the courts. This point, and a few others that have been made by other speakers, may be illustrated with data in Table 12.1.

TABLE 12.1. Estimated total income of males from the year of completion of specified number of years of school through age 64, U.S.

Years of School Completed	Nonsouth		South	
	White	Nonwhite	White	Nonwhite
	(thous dol)			
8	224[a]	172[a]	197[a]	115[a]
12	300[b]	195[b]	274[b]	138[b]
16	371[c]	215[c]	346[c]	157[c]

Source: (1, p. 20).

[a] Assumes that 8 years of school are completed in the year that the person is 14 years of age.

[b] Assumes that 12 years of school are completed in the year that the person is 18 years of age.

[c] Assumes that 16 years of school are completed in the year that the person is 22 years of age.

The implication of the data is that at each level of schooling, it would "pay" the nonwhites in the South to migrate rather than to continue to the next level of schooling. This may explain the high dropout and migration rates among nonwhites in the South at a time when many persons appeared to believe that the high dropout rate was a noneconomic matter and were advocating more education as a solution to the poverty problem. Note also the differences between the estimated income for whites and for nonwhites at each level of education within the South. In large part this difference probably could be accounted for by unequal quality of education and barriers to entry into the higher paying occupations. It appears to me that the university, in its primary roles of education and research, should be at the forefront in reducing the social and economic barriers to migration from lower to higher paying occupations. A college education is not very useful when one is using a shovel or a hoe.

ORGANIZATION AND SCOPE OF ACTIVITIES. Castle suggested that research and education should encompass disciplines in the other social sciences in addition to economics. I certainly agree with this suggestion. The problems of rural poor people are not all of an economic nature and neither are they all of an agricultural nature. Thus the scope of work must be extended well beyond the traditional bounds of economics and agriculture. But agricultural economists should be able to play a key role in synthesizing knowledge from several disciplines—a role similar to the one played by the farm management specialist with respect to production. We need a more comprehensive approach to get at the foundations of the problems rather than to spend all of our efforts on a piecemeal approach of continuously patching leaky roofs. I share Castle's concern for the matter of how such multidisciplinary activities should be organized and administered. Castle suggests that the rewards structure as oriented around discipline departments may be a key problem. But casual observation has led me to believe that agricultural economists in the areas of production economics and farm management have developed much more effective cooperative relationships with agronomists and animal scientists in separate departments than have been developed between agricultural economists and sociologists when administered together in a single department. I suspect that this is due to the fact that production sciences, but not social sciences, were included in the educational programs of agricultural economists and thus they feel more at ease in communicating with production scientists. Regardless of the organizational system, I do not believe that the efforts will be very successful unless the individual participants are quite willing and possibly anxious to cooperate. In the latter case the work probably would be rather effective regardless of the administrative arrangement.

SOME AREAS FOR PROGRAM EMPHASIS. A review of the chapters throughout this book will reveal many areas in which research or education or both are needed. Here I list a few additional ones that have come to mind and emphasize some of those that were mentioned.

The emphasis in the book has been placed on ways of increasing and distributing incomes. In addition to this concern, I suggest that work needs to be done on income expenditure—can utility be increased by changing expenditure patterns, espeically in such areas as nutrition, mental and physical health, housing, legal services, and credit? And to what extent are there opportunities for developments in goods and services, housing for example, that would lead to increases in utility per dollar spent?

While our most immediate concern is with problems of the existing poor, we should be concerned with matters of discovering and eliminating the basic causes—we must begin to work on the foundation, in addition to keeping the leaky roofs patched. We must go beyond the felt needs approach and head off problem situations before they arise.

In the more basic areas much work is needed in individual and social behavior and institutional change. In this connection I would like to comment on the matter of neoclassical and radical economics. If a radical economist is one who believes that neoclassical economics is not adequate for explaining past and present conditions and for predicting the future and estimating consequences of alternative actions, then I am a radical economist. But if a radical economist is one who believes that neoclassical theory is totally useless and that the only alternative is a theory of two-class conflict, then I am not a radical economist.

If one accepts the assumptions, both explicit and implicit, in neoclassical theory, then one accepts the conclusions. But I see nothing sacrilegious about questioning assumptions. For example, one neoclassical assumption with regard to the market is that individuals, when left free to behave as they see fit, will behave as individuals. Then the competitive process forces the individual to behave in the public interest even though he is seeking to maximize his own income in a self-interest way. This self-interest, however, is modified by Adam Smith's theory of moral sentiments that motivate individuals to be good neighbors (see 3).

On the other hand, observations show that individuals, when given the opportunity to do so, form groups, and we can no longer depend on the competitive process to insure that the group will perform in the public interest. But, in place of the Marxian model of two classes, numerous interest groups are formed. In fact, most adults, except those in poverty, are likely to belong to one or more interest groups. In a structure of collective action, we may not be able to depend on a free market as a means of insuring that the group will behave in the public interest.

Some years ago economics was broken into two groups—the "theorists" and the "institutionists"—as though there were no institutions with respect to theory and no theories with respect to institutions. This split, in my opinion, was extremely unfortunate. To deal with questions of the poor I do not believe that we can move very far without a synthesis of theories and institutions.

One final comment—in many program proposals there is a tendency to create an imbalance between supply and demand. The program is likely to do more toward increasing demand without adequate provisions for increasing supply. This point merits much more research and education than it has received in the past.

REFERENCES

(1). Lassiter, Roy L., Jr., "The Association of Income and Education for Males by Region, Race, and Age," *Southern Economic Journal* 32 (Part 1): 15–22.
(2). Marshall, Alfred, "Three Lectures on Progress and Poverty," *Journal of Law and Economics* 12:184–226.
(3). Schneider, Herbert W., ed., *Adam Smith's Moral and Political Philosophy*, New York: Hafner, 1948.

C O N T R I B U T O R S

BAWDEN, D. LEE, *Professor of Agricultural Economics and Economics, University of Wisconsin*
Dr. Bawden received the B.S. and M.S. degrees from Montana State University and the Ph.D. from the University of California at Berkeley. He has held joint appointments in the Departments of Agricultural Economics and Economics at the University of Wisconsin as Assistant Professor (1963–67), Associate Professor (1967–71), and Professor (since 1971). He was a Research Economist with the Institute for Research on Poverty (1968–71) and Institute Fellow (since 1971) at the University of Wisconsin. Dr. Bawden is currently on leave of absence from the University of Wisconsin as Principal Research Associate and Director of Income Maintenance Division with the Urban Institute, Washington, D.C.

BOULD-VAN TIL, SALLY, *Assistant Professor of Sociology, University of Delaware*
Dr. Bould-Van Til received the A.B. and M.A. degrees from the University of California at Berkeley and the Ph.D. from Bryn Mawr College. Dr. Bould-Van Til was an Instructor at Cheyney State College (1966–67) and Consultant to the President's Commission on Income Maintenance Programs (1969). She has held her current position since 1972. Her fields of specialization are industrial sociology, sociology of poverty, demographic aspects of the labor force, and social stratification.

CASTLE, EMERY N., *Vice President, Resources for the Future, Inc.*
Dr. Castle received the B.S. and M.S. degrees from Kansas State University and the Ph.D. from Iowa State University. He did postdoctoral work at North Carolina State College (1956). He was Assistant Professor at Kansas State University (1948–52) and an Agricultural Economist with the Federal Reserve Bank of Kansas City (1952–54). Dr. Castle joined the Agricultural Economics Department at Oregon State University as an Assistant Professor in 1954 and became Professor in 1959. He has held numerous academic and administrative positions, including Visiting Professor at Purdue University (1962); Dean of Faculty, Oregon State University (1965–66); Head, Department of Agricultural Economics, Oregon State University (1966–72); Director, Water Resources Institute at Oregon State University (1966–69); and Dean of the Graduate School, Oregon State University (1972–75). Dr. Castle has held the offices of President, American Agricultural Economics Association (1972–73); Past President, Western Farm Economics Association; and Past Vice President, American Farm Economics Association. Dr. Castle assumed his present position in 1975.

COPPEDGE, ROBERT O., *Associate Professor of Economic Development, Cooperative Extension Service, New Mexico State University*
Dr. Coppedge holds the B.B.A. and M.S. degrees from New Mexico State University and the Ph.D. from Oregon State University. He was a Research Assistant in the Department of Agricultural Economics at New Mexico State University from 1965 to 1967, and an Agricultural Economist with the Economic Research Service, U.S. Department of Agriculture, from 1967 to 1968. Dr. Coppedge was an Extension Economist in the Department of Agricultural Economics at Oregon State University from 1968 to 1974. He joined the staff of the University of Florida as Assistant Professor of Food and Resource Economics in 1974, and returned to New Mexico State University, where he holds his present position, in 1976. His areas of specialization are economic development, human resource economics, and community development.

DAFT, LYNN M., *Senior Economic Analyst, Congressional Budget Office*
Dr. Daft received the B.S. degree from the Ohio State University, the M.S. from the University of Massachusetts, and the Ph.D. from Michigan State University. His areas of interest are agriculture and resource policy, regional economic development, and human resource development. He was Assistant Deputy Administrator, Economic Research Service, U.S. Department of Agriculture (1971–74); Rural Affairs Coordinator in the Office of the Assistant Director for Special Programs, Office of Economic Opportunity (1970–71); Special Assistant, Office of the Assistant Secretary for Rural Development and Conservation, U.S. Department of Agriculture (1970); Staff Economist, Office of the Secretary, U.S. Department of Agriculture (1967–70); Staff Economist, National Advisory Commission on Rural Poverty (1967); and Staff Economist, National Commission on Food Marketing. Dr. Daft was Senior Economist in the Office of Management and Budget from 1974 to 1975, when he assumed his current position.

DAVIS, CARLTON G., *Associate Professor of Food and Resource Economics, University of Florida.*
Dr. Davis received the B.S. and M.S. degrees from the University of Nebraska and the Ph.D. from Michigan State University. He joined the Food and Resource Economics Department at the University of Florida as an Assistant Professor in 1970. He held a civil service appointment in the Ministry of Finance, Government of Jamaica, from 1956 to 1959. From 1964 to 1968 he held Graduate Research Assistantships at the University of Nebraska and at Michigan State University. Dr. Davis was a Ford Foundation Research Fellow in the Department of Agricultural Economics and Farm Management, University of the West Indies, Trinidad 1968–69), and an Instructor in the Agricultural Economics Department at Michigan State University from 1969 to 1970. His areas of specialization are human resource development, economic development, and public policy.

EDDLEMAN, BOBBY R., *Professor of Agricultural Economics, Mississippi State University*
Dr. Eddleman holds the B.S. degree from Texas Technological University and the M.S. and Ph.D. degrees from North Carolina State University. He was an Instructor in Agricultural Economics at North Carolina State University from 1962 to 1964 and an Assistant Professor at Texas A & M University from 1964 to 1966. In 1966 Dr. Eddleman joined the faculty of the University of Florida, where he held the ranks of Assistant Professor, Associate Professor, and since 1974, Professor. His areas of specialization are

regional economics, rural public facilities, and economic development. He has published extensively on the subject of rural development and has served on numerous task forces and committees dealing with domestic and foreign rural development problems. He served as Director of the Center for Rural Development at the University of Florida from 1973 to 1975. Dr. Eddleman assumed his present position in 1975.

EMERSON, ROBERT D., *Associate Professor of Food and Resource Economics, University of Florida*
Dr. Emerson received the B.S. degree from Cornell University, the M.S. from the University of Chicago, and the Ph.D. from Purdue University. He was an Economic Assistant with the Economic Research Service, U.S. Department of Agriculture (1965), and Research Assistant at the University of Chicago (1965–66) and Purdue University (1967–71). He joined the faculty of the University of Florida as an Assistant Professor in 1971.

GORMAN, BENJAMIN L., *Professor of Sociology, University of Florida*
Dr. Gorman received the B.A. and Ph.D. degrees from Tulane University. He has held faculty positions at Tulane University (1958); West Texas State College (1960–62); Central State College (1962–65); Oklahoma State University (1965–67); and Boston University (1967–68). He joined the faculty of the University of Florida as an Associate Professor in 1968 and has held his current rank since 1973.

JANSMA, J. DEAN, *Professor of Agricultural Economics, Pennsylvania State University*
Dr. Jansma is a Professor of Agricultural Economics at the Pennsylvania State University. During the 1974–75 academic year he was a Visiting Professor in the Department of Food and Resource Economics at the University of Florida. Dr. Jansma received the B.S. and M.S. degrees from Iowa State University and was awarded the Ph.D. degree from Oklahoma State University. He has been employed by the Economic Research Service, U.S. Department of Agriculture, and has been a faculty member at Pennsylvania State since 1964. Dr. Jansma has written numerous articles in books and journals and has authored several agricultural experiment station bulletins. His professional area of interest is rural development policy and natural resource economics.

LESLIE, GERALD R., *Professor and Chairman, Department of Sociology, University of Florida*
Dr. Leslie received the B.A., M.A., and Ph.D. degrees from the Ohio State University. He held Instructorships at Ohio State (1949–50) and Purdue University (1950–52). He held the ranks of Assistant Professor (1952–53), Associate Professor (1955–56), and Professor (1957–63) at Purdue University. He has held Visiting Professorships at the University of North Carolina (1953–54), Columbia University (1956–57 and 1960), and the University of California at Berkeley (1959). He was Professor and Head, Department of Sociology at Oklahoma State University, from 1963 to 1967. He has been Professor and Chairman of the Department of Sociology at the University of Florida since 1967.

LOEHMAN, EDNA T., *Associate Professor of Food and Resource Economics, University of Florida*
Dr. Loehman received the B.A. degree from Rice University. She was awarded an M.S. degree in Mathematics and an M.S. in Economics from

Purdue University. She holds the Ph.D. in Economics from Purdue University. She joined the faculty at the University of Florida as an Assistant Professor in 1970. Her areas of specialization are natural resource economics, regional development, welfare economics, and operations research.

McPherson, W. W., *Graduate Research Professor of Food and Resource Economics, University of Florida*
Dr. McPherson holds the B.S. degree from North Carolina State University, the M.S. from Louisiana State University, and the Ph.D. in Economics from Harvard University. He has served with the Bureau of Agricultural Economics, U.S. Department of Agriculture, and has been on the faculty of North Carolina State University (1949–59). From 1955 to 1957 he was advisor to the Planning Board of Pakistan with the Ford Foundation-Harvard University Advisory Team. He was Head of Economics and Statistics Research (1959–61) and Assistant Scientific Director (1961–62) with the Division of Tropical Research, United Fruit Co., and worked in Honduras, Guatemala, Costa Rica, Panama, The Dominican Republic, Colombia, Ecuador, and Nicaragua. In the spring of 1963 he served as consultant to AID in Trinidad and Tobago, and in the summer of 1966 he was with the International Research Institute in Brazil. Dr. McPherson joined the University of Florida faculty in 1962.

Owens, Emiel W., *Associate Professor of Finance, College of Business Administration, University of Houston*
Dr. Owens received the B.S. and M.S. degrees in Agricultural Economics from Prairie View A & M University and the Ph.D. from the Ohio State University. He joined the faculty at the University of Houston in 1971. He was Visiting Professor in the Department of Agricultural Economics at the University of Minnesota from 1959 to 1971 and Professor of Agricultural Economics at Prairie View A & M University from 1960 to 1969. Dr. Owens has held numerous consulting positions, including Economic Advisor in Rural Development, Government of Liberia, West Africa; Member, Task Force on Rural Development, USDA, 1969–70; and Consultant, International Agricultural Economics Conference at Sydney, Australia, in 1967 and Minsk, Russia, in 1971. He was also Guest Scholar at Rutgers State University from 1965 to 1966 and at the University of California at Davis in 1963.

Padfield, Harland I., *Professor of Anthropology and Director, Western Rural Development Center, Oregon State University*
Dr. Padfield received the B.A. degree from San Diego State College and the M.A. from Arizona State University. He holds the Ph.D. from the University of Arizona. He was a Research Specialist in the Bureau of Business and Public Research, University of Arizona (1962–64), and held a similar position in the Bureau of Ethnic Research, Department of Anthropology, University of Arizona (1964–72). He was an Assistant Professor in the Department of Anthropology at the University of Arizona (1965–69) and Associate Professor (1969–72). Dr. Padfield served as Visiting Senior Research Fellow at the Institute for Development Studies, University of Nairobi, Kenya, from 1970 to 1971. He has been Director of the Western Rural Development Center and Professor of Anthropology at Oregon State University since 1972.

Persky, Joseph J., *Associate Professor of Economics, University of Illinois at Chicago Circle*
Dr. Persky holds the B.A. and Ph.D. degrees from Harvard University. He was formerly an Instructor at Yale University and the National Bureau of

Economic Research and an Assistant Professor at the University of Alabama in Birmingham. Dr. Persky also held the position of Senior Staff Economist to the New York State Council of Economic Advisors.

SCHUH, G. EDWARD, *Professor of Agricultural Economics, Purdue University*
Dr. Schuh received the B.S. degree from Purdue University and the M.S. from Michigan State University. He also holds the M.A. and Ph.D. degrees from the University of Chicago. He has held the ranks of Assistant Professor, Associate Professor, and Professor in the Agricultural Economics Department at Purdue University. He was Program Advisor to the Ford Foundation, Brazil (1966–72), and has served as Consultant to the Ford Foundation for Latin America and India (1972–75). Dr. Schuh has authored or coauthored three books on Brazil and won an award for Best Published Research from the American Agricultural Economics Association for his book *The Agricultural Development of Brazil*, 1971. He was on leave of absence from Purdue University to serve as Senior Staff Economist with the Council of Economic Advisors from 1974 to 1975.

SCHULTZ, THEODORE W., *Charles L. Hutchinson Distinguished Service Professor, Emeritus, University of Chicago*
Dr. Schultz received the B.S. degree from South Dakota State College and the M.S. and Ph.D. degrees from the University of Wisconsin. Professor Schultz holds honorary degrees from Grinnell College—LL.D. (1949); South Dakota State College—D.Sc. (1959); Michigan State University—LL.D. (1962); University of Illinois—LL.D. (1968); and the University of Wisconsin—LL.D. (1968). He is the author of numerous books and articles, many of which are considered classics in the economics profession. The breadth and depth of his contribution to the profession is illustrated by the following books which he has written: *Redirecting Farm Policy; Agriculture in an Unstable Economy; Production and Welfare of Agriculture; The Economic Value of Education; Transforming Traditional Agriculture; Economic Crises in World Agriculture;* and *Investment in Human Capital.* In addition to other books for which he is sole author, he has edited more than five books and authored and coauthored hundreds of professional articles and papers. He is Past President of the American Economics Association and the American Agricultural Economics Association. He is also a Fellow of these two professional associations. Professor Schultz has held numerous nonacademic and academic offices and has served as advisor and consultant to private and public, national and international organizations.

TWEETEN, LUTHER, *Regents Professor of Agricultural Economics, Oklahoma State University*
Dr. Tweeten received the B.S. degree from Iowa State University and the M.A. and Ph.D. degrees from Oklahoma State University. He joined the staff of the Agricultural Economics Department at Oklahoma State in 1963 as an Assistant Professor. He is currently Regents Professor of Agricultural Economics, a distinguished title awarded in 1972. He was Visiting Professor at Stanford University in the academic year 1966–67 and at the Institute for Research on Poverty at the University of Wisconsin in 1972–73. He has served as consultant to the National Advisory Commission of Food and Fiber, the U.S. Department of Agriculture, the Harvard Development Advisory Service, and the Center for Agricultural and Economic Development. His research emphasis has been on problems of regional and national economic development, the economics of human resources, and public policy for agriculture. He is the author of several books and numerous journal articles.

UPCHURCH, MELVIN L., *Professor of Food and Resource Economics, University of Florida*
Dr. Upchurch holds the B.S. and M.S. degrees from Texas A & M University and the Ph.D. from the University of Wisconsin. He joined the faculty at the University of Florida in 1972 after retiring as Administrator of the Economic Research Service, U.S. Department of Agriculture, a post which he held from 1965 to 1972. Dr. Upchurch was Director, Farm Production Economics Division, Economic Research Service (1963–65); Staff Economist, Office of the Secretary, U.S. Department of Agriculture (1962–65); Assistant Director, Farm Production Economics Division, Economic Research Service (1960–62); and Assistant Chief, Agricultural Adjustment Branch, Economic Research Service (1958–60). Dr. Upchurch held positions as Agricultural Economist-Administrator and Professor at the University of California at Berkeley (1948–54) and at Oregon State University (1946–48). His area of specialization is public policy.

WALKER, O. NEAL, *Research Fellow, University of New England, Armidale, Australia*
Dr. Walker received the B.S. and M.S. degrees at Texas Technological University and the Ph.D. from Oklahoma State University.

YOUNG, JOHN A., *Assistant Professor of Anthropology and Research Associate, Western Rural Development Center, Oregon State University*
Dr. Young received the B.A. and M.A. degrees in Philosophy from Macalester College and the University of Hawaii, respectively. He holds the M.A. and Ph.D. degrees in Anthropology from Stanford University. He was a Teaching Assistant at Stanford University (1967–68) and an Assistant Professor at California State University, San Diego (1970–72). He joined the faculty at Oregon State University in 1972.

INDEX

Age and poverty, 21–23, 25–26, 83, 153
  See also Children
Agricultural Act of 1970, 26
Agriculture, Colleges of, 76, 199, 205
  See also Farm
Aid to Families with Dependent Children, 74, 153–54, 186–89
Aid to the Blind, 153
Aid to the Permanently and Totally Disabled, 153
Anthropology and economics, 6–7, 131–32
Antipoverty programs. *See* Government; Welfare
Assimilation, 133–34
Assumptions
  of economics, 4, 6–7
  of neoclassical theory, 88–89, 111
  of the university, 196–97
Attenuation, community, 141–44, 146

Behavior. *See* Human behavior
Benefits of poverty to nonpoor, 72–76
Brazil, poverty in, 97, 105, 107
Bureaucracy, university
  and poverty research, 199–200
Business
  NAB/JOBS, 135
  See also Industry

Capital gains, 173–74
Capitalism, 116–24, 126–27, 138
  and labor surplus, 139
Cash transfer programs. *See* Income maintenance
Ceteris paribus, 5–6
Charity, 72
Children, 25–26, 83
  and farm poverty, 89, 112
  and time, 97
Class structure, 61, 73, 79, 115–23, 134, 140, 149
  See also Lower class
Community Action Program, 82

Competition, 99–100, 112
Cooperative extension services, 76, 202–3, 207
Cost of poverty, 45–67, 69–70
  See also Social cost of poverty
Credit, 93–94
  and rural black poor, 168–71, 181–82
Culture of poverty, 16–17, 131–34, 165, 168
  outside U.S., 36
  See also Lower class

Debt. *See* Credit
Demograms, 176
Diet and poverty, 14–15

Economic Development Administration, 50
Economic growth, 17, 31, 38, 56, 59, 90–91
  to eliminate poverty, 79–80
  and technology, 98–99
Economics, 4–8, 70, 132
  research on poverty, 8–10, 201, 204, 208–10
  theory of poverty, 35–36, 38, 41, 92–105, 137
  See also Neoclassical theory; Radical theory
Education, 51–52, 94–95, 97, 104–7, 143, 151
  dropouts, 49, 51, 208
  and employment, 155
  human resources, 134–36, 139–40, 149–50
  and income, 39–40, 48–49, 51–52, 207–8
  and parents' income, 69
  and poverty, 30
  rural black poor, 167, 178–79
  See also Research
Elementary and Secondary Education Act Title I, 49, 154
Employment, 17–21, 23–25, 40, 46–52, 142, 144, 147

Employment *(cont.)*
  beliefs of nonpoor, 76
  disincentives to, 53–54, 102
  farm, 100–101, 113
  income maintenance programs, 55–56, 174, 177–79
  labor market, 135–36
  and negative income tax, 52–56
  pleasure in, 101–2
  policy for, 105–6
  public programs, 192–93
  and rural poor, 152–59, 165, 166–67, 181–82
  technology's effect, 98
  See also Labor
Engel's Law, 14
Extension Service. *See* Cooperative Extension Service

Family
  as economic unit, 93–94, 96, 112, 137–38, 149
  planning, 51
  size, and poverty, 12–13, 25, 36
  structure, and poverty, 24, 35–36, 144, 174, 177
Family Assistance Program, 74–75, 79, 154, 178, 184
Farm
  as economic unit, 93
  incomes, 13, 89–92, 101, 106
  poverty and programs, 12, 35, 73–74, 78, 84, 89, 112
  workers. *See* Labor
  See also Rural
Farmers and capitalism, 118–22, 126–27
Farmers Home Administration, 78–79
Finances for poverty research, 204–5
Food expenditures
  to determine poverty, 13–15
Food stamps, 99, 106, 154, 187, 188

General assistance, 153
  See also Public assistance
Geography
  and estimated total income, 208
  and income maintenance programs, 174, 178, 188, 190
  and poverty, 21, 29, 100, 101, 164
Ghetto, 144–45, 151
Gini ratio, 59–60, 61, 63, 64
Government
  antipoverty programs, 31–32, 78–79, 133, 150
  and income distribution, 115
  market policy, 105
  and research, 130
  and rural development, 26
  See also Politics; Welfare
Graduated equality model, 61–64
Growth, economic. *See* Economic growth

Head Start Program, 49
Health
  Medicaid and Medicare, 189–90
  national insurance, 189, 191–92
  and poverty, 23, 30–31, 40
Hick's Law, 38–39
Housing, 29–30, 154, 192
Human behavior
  relation to income, 5–6, 7–8, 96, 131–40, 142
Human capital, 38, 40–41, 94–95, 96–97, 104–5, 106, 107
  development programs, 52
  and income, 38–41
Human resources, 46, 51
  development programs, 174
  investment in, 134–36, 150
  marginalization of, 142–45, 146
  processing of, 130, 135, 140, 145
  rural and urban, 140–41

Incidence of poverty, 17–21, 23, 32
Income
  and education, 39–40, 48–49, 51–52, 207–8
  factors determining, 4–8, 38–40, 93, 208
  farm, 15, 89–92, 106
  growth, 57–58
  and human capital, 38–41
  indebtedness, 168–71, 181
  level, 17–20, 165–67
  noneconomic factors, 64–65, 138
  rural, 112–13
  for unemployable poor, 153–55
Income distribution, 35, 52, 56–57, 59–65, 173–74
  functional and personal, 111–12
  and human capital, 104–5, 107
  and income support programs, 175–79
  neoclassical theory, 87–108, 111–13
  and politics, 115–16, 125–26
  and technology, 87–88, 97–99, 107, 112–13
Income maintenance, 50–51
  cash transfer programs, 153–55, 186–89, 190, 194–95
  existing programs, 182–83
  Iowa-North Carolina experiment, 52–53
  negative income tax, 52–56, 61, 176–78
  New Jersey experiment, 55–56
  reform suggestions, 175–79, 184–85
  and rural poor, 165, 171–75
Income Supplement Plan, 187–89
Income tax, 64–66. *See also* Negative income tax
Industry, 140–41, 146–47
  and farm income, 91–92
  location, 49–50, 51, 156–57
Insurance, national health, 189, 191–92
Investment, 49, 56–61, 69–70
  and income transfer, 56–57

in human resources, 134–36, 140–45, 147, 150
theory, 88
of society, 95

Job Corps, 48
Jobs. *See* Employment; Industry

Labor
  agricultural, 89–92, 116–17, 119–24
  market, 24, 100–104, 135–36, 138–44, 147
  mobility, 47–48, 51, 105
  poverty, 73–74
  supply, 8, 39, 52–56
  transfer from farm, 89–90
  See also Human capital
Land and poverty, 37, 100
Landlords, 38–39
Legal Services to Poor, 82
Life span and poverty, 37–38
Lower class, 131–40
  culture, value of, 77
  lack of success, 138, 149
  See also Class structure; Culture of poverty

Manpower Development and Training Act, 48, 154
Market
  government policy, 105
  labor, 100–104, 135–36, 138–39
  transactions, 114–18, 124
Marginalization
  of human resources, 142–45, 146
  rural-urban, 142–45
  See also Social marginalization
Marginal productivity theory. *See* Neoclassical theory of economics
Medicaid, 190
Medicare, 189–90
Middle Class. *See* Class structure; Nonpoor
Migration, rural-urban, 143, 163–64
Minimum wage, 74, 123, 182
Mobility
  and employment, 47–51, 105, 155–57
  and rural black poor, 167, 179
Modes of production, 120, 126, 127
  capitalist, 116–19
  noncapitalist, 118–19
Monopsony-monopoly exploitation hypothesis, 99

National Alliance of Businessmen/Job Opportunities in the Business Sector, 135
National health insurance, 189, 191–92
Negative income tax, 52–56, 61, 176–78
Neoclassical theory of economics, 8, 87–113, 125–26, 209
Noneconomic factors of poverty, 6, 13, 16–33, 45–46, 65, 71–84, 95–97, 101–4, 165
Nonmetropolitan
  industry, 50
  poverty, 26–31
  schools, 48
  underemployment, 46
  See also Rural
Nonpoor
  beliefs of, 76
  social costs and benefits of poverty, 71–77, 79, 81, 150

Office of Economic Opportunity (OEO), 76
Old Age Assistance, 153

Payment-in-kind programs, 154–55, 174
  See also Food stamps; Health; Housing
Plantations
  as modes of production, 118–20, 126
Policy, 137, 146, 152–59
  economic equality, 33
  implications, 105–7, 145, 153, 155, 179
  neoclassical theory, 105–7
  research, 129–33
  welfare, 65–66, 73
Politics and poverty, 75–76, 78, 115–16, 125–26, 136, 205
Population-land ratio and poverty, 37
Populism, 120–21
Poverty
  cost of, 45–67
  children and, 25–26, 83, 89, 112
  culture of. *See* Culture of poverty
  definition, 11–13, 16–17, 45, 69, 72
  food expenditures and, 13–15
  hope to eliminate, 78
  outside U.S., 35–37, 97, 105, 107
  programs, 9, 31–33, 47, 76, 79. *See also* Welfare
  research 129–33, 145–47, 149, 196–210
  and rural development, 3–4, 26, 47, 75–76
  statistics, 12–13, 15–21, 25, 35–36
  variables affecting, 165–71. *See also* Noneconomic factors
  See also Rural poverty
Production, modes of, 116–20, 126, 127
Property assets and income, 38–39, 41
Psychological aspects of poverty. *See* Noneconomic factors
Public assistance, 47–53, 60–61, 153–54, 178, 186

Race
  and capitalism, 119–21
  and estimated total income, 208
  and poverty, 17–21, 23–26, 29, 30, 75–76, 81–82, 84, 101, 102–4, 107, 164–67
Radical theory of economics, 7, 8, 10, 114–28, 209

Research
  and poverty policies, 129–33, 145–47, 149
  university, on social problems, 26, 196–210
Resources, 88, 93–95, 98, 106, 108, 112, 114
  See also Human resources
Rural development, 3–4, 26, 47, 75–76
Rural poverty, 26–31
  and capitalism, 118–20, 123–24, 126–27
  and employment, 74, 100–101, 152–53, 155–59
  income maintenance, 165, 171–75
  industry location, 156–57
  research on, 129–33, 145–47, 149, 196–210
  and social disruption, 73
Rural-urban contrasts, 92
  health care, 30–31
  human resource systems, 140–41
  income maintenance programs, 174–75, 178–79, 183
  levels of living, 26
  marginalization, 140–45
  migration, 143, 145, 163–64
Rural-urban poverty, 29, 32
  cash transfer programs, 187–89
  employment programs, 192–93
  health insurance, 190, 192
  housing allowances, 192
  problems, 205

Schools. *See* Education
Sex
  cash transfer programs, 188
  and employment, 53–56
  and poverty, 21, 23–25, 164, 167
Social aspects of poverty. *See* Noneconomic factors
Social cost of poverty, 45, 71–84.
Social marginalization, 8, 133–35, 138–39, 140–47, 149–51

Social science research. *See* Research
Social Security, 172
Social service of universities, 196–210
South, 74–75. *See also* Geography
Supplemental Security Income, 186–87

Taxes
  and employment, 53–55
  income, 64–65
  See also Negative income tax
Technology, 73, 91, 137–38, 140
  and income distribution, 87–88, 97–99, 107, 112–13
Time, economic analysis, 95–97
Training. *See* Education
Transfer of income. *See* Income maintenance

Underemployment, 23, 46–47, 51, 144, 146, 152–58
Unemployable rural poor, 152–55
Unemployment. *See* Employment
Unemployment Compensation, 74
Unemployment Insurance, 187
University, and poverty research, 26, 33, 130, 196–210
Urban-industrial impact hypothesis, 90–92
  See also Rural-urban
USDA economy food plan, 13–15

Value of poverty to poor, 77

Welfare, 15, 51, 141, 145
  benefits, 56–57
  expenditures, 45, 46, 56–57
  policies, 65–66, 73
  programs, 31–33, 60, 63, 73, 74
  See also Government; Income maintenance; Payment-in-kind; Public Assistance
Western Rural Development Center, 146